T0366301

WARS
OF THE
MIND

VOLUME 1:
(*Upon the Road of Leaves.*)

By: Jonathan *W.* Haubert

Edited By: Rebekah Almogabar
Additional Editing By: Jonathan W. Haubert

8	X	8

Order this book online at www.trafford.com
or email orders@trafford.com

Most Trafford titles are also available at major online book retailers.

Printed in the United States of America.

ISBN: 978-1-4669-6316-0 (sc)
ISBN: 978-1-4669-6315-3 (e)

Trafford rev. 02/04/2013

 www.trafford.com

North America & international
toll-free: 1 888 232 4444 (USA & Canada)
phone: 250 383 6864 ♦ fax: 812 355 4082

"All great journeys begin with one small step
As for this one
A Revolting "Twist" of Self-Inquiry..."

(Jonathan W. Haubert)

Wars of the Mind Contents:

CHAPTER 8- *Numb Nerves*

CHAPTER 12- *Forever Wasn't So Long...*

CHAPTER 13- *Upon the Road of Leaves*

Chapter 1

First Steps

Pride.

If it's likely for someone "else" to have a true black-heart.
Then it's likely for me to breathe under water.
"Think about it..."

Have You?

Have you ever thought of what would've happened?
If you had said or done something else, have you?
Sometimes I wonder.
If there will ever be a better way to scream.
Sometimes I wonder.
If I pushed hard enough, would it bleed?

Inside I weep the nothing I held for you, the one I loved.
Inside I wonder, have you ever thought of me again?
Have you ever wanted to rip out your own eyes?
Have you ever thought of what could have happened?
If you had said or done something different, have you?

I have only one more thing to say.
"In this Never-Mind, you shall find the things to be."
Have you ever thought of what we could have been?
Have you?

Heated

The evil inside could burst out and hurt someone.
"If to that point I am heated."
So many people try to push me over the edge.
So I stand here leaning over the ledge.
Screaming and beating my own head.

If I am heated, who will wind up dead?
If I am hated, for being only myself inside.
The pain could grow and fall deeper within.
If I am heated, then who is it that is left with sin?

I Must - In Me

Why can't I have true love?
Why can't I have a real friend!?
I need to have some... "No, fuck it!?"

Let the blood drip onto the demon's wings.
Sing in a new voice that only God can hear.
Fearing the last - I hate the untrue.
Still you can't see, I need more.

You reject piece of shit, "you stupid bitch."
"I win - I am right - this life - I see."
I need to remain forever inside.
Because you do hate me.
The creatures in my head are all now dead - in my mind.
In my mind we all die to see one fear in me - "Me."

If yet never to see, die for you and die for me.
Or always to be, cry a Never-Soul...
A hole in the walls of a mind from hell.
I must find the light. "The light in darkness."

Beyond

Further away from everything I ever knew.
Deep in her eyes, my soul they consume.
The forever I wish, I could be at her side.
Further into grace, and deep within her mind.

Beyond everything I ever knew.
Oh how I wish I were with you.
How could I tell you how I feel?
Only with this rhyme, your heart I shall fill.

Beyond the doors of what I've felt.
Soon again, I kill myself - for you my love be true.
"I don't know what to do."
Forever and a day, I love you...

Anarchy

So I begin this little story with words of what I feel.
Hate is only in your mind but I find, there is no way to stop it.
As much as I could, I fought the demons of my own hell.
Yet still I am lost.

The story started when I was but an innocent child.
So there I sat, no deep issues, "so you'd think."
Who would have thought that such a sweet kid.
Could grow to have a mind from hell?

"Someday I shall bring all to fall before my feet..."

Cry

Drip - drop, so I cry.
As I look into your eyes.
I see something I must have, love true love.
It must be only for the person.
Who sees what he must see and feels what he must feel.

And I will never awake from this dream I call life.
I cry from my eyes, I look up and reach.
I reach out to a love that does not care.
As I sit here and rip out my hair with broken pride.
I cry.

Eyes

As I sit here and let my life pass me by.
I seem to have the time to look into your eyes.
I gaze into a dark room in which reflects my life.
"A reflection of things to be." Love, hate and insanity.
As I seem to be lost, always am I found.
I am bound to screw it up.
And hate into me – but.
"It's only evil, to an evil eye."

FUCKING HATE YOU

In a world of faces, in which can stop all that is good in me.
They are the fuel to my insanity.
"You hate me because I'm me."
Why must they see only *Death and Insanity* in me?

"DON'T SAY SHIT UNLESS YOU KNOW ME!"
"I FUCKING HATE YOU, BECAUSE YOU HATE ME!"

I've killed the inner me only to see, I am nothing.
So in a soul of nothing I cry.
"I fucking hate you... I wish the world would die!"

All this hate and insanity! All this hate - Oh this fate.
It crushes down onto me - crushes down into me.
I fucking hate you because you hate me!

Hold on tight, never let go.
Let out the air, Eyes to God, forgive us please.

"DON'T SAY SHIT UNLESS YOU KNOW ME!"
"I FUCKING HATE YOU, BECAUSE YOU HATE ME!"

Guinea-Pig of Society

I don't know where I'm going or what I'm doing.
But I hope I get there soon...
If it were into my soul, "suicide was once of me."
An owl cries into my face, and I see hunger in my body.
So I laugh out at it all, and try to pull the pieces together.

Lost in my own mind, *I find it all again.*
I seem to go back to what I was, I just can't be myself.
"No more, no - no more!"
Guinea pig of society - socially I am dead.
Lost into it all - into me.
I'm just another, guinea pig of society.
Grown on hate, without love - numb because of you.
Forever now I am done and confused...

Can't Take It

Over time, I've let the devil win.
The end is here and the light is gone.
I fear of my "*last song.*"
Will I become something I am not?
So will I still fuck it up?!

Just end me please, I must die!
Because I tried to remain the same.
Yet still I grow in pain.
Just end me, I can't take it! *In all in which I've come to learn.*
I find the most difficult battle I'll ever fight, is the battle within myself...
"*I can't take it.*"

Shooting At Bottles

Lost and have nowhere to be, lost and I cannot see.
"I'm lost inside of me."
Run into nothing, just like me.
Shooting at bottles, lost indeed.

Well me - I'm fucked! And cannot be!
Without love, death to me...
I'm so cold, I cannot weep.
Shooting at bottles, death filled dreams.

Run to nothing, I am dead.
Running lost, inside my head.
Kill the light, of a friend.
Endless thoughts, insanity begins!
Shooting at bottles, I cannot see.
This world is caving onto me.
It's funny to think there's nothing left for me.
Inside of my head, is death filled dreams.
You're shooting at bottles, shooting at me.

"*Still - I cannot weep...*"

I Am Found

I was lost but didn't want to be found.
Always running around.
"Looking into nowhere."
I see what made me, Me!
"Insanity."

A symbol of something in me.
It's all a part of my childhood.
Something lost, left behind.
But no one can see.
I have found the inner me.

Years back, I saw in a dream.
A little child, so - so sweet.
A nice kid, everyone could see.
But a dark cloud began to loom over me.

"What they didn't see."
Was a future of suffering.
Just because I didn't get along with the teachers.
And decided to ignore them...
And happiness in my life, I am to see.
Was the biggest knife into my side.
Knife - symbol of a pill.
"Nothing could heal, this sadness."

"But I am found."

Jingle In Me

Jingle bells - jingle bells - my life's hell - I tried to kill myself.
Something stopped inside of me, only to see - I've killed the inner me.
Oh, jingle bells - jingle bells - I'll go to hell, please God forgive me.
Never die - always cry - loving you and me.
Welcome to a Christmas time - raise your glass and drink the wine.
Loving you and me - "forgive my soul please."
So jingle bells - jingle bells - jingle-in-me.
Forever lost, I shall always be...
Child-minds, crying out to you and me...

"Forgive my soul please."

Deadicated

I've never sat down and took the time to reflect.
On all my neglect for my loved ones and myself.
So now I sit down and thank everyone that matters in my life.
I now put down the knife and reflect on love and light.
The light of love and happiness too.
To you the un-named, "I deadicate this to you."
If I never say it out loud, I now will "I love you".

So I deadicate this one to you, forgive my neglect in the past.
Forever I wish our love to last, so I deadicate this one to you.
Everything I do is for you. Forever I wish to never neglect you.
I deadicate myself to you. Forever I'll live to love you more.
"Because I am deadicated to you..."

Ever through the times I tried and the times we cried.
Sorry if I ever caused you pain.
I deadicate myself to you, the one person I love.
I hold you closer than you ever could know.
I need you more than I have ever needed you before.
I love you now and always will...

Still, I feel that with all of this love and deadication.
That I hold for you and for what I believe in.
"I will never leave you again."
I deadicate myself to you, everything I do now is for you.
I live only to see your face once more.
I breathe only to hold you in my arms forever more.
With love deep and true.
So now and forever - I am deadicated to you.

"Me!"

What was it, what could it be? What events in my life had made me, Me?
Once in this life I was happy - now fighting my inner demons.
"Can you help me!?"
These are the chronicles of 3 Angels that were sent to save my soul.
"And how they all had failed..."

First it was all, "Me!" A happy child, *everyone could see the light within me.*
But still! Yet to find the thing to be.
The one thing in my life that had made me, "Me!"
#1 Oh so sweet, "green," nice to me.
It was there when the pills went away, it was there every day, "but!"
I was only to see that *Angel #1 in fact* never helped, "Me!"
Now Angel #2 cried for me, it was only to be, the love inside of me.
She was there when I needed to talk.
The last thing to my mind was to put up and "Walk!"
She was there for me every day and my only wish was for her to stay.
Angel #2 Oh so sweet. Angel #2 was everything I did need.
But as it was to be, Angel #2 had left me...

So... as I watch my hands melt and the walls seem to breathe.
Soon it will come to pass.
I shall see the one thing in my life that had made me, "Me!"
Soon you will see the true inner "Me!"

Okay... it's time to end this shit! Angel #3, God what is it!?
It's time to reflect on the other parts of me.
The snake - the voices and demons within me.
Demons in my soul that make me - kill me - want me!
So these voices are the only things that help.
I still can't see Angel #3. While their eyes hold over me.
What the hell could it be!? Who is Angel #3?
So I'm only to find the nothing in me.
Evil Angel, don't cry for me, forever black is the color inside of me.
The evil angel is all that's left in me, the evil angel. "It is Me!"
True as can be, it's only the evil inside of me.
So I'm left behind only to find no one can help me.
So I cry, so I die, so the angels never helped me.
#2 had left me, and #1 was hell.
So only for me, deep as hell I fall into this *Never-Mind* to see.
The Angels were all along just a reflection of "*Me!*" Nothing...

Me Into Me

Now all these things in my life.
Just seem to be another knife to pull out of my heart.
I am to see it is all a part of me but as always you just look through me.
I know you hate me, so I sit here.
Looking into a dark place in my mind to find a way out.
Because never will I find out what this life I live is for.
Always the door to my soul is shut from you.
Never will I cry for you, never will I know what to do.
"I just don't care!" Always no more air!
So I just die, so I cry and scream out to the sky.
As the blood from my eyes pours out onto the floor.
So never no-more for you - always your knife into me.
Because I fear the things to be and alone I am dead for nothing or something?

So you look through me and think I'm nothing.
So I sit in a dark room that reflects my life.
With all these things in me, I pull out the knife.
But I'm only to see, you put it back in.
This life will end... I will always end with hate and insanity.
Love is no more and death fills up into me.
So I'm happy to see I'm left with only insanity and Me.

I'm so alone, love's in the air for you, hate in this life for me.
Me into me, so I'll always be a sad kid, I am so misunderstood.
Now in the spotlight I fight myself. So I sleep and dream of a land.
A land in which I have everything I want yet nothing I need.
So I wake up to see - my life is a dream.

So Me into me, these words are the only thing and way to stop the pain.
Paper and ink are my only loves, "*that*" and the dark sky above.
In my mind I find I'm nothing.
So what, I don't care, this life can take me "anywhere!"
Me into me, why must I fall deep as a well into hell, *just to make you happy?*

Die or cry in a world of hate, so long - after "*13*" just another song...
In the mirror I'm going insane, I'm crying to a love that does not care.
Yet somehow, somewhere - I will find a way out.
Me into me and love into you, I'm left to see, *"I have everything of nothing."*
No one can help me and no one will. So I die and cry and try and try,

Yet I'm left to see you took everything away that I need.
Left with nothing, I'm always left behind.
Looking to a dark place in my mind and only finding ways to kill.
Not a thing in me, "you've never cried for me."
I feel your knife in my eye and a sharp pain in my heart.
As I bleed, I see God will never forgive me.
Because I don't want to be forgiven.
I feel a dark cloud cover me and I see no light.
Only heat and hate and pain into me, Me into me, "so it is to be."
I wake up to see - my life is the biggest dream...

The Light

I'm now to see the light of my life and the darkness of yours.
So I'm now giving my true inner-feelings.
A list of everything I hate about you and "your" friends.
First of all you look at me as if I were a freak.
You never talk to me, "Love?"
I once thought was the only way of life, but now I've seen the light.
There is no such thing as love.
I hate the way I had sung a song of singing to a love so true.
But soon to show, the light of my childhood.
I once had a life, I once had love.
I once looked to the sky above to see... "I'm nothing."
Forever now I've seen the light.
The light of a love that cannot win.
So I've sinned in a world of hate, kill the light - forever I hate.
I hate the world of love, I look to the light.
The light above.

I've seen you walk with "your" friends,
I've seen the ways you've been - the way you sin.
The way you talk behind my back...
"I will not take this shit!"
No more shit, because I've seen the light.
Yet the flames of hell burn brighter than heavens glow.
So I'm stuck not knowing where I should go.
Stuck in nothing, just nothing.
I've seen the light, the light of nothing!

I've killed the inner-me only to see I am nothing!
So in a soul of nothing I cry.

Broke

The cat claws at my grave, the dog barks at the moon so bright.
This is the night I die and cry, because I'm broken.
And the life you lived has set me free. So I am dead and you grab your head.
This is not the day for you. The razors shall consume me soon.
So the pain will grow and never.... never! No you won't be like me.
My death will hopefully free all this insanity.
You might feel bad for the first few days but I'm broke, don't sob for me.
Forget everything about me, I'm so.... so sorry.

Leave the past in the past we lived. Move on! "I move on broken."
My tears so red, I soak in the blood of whom I dread.
With all these years of pain and un-truth.
You break me down until nothing's left. So leave all I did in the past - past.
Dark winged *Mother-Death* call my name and bring me freedom.
Free my pain, "not yet am I free now?" Please!
So broken and gone, lifeless body laid on the floor, torn-away.
Still! The cat claws at my grave! I wish to sleep.
Creeping deep into the abyss.
Past the past – I am broken.
Broke?

Within

I've been places, so many places. I've seen faces, so many faces.
"I feel a masquerade within my soul."
Cold as ice, it's nice to think within my mind I shall find demons...
Demons of monstrous things!
Within my soul "me be insane?" Death as rain, with such pain.
Lost is forgotten, for me it's all the same?
So come forth my brothers to see it now.
The time has come, for what has been done?
The great soul did fall, so we crawl out of the pit "This is it!"

Darkness falling upon a good land, within the mind of a man.
"The soul of me shall come forth with words of life."
This is my new knife, "within my eyes."
In the knowledge of being re-born, there comes a storm.
Hell brought soon, help brought soon. "Welcome to Noon."
A life of hate - brought by the snake.
"It's too late, time to die - in my mind,"

Your soul I keep.
Human as sheep.
Kill till dead.
Destroy lost head.
Found in bed.
Cry out dust.
Must it be?
Without love.
Death to me.

See - the religion of me shall always be.
Lust has fallen onto you, my toy called humanity.
Within my hands lies the tool of God or the devil.
"*It will be terrible!*"
I understand you're just human. I ask you now, "Can you take it?"
Sick as a dog, the fog over the roads - lust in snow.
Dust covers eyes, lost in mind, you can't kill!
You must embrace the only thing that keeps you sane.
Within her love lies the truth of one...

"You."

A New Darkness of Me

Dark devilish things soar above me and I see murder is all I feel in my hands.
"*I sing it to myself...*"
So I ran into a life that fucks up every time I turn around, "so I see."
If I stand still I could feel love, bliss and happiness too.
"So what the fuck could I do?!"
Stand still my whole life or move and feel another knife into my heart?
"I'll never find the one."

Too many in my life, just another knife!
I love what loves me and hate what hates me.
I see what you see, and you think I'm nothing!
So as the angel cries and my soul dies, this world crushes onto my chest.
So as I let out my last breath, I was tempted to stay, every day lost in you.
I'm left behind one last time but no longer will I feel lost.
"I've found myself."
So the quest to find the light is over, "and I win."

So I sing it to myself and never sin,

No longer will I be tempted to be left behind.
Because I know just now, what you want to find.
A weakness, you'll just need this to leave me.
But you'll want me back again.
"And then the darkness sets in...."

Such a new feeling, so overdone. "I was used."
Evil on my mind, I find no way to free this strain.
What a pain I feel in my heart. Ice-warm on my tongue.
"Death is all and all is dead."
You dread the day when I awake.
I'll free the power and unleash all my hate.

A little place in the back of my mind.
Such a new darkness of me. *"Love so over done."*
I see you burn alive in front of my eyes.
I smile while you melt - I'm left in the dark about everything.
I'll never stop, I feel the end drop in front of my mind.
My eyes so dark and gone...
Of all that you've said, I believed only one thing to be true.
You hate me, "yes you do!"
Such a new darkness of me – so on I stay alone for an eternity.

What I've Become

A child with nothing, I'm forever dead.
So lost in a hell filled mind. I cry only to die in a soul of pure insanity.
So I'm lost for something and I'm now here. I've seen what I've been.
A mind of nothing but inquiry and I love what I've become.
"So what the fuck do you think I'm going to do?" "Well fuck you!"
Lost into hell as deep as a well, I love what I've become, "Don't you?"
So I cry about it all! Hell filled mind but damn I love it... "Don't you?"

Could you ever kill this soul or would you be too in love with me?
So I see this life is nothing and you're just shit to me.
Well can you see I love nothing but, "Me!?"
So the devil looks into me and you cry for nothing.
So I'm too evil for you and too good for them?
So I love what I've become, "don't you?"
With God's eyes gazing into my soul, so I'm cold in a mind of hate.
What should I do... Do you like what I've become, "well do you..?!"
Well I'm lost in a maze of hellish toys and can't find my way out,

So I'm lost within your soul.
So lost in your eyes I can't find a thing, "Can you?!"

So what! I don't give a fuck about you.
Or anything – anyone – everyone around me!
So lost in myself, could you love me? Well I don't think so.
Could you ever be like me? Could you ever kill me?
Just kill me because forever I am nothing, "So fuck it."
So could you, should you? Do you like what I've become?
Do you like it? "Well just remember, you made me this..."

EuQiNu

I'm not a scared little child anymore but I fear what I've become.
I'll take matters into my own hands.
And crush this world around me, kill all that matters to me.
Because I feel no love, only regret. "So I'm unique you say?"
Every day I seep the pain. I find it is you who are EuQiNu. "*Or is it me?*"
Your Godless eyes are nothing to me.
The devil I've fought once and again, my mind fills with sin.
Unique, it is me - EuQiNu "who are you?"
What makes you the thing to be?
Who said you control this world of suffering?

I see purgatory into me.
My heart has broken, to God I pray for the light of day.
So as a black sun rises the razor lowers onto me.
So rise your glass and drink the wine. Deep in hell I lose my mind.
For I am unique but I see the demons to be.
I control my mind and destiny.
Because I have the choice to take it all or let it out.
From my mind, through my mouth.
So I'm unique you say? EuQiNu is to be.
So forever now I live my life in purgatory.

"*This is just the beginning.*"

Fork In The Road

So I'm at a fork in the road and I have no clue as to where I should go.
Which life should I live? "Now I see this is it."
First of all I could just stay the same and live this life of going insane
"And just keep losing everything."
I step one up, I fall to hell. I step one down, I fall to hell.
And if I don't move at all. Deeper I fall through you.
Yet have I fallen for the wrong person?
The angel was just a demon sent here to keep me down.
I have found that I am lost.
Well let's think now. I could just follow through and love again.
I could be forgiven for all my sins, but the curse has consumed me.
And now I'm at a fork in the road and "I don't know..."
Should I stay in this state of madness, or fall to hell?
So should we all go through hell to prove ourselves to God?
"Well I believe I should."
I feel I'm not good enough for our lord, yet still he forgives my sins.
Heaven I wait for, yet hell calls to me.
Millions into one, this demon within my soul.
I find no way out, nowhere to go!
The first road, "hell no." The second road? "Fuck you!"
Do you want to know what I say? "*I turn away.*"
I'll go back and look to the past.
The only way to end this day is to find myself.
I need to find what it was, I end this now and I mean it!
"Never should I love again..."

You're Not Shit to Me.

Love the pain, to kill in me. Soon to see the hate in me.
Why I fall? But soon to crawl, out of hell.
Deep into our hearts, it falls apart.
I do kill soon. Love the pain to kill soon, so soon - so soon.
A child you think, yet wrong again!
You don't know me, and I don't give a shit!
You're not family, no you don't mean shit!
And so I rise out in dark, it falls apart again!
This life, your sin. Never again, never no more!
The pain is "you" fuck you!
You think I'm a child, hell no! Just a child? FUCK *YOU*!!
"*Welcome to my life bitch.*"

Love No Love

If I think about it long enough, I see that I love no love ever for me.
I push away, get out of my face! I've screwed up and I didn't think straight.
And if I hurt you, well then "hey?" You screw up too, everyone does.
As above I kill the light of love, I'm just a child? And I love no love.

Because I'm not the right person for you.
I need not to feel these kinds of things.
All the love in the past has driven me insane!
I see the nicest people throwing their lives away...
Just because he or she may look good, hot, fine.
I see that's your knife but I try to help.
I've seen that road, even now you don't listen to me.
And no time will I cry for you. "Yet I do."
I feel I could help, you're right in front of me, yet I just can't reach.

So I sleep and feel the demons creep into my dreams.
I fear what has become of you.
I hate myself because I wish I could have helped and now I never can.
Ever will you feel what I feel? Never will I forgive what you do!
"I'm just a child, that loves no love."

See No Love - Feel No Love

Lost in a world where everything is found.
I am truly bound to see, everything in my life is nothing!

Lost in love, lost in you. I'm forever lost, so what could I do?
Always in this mind, I will soon find. How could anybody love me?
And so I see, there is no love for me! Always can I see, no love for me.
True as can be, no love for me. Only for you, only for them.
Only for all, just not for me...

So I'm lost in a world where everything is found, but me.
Forever now I see, love no love - ever for me "Now I see."

Never Again

So you see it every day, you see it right in my face.
I'll never ask for it again, love so forgotten and I sin.
"Everybody has it." I walk down these same old halls and feel so disgraced.
Every day I feel it slip, with no more inside, *never again, never no more.*
I've closed the door to it all, should I have done what I did?
Always so much is closed to me. I feel no love ever again, never again.
I've held back for far too long. I feel I've done so - so wrong.
I'm sorry I did that to her. She felt love inside of me.
"Forgive me lord, for I have sinned. Pride has taken over my conscience."
It all started with her on me, and then it soon became all my game.
Every time it felt the same...
"She loved me, I liked her - the wrong words said and the rest was a blur."

All her friends came to me, a slap in my face.
For what I don't know? I hear crying all around.
"Forgive me lord for I have sinned, never again, never again."
I shouldn't have done what I did, never again!
Who would have known that she was the fuel to the fire?
She the seed, not the first nor the last but for her I look to the past.
She was the one - the cure to me. What a sickness I hold, love true love.
I look into her eyes and see, so much that could never be.
Now the razor on her soft wrist, and I know now why they're pissed.

Oh, the middle people help my sense of loving you. *"Oh, loving you!"*
So my friend you lay your head back on your day - in your soft parade.
You need to be ready for the end so soon in noon.
Now how will God forgive me?
Never again, never anymore. So sorry for denying you. Sorry I rejected your heart.
So I'm sorry for the moment in which you died.
Thank God it was not your time, but only he knows why I didn't cry.
"Never again, never again."

Blood pours out of my mouth...
And I cannot find the light anymore, how will I end this night?
"Forgive me friends for I have sinned. All of this has clouded my judgment."
And you died, so what should I do?
I haven't yet cried, "yet I've died within," *oh so many times.*
I've killed myself - changed my life.
All that was, just seems to be another knife into my spine.
I'm still yet to cry, "God what is this, *a voice in me?" I scream out to him.*
"Forgive me lord for I have sinned. Never again - never no more,"

I awake on the floor today with a memory of the past.
Damn my head... These voices scream out to God.
I have sinned, never again, and it begins.
All of everyone around me seems to have love.
The one person that turns the others tank. "*That one person!*" *I do not have.*
Please Angel forgive me. I didn't mean to put you through what I did.
I wish now to love no love ever again.
Because I destroyed the first. I hope to God she's doing well.
Two years have passed, and I've held back.
I've never told anybody of this till now.
The strain was more than I could bear.
How will God forgive me? Never again, never again.

So she died but was brought back to me.
Yet I know she will never forgive me, it is all my fault.
I was the one who did what I did and said what I said.
How could I have known that it was her first - and my last love?

I'm Broken

So there it is, I'm now broke. I soak in my own blood from out of my eyes.
I cry because I fear what I have done. Once - twice yet never again will I sin?
Hate till death, I feel my chest caving in. And holding my breath as I sin.
I close my eyes and think no more. As the door to hell opens.
And deep as a well, I go into this *Never-Mind* to see...
I'll live the rest of my life with hate and insanity.
Nothing will ever love me, because I just hate the inner me.
I'll never let anyone in because I do fear what could become of me.

I'm broken and I'll never be fixed. *The tool called love was pissed away by me.*
So I live with my hate and insanity.
I've been broken and I just see I'm forever nothing.
As the seed has been planted, the tree of life will grow.
And no one cares to know how much evil its fruit will bestow.
My new life has come to a fork in the road, which way should I go.
Only God knows.
"So that was it, I'm now broke." As I soak in my own blood, it will flood.
And the angel licks her knife, as by the sword I die.
I live and hate, I feel the snake crawl up my spine.
Every time I feel love - I am broken.
So I kill and so it was that. The salt has spilt onto the ground and I have found...
Ash to ash and dust to dust,

Must I live to see or will you please forgive me?
I didn't know and still I do not. Can't see out of my own eyes.
But you mean so much to me.
So I seep into my life of hate and insanity. So I scream out to God in my sleep.
A field of grass stained red and on dark wings I find death.
I see you know, you truly despise me and I see no love for me, *I am broken.*
I am broke and you soak in your own tears.
As you cry yet die, suicide has once consumed me.
With **8** I hold the light as I die. So down this tunnel of madness I fall.

The demon-snake wraps around me. I've now killed this life of insanity.
Sorry that I left you behind. You will find the light of heaven.
True love will come to you, as I sit here and pray to him.
God will see... And help you through all the hard times.
When you lose your mind. "Stop!"

"And I see in the distance, a breath of life."

Angel

As I reach my hand to a love true love. I can feel the light above.
As I crawl on the floor I feel no more and so I cry but I've tried.
I looked in deep. Your heart so pure, I feel butterflies inside.
I look into her and feel so loved, but still I feel it kill my soul.
A demon within my head, blood pours out of my eyes as I weep.
I feel hate and pain grow deeper in me. So I die to see nothing!
"So the one girl who loved me had killed herself." It's all my fault!
She I rejected and so then the razor to her wrist. "Now I am pissed."

I see suicide in my eyes because. No love, no hope ever for me.
I am hopeless, full of evil and hate. Still I feel no love in my heart.
"I know why!" Because of a memory that lies in the back of my head.
So I feel I wish to be dead.
As I reach my hand to a love true love, I can feel the light above.
Yet I fear it's not for me, I crawl and fall forever in a Never-Hole of the truth.
It was only youth and most likely not what I think it was.
But she will live with the pain and I will live with the scar so...

Within a demon's dream of all time ending.
"I know the way..."

Chapter 2

Forgiven?

My Curse

What have I done to you? Never into me, always into you.
Curse I've brought upon the world. Of what I've sinned and what I've been.
Forgive the things I did... Out from this demon's eyes.
I feel the pain grow upon what I have done to you.
An angel in whom I see? The angel can never help me.
I'm lost to see - death of me - hate to be, "*never will I love again.*"
Because of a curse that has been cast unto me.
So I see God will never forgive me. O what have I done to you!?
Damn this curse I've brought into your life.
I wish to awake and see the light of day.
As to God I pray every time, "I lose my mind!"
Curse when the dark-crow flies past and the insects all scurry.
As the first sin brought upon him. God will always see the curse in me.
I crawl deeper into a world of shit. To you the un-named.
Please forgive the curse I've brought upon you.

A devilish thing flies above head.
Forever now the world be dead to a mind from hell.
Only for you - forgive my curse I've brought into your life.
Can you see? There can never be love in me.
For what I've done to a love I never had.
Upon that, the curse grew to an unbelievable size.
Forever now, all dies within me...
Yet I and the curse grow on and on. "It will never quit!"
Because I see further than the doors of hell.

I killed her and one more to be. I'll never let anybody love me!
Because I know I will fuck it up, the next and the next!
I'm so mixed up but what am I to say?
The curse will be cast on me till I end this day!
Out from this window I fear what I see, this curse upon me.
A curse in which stops all to be. "So mixed up, I can't see."

Now the sound in my head, I feel it in my feet.
A million into one - a million into me.
My soul so cold, the ice on the walls of my mind so thick.
I find nothing, I am just nothing!
Love is for everyone but me, all I know is hate and all I feel...
Is I've killed the first person who ever loved me.
Now alone I fall back and back, my soul and heart crack in two.
What in God's name could I do to cure the curse in me,

I found the cause to all of this. It was just that child I hated and killed.
It's just that little child I killed! "The child was me."
The curse I've brought upon you, I will soon fix. A mix of everything within me.
Voices, hate, death, and a dark demon into my heart.
As I fall apart I kill myself! I don't feel love because I fear what I could do.
"Fuck it up or it be true."
I cure the curse I put onto you, you are the one I must save.
This is the only way to end this day.
As this razor to my neck, I laugh as much as I can.
Hell awaits me now, "*suicide*?" O God forgive me!
For the curse will remain, I love this love of going insane.
No one loves me because of me.
I cure the curse of me, my cursed love is done and I kill it all at this time.
"Yet still I'm losing my mind?"

Forgiven?

As in your eyes I shall see, you've forgiven me.
As into a demon's eyes I see, "Evil is me."
I'm my own devil, so I weep and reap what I have sown.
I so hope this is the last. "So I'm forgiven?" Yet I turn away.
I fall to my knees and pray, even if it is to be, "I don't forgive me."
For what I did that day, I see from then on I've gone insane.
Never again will I think of love the same and you're driving me insane!
"Yet I'm forgiven for what I did?"

I was just a kid and didn't know what I was doing;
"*Father shall I not be someday?*" I love the love of going insane.
The one to be, lost in me, "I can't feel a Goddamn thing!"
Forever now I feel I'm insane and forgiven for what I did.
Everyone around me has love. They fall into it so easily but not I.
You and she forgive me...
One step away from the light and I will kill myself tonight.
Then we shall see, has God forgiven me? Could you forgive me?
By the time you read this, I will no longer be around for you to see.
"Forgiveness is such a funny thing."
I ask you though, "how could you forgive the insane?"
And she came to me - I was weak at the knees.
My arms opened to her, and I got the second biggest slap in my face.
I am still the disgrace, with blood on the floor, on the ground so sweet.
I shall see, truly in me... "Am I forgiven?"

Thank You.

Like a slap in the face, I feel I've done wrong so wrong.
Forgive me because I must have done something to you, "Something."
I do now see the light within-side me, "you do hate me."
I thank you for leaving me.
I see the light of darkness now for the very first time.
Thank you for showing me who you truly are.
Thank you for showing me that I'm just shit...

I'm nothing; sorry to you my friend, for driving you insane.
So sorry, sorry for feeling love.
Sorry for going above to be something I am not.
Thank you my friend, I know it will not get better.
The darkness will overwhelm my life, "I have no life."
Nothing, I am NOTHING!!!
So I thank you for everything of our nothing.
Thank you everyone, I thank the one person I love.

I've once felt bliss but I messed it up. Now years later I'm all alone.
There can't be love for me, call it destiny. Call it shit - I'm just SHIT!
As I sit here in my room, soon it ends and suicide will only make the pain worse.
Still I feel the razors onto me. Sorry, so sorry and "Thank you..."
Like a slap in the face I wake up to see reality, "Good morning to me."
As if there is anything good in life, "I need to die."
God let it end! It's not likely for me to feel love with this curse.
The first moment it's heard of it falls apart.
With all these damned demons around me, I see my life gone and yet you're so happy?
"To you and my friends, I thank you..."

Reject: Thank You #2

Once upon a time I felt love, I felt happiness, bliss and I thank you.
"To all in my mind," I find myself in a time.
A time where my friends lie straight to my face.
Hand me the razor and soon I die. I have found I've lived a lie.
I am nothing to you, I love my, "8" voices, demons, angels.
My world of purgatory within my mind.
I'll soon find I lost it all! "love, bliss, friends, family."
So tell me now - what have I to live for!? No love, no friends, no, no family.
I have NOTHING! I am nothing...
I'm just a stupid, dumb reject from a lie I call life, " *Yet I thank you,*"

So, so, so I'm sorry my friend. I'll think of and thank this to the end.
It's over, "suicide?" Well it is a good day to die.
The end is soon, the end is noon rising, "I'm trying..." To think straight.
On that un-forgettable day I saw the light of life.
And today I will die. "Right?"
It's over to all and thank you for hating me.
Sorry I rejected you. But you had rejected me.
"Reject."

So Alone

Forever now I'm alone, alone in a world of hate and death.
So alone, I'm only to find I will cry.
Why must I cry only to make you want to lie?
So alone, I will never live in this heart of hate and death.
So I will be left behind for the last damn time! So alone I will weep.
So alone, so alone, so I hate this love and my heart.
Why must I cry only to die?
So I try to get some affection from above in the light, so alone, so alone.
"I can't take this shit in my mind!" I must find a way out, so alone, I'm alone!

Oh I'm alone and I sit looking for someone to help me.
"So alone," and you hate the way I look and dress.
You hate me because I'm a little strange, so alone, I'm alone.
Demon, devil, melt of my flesh; so all of you will die like the rest.
And hate to kill this soul of love, and I look to the light above and die, so I cry.
So alone, so I'm left behind one last time.
So alone I watch the world around me.
In my soul I feel the break; alone I make up a little friend in my head.

I forever die in a hate filled mind.
So many people around me, yet I'm alone.
So alone and I die in my mind in which cannot hurt a fly.
So I die and forever I'm alone. 3:00am and I can't feel shit.
Left alone and I can't feel shit!
I'm alone, so alone that I've made up a friend, little friend in my head.
Oh, so much time and time we all lose.
Alone into death with belt up hate and insanity.
So alone and I die, why must I cry in this life so broke?
Alone in this mind, so alone and I die, cry, why?
In this rain - oh this pain - endless pain - oh my pain - I'm so alone.
I am dead, so I look back and back, think about my life,

"What was that?" IT'S OVER!
The little kid that I've killed, bloody death, so I cry.
Little kid you must die! So alone I cry...
Yet I always seem to find someone which has had it worse off than me.
I can't feel in my heart, it's all a part of my mind.
Of my soul, in this heart of coal. I cry, so alone I will die?
I die, I'm just so alone in this mind. I find now I'm forever alone.
Yet to see all the demons of my heart.
It's just another part of me. So alone in a world of insanity.
So the flame will grow till everyone knows. Why I feel like this.
It's just BULL SHIT!
"So I end it," a life with a knife and the voices ring into me.
Sounds far from sweet, a sound like...
"You're nothing, you're a WORTHLESS FREAK!" "Your life will go nowhere."
These are the things I hear, what devilish things I hear, I don't care!

No longer will I care, "This life?"
Never will I care, so from what I think, God will never forgive me.
So why do I feel this shit? Hate is all I love and love is all I hate.
So enter the mouth of the snake of evil.
Because the darkness of my soul makes me so alone.
I'm now and forever alone and hate to kill you, love to hurt me.
I can see no love for me.
"I'm empty," so alone because forever now I am broke, so I kill myself.
This life is over and so I'm done with me. I'm no longer fine.
No more jokes, no more smiles, no more at all forever now and always I am alone.

Blank.

If it were right in my face, soon I will be a disgrace.
I grab the bulb and kill the light, because I will now win this fight.
Nothing in my soul so blank, so I'm cold and forever blank.
I crawl on the floor and cry, yet soon to rise.
I beat on the floor and kiss the sky. *Forever live yet never die.*

Blank - into a soul so cold. Kill a love inside my chest.
Cut the arm and scream out the last breath.
Blank - I'm just so numb without you.
Nothing into me, bullet tip on my temple.
I laugh out loud and feel so blank.
Nothing into me, and I see no one will ever care,

So soon it dies and screams out to me.
I'll stand right in front of you, yet you walk away from me.
I try to feel love every day yet I am blank.
Cold and blank, I scream out!
Right in your face and I see you're the disgrace.
And I am dead, I dig so far, oh so deep.
All of you, so I fall asleep. Kill a love inside of me.
Forever now I will scream. Blank, into my soul and cry!
Forever live yet never die.

If it were right in my face, soon I will be a disgrace.
Kill a love inside my soul. Forever now I am cold.
Blank, I feel so numb and cold. So blank, forever now I am cold.
"And you're nothing."

Torn Apart

The dark eye inside my mind, the walls of my soul seem to get hotter.
Out of the shadows, the beast will creep into my sleep.
I dream of murderous toys. *Just remember I'm still that little boy you killed.*
I found him, bloody death. *As I took my last breath, now all of us into one.*
With the dark eye inside my soul, behold - this is what you killed.
One step away from love yet deep as a well I fall to hell for you, *"For you."*
"See it in me." Only to be, no one loves me.
And the darkness from my mind crawls down my spine.
To find, "I am nothing."

The cold razor, the hot death and my last breath.
So many lives in this mind but all of us into one.
A million demons into my heart, it's all apart from me.
"So say it to yourself." You don't love me.
You just say it so you won't feel bad when I'm gone.
So as my last deliberation to paper - thought to be apart from me.
I lost my mind in a world where hate is love and love is hate.
So enter this snake of something; because I am nothing.

You think you're my friend?
Look to the past and see, you have always hated me.
So I see as I write - my only love; a #2 pencil.
All I see, enter a world of insanity and me.
And kill my heart as I fall apart. I fall into you yet you push me away.
Every day I'm lost and alone, I cry for you - love and me;

"Can't you see, you hate me?"
Hands to the sky, as now I die; you've forgotten me?
You hate me, you think it's love, yet it's only sympathy.
That's all you have for me, I'VE KILLED MYSELF!
One to hell, the other to heaven, I'm lost in me.
I'VE LEFT FOR PURGATORY!
I hit the ground, that's all I've found. Nothing in me or something to be.
I run away every day, cry to me, in my soul oh, so cold.
Yet hell in me and bliss in you.
Who are you to say; every day I cut myself in my heart?
You ask me why, I have found the pill of hell and the song of life.
EVERY KNIFE INTO ME, GIVE FORTH *INSANITY!*
Blood out of my head today and you still say that you love me!
All I feel is hate in me, I cry out of my dark evil eyes.
I'm lost to see that I've had it, so you hate me!

"I'M JUST *NOTHING!*" So I spin around to God himself.
I ask for love, forgiveness too. So what could I do?
"He won't forgive me for killing you."
I look into this mirror and see. I know my fears, to be left alone.
So one more time, I start this new life. "How will I survive this?"
Hate to me, you now see, "I am forever me."

Last List:

So I write this letter to you my friend, "I'm lost again." Sorry I didn't take the time to talk to you. These are my last words and a list of what I left for you. First I leave to you whatever you want from my room that my parents don't want to keep. To you I leave everything. You were there when I needed to get away; "now I am away." I remember when we'd turn up the volume to kill the pain. "With your life, how do you keep sane?" Your way with words helped a lot. Just put up your middle finger and watch the world rot. I loved the way you had sung a song about singing to a one true love. "Tell my Ex that I still love her," and I'm watching over her now. "Watch her for me, please; mess-up and you'll soon see what the afterlife can bring." Tell her I still love her oh so true. "Can't you see where I'm going with this?"

As you know, I am pissed and can't see further than my own two eyes. So I kill the pain of going insane, if only I could do what you do and,

Then maybe I could just move on and leave the past in the past. Like you, I need to get it out! This pain deep within my soul burning me alive. "Soon I'll be at home in the grave." It's been so long since everything in my life went wrong. Sorry but I must kill the pain before I hurt someone else. So this is the last list I leave to all. Everything I leave is yours and our friends can take what they deserve, "you take care of that for me, okay." Tell all the guys I said hi. As I sit here and cry, I have only one last thing to say.
"Goodbye."

PS: I'll see you soon.

To: The World

I hate the world around me.
I see everything I thought I knew I will never know.
I would cry, but why must I pity myself?
I've tried to understand it all but I don't want to care.
I don't know my friends or family anymore.
My one and only love has been untrue. "Truly my life is a lie."
I've tried to live it but still...
I seem to love the sweet glimmer of the warm red razor.

I hate the world around me.
I no longer know what to do.
I'll let them decide what happens from here on out.
So I shall let all die to me, sorry but this world is dead to me.
"You know it's funny..."
How when I think all the worst will happen to me, and it does.

"Only to me..?"

46

To: The Un-named Love #1

It's me again - so I would like to say hi and hello, well what do you know? I finally write to you yet I have nothing to say. In this letter you can say I'm going insane but love can make people do these things. Love itself is insane. Yet to you the un-named - could you go insane? Or is your mind so strong that you could help both you and me?
"Well I'm just writing this to say hi and the one thing I fear - bye..."

Love: John

PS: I do love you, so true.

To: The Un-named Love #2

So I'm writing to you for another time. You my love, the girl I hold in my mind. This letter is to say once again I'm going insane. I can't feel my own legs, I'm lost but don't want to be found. I've gone insane and again you are the only one person I could talk to. My love, "what should I do?"
You, you're there for me every day; you help me but I've gone away. So my love never more will I change. I'll watch the world around me change and crumble away like me. Deep down I know you love me. And I love you too.

Love: John

To: The Un-named Love #3

To you the un-named I write this to say I love you and I don't know what to do. I am lost and cannot see. "If only - if only." Still I don't know what to do with all this in life. Tell me what I should do! Love is in the air for everyone and you. I am so lost and alone in this mind. I find now only nothing. So to you the un-named I sit here and scream in pain. Lost in love, lost in you. I'm so lost, so what should I do? Lost and I cannot see. "If only – if only." If only you were real, then I could feel true love. So I'm lost in nothing! I love nothing, so to you the un-named, I am forever now and always insane.

From: ME!

PS: This life is over.

To: The Un-named Love #4

Damn, I'm writing to you again. I thought if I could hold you one last time before I lose my mind, I'd be happy. Could you ever forgive me? Sorry you loved me. I know I'm just an evil heartless son of a bitch that doesn't give a shit about life. I will die but I ask you not to cry for me. As six feet under I will lay asleep. The pain will creep; the dream will be brought back to me and I don't know any other way to end this day.

To you my un-named love, I hope you understand where I'm coming from. So I see, every time you see me you start to cry. Please, no more tears from your eyes. "Don't let it get to you." I hope you meet one true but this is the final kiss I bring to you. I'm writing this just to say bye, and so I die - forever *good night*.

Love: John

PS: I do love you too much, but we cannot be...
Sorry I caused all this suffering. "Sorry."

The Final Kiss

So I let it all fall down to the ground.
I feel the monsters within me rising to the surface.
I see the angels cry - for as I die - I won't be forgiven.
So I sin, as I let it all in. I fear what I've become.
I let the feelings take over my mind. I feel I love you too much.
"So my final kiss to you." This is the last kiss from me.
I can't let this life begin, because I fear the end.
I fear what I could do. I am my own devil.
And I fear the voices have taken over my soul.
I'm so cold, and alone I will be.
My Angel please don't cry for me, "I'm lost in insanity."
And I will never be free, because I don't want to be.

I asked you why you love me.
As I sit here and stare into your face, I feel like such a disgrace.
I made you feel something that I wish you did not.
If I were not here everyone could live their lives better.
This is hell we live; it would be easier if I would just die.
Not one tear would fall from their eyes.
The joke I made about him;

It wouldn't have been the same if it were me.
Not one thing would change. Everyone would move on with their lives.
Just an empty desk, as I hold my breath, I know you're not that way.
If only I could love you, this life you could change.
So my final kiss to you, the last kiss from me.
I love no love because no one loves me.
Still you're there, your mind so strong and your soul so sweet.
Me, I sit in a dark room that reflects my life.
And I wish for the light, "I know you care for him."

I feel you and they, are the knife in my side.
I wish I had what he has, "you."
But I don't and I won't. I have a mind from hell.
A heart from heaven and a soul from purgatory.
I EuQiNu - the thing to be. I live in my own insanity.
And I hope you never do. I wish me not for you.
With me out of the way it could be true.
But if I died it would hurt you too.
"Damn..."

Dream Of You

I've sat down and gave it time, without you I lose my mind.
I cannot sleep; when I do I see there's nothing left for me.
I dream of things, oh so sad, "without you I'll go mad."
I've had time without you, "girl of my dreams," it seems I need you.
In a ball of pain I go insane, my angel I need you.
I feel hate rise up into me. You're my angel, oh so sweet.
I dream about you every day, I hope you feel the same way.
I've cried - tried - why? I'm just so lost without you.
Tell me, what would I do without you?!

I dream of things about nothing but you. I so need you!
I eat, sleep, *dream*, think, drink, need - see I love you...
When I was with you I felt something that will always be.
Can't you see, without you I am nothing?
"So for now I dream of you."

Fight Myself

As I have fallen onto the ground, it is you who I have found.
You were my angel, all this time you've been in front of my eyes.
And now I cry? Fight myself as I do, because I don't know the end.
I said I would never hurt you - yet I did.
I said I love you and I do but you'll never forgive me, "forgive me you."

So I try to lie down and die, just cry myself to sleep.
The inner fight creeps onto my back, up my spine and into my mind.
I still love you, the world could end and I'll never win.
The things around us keep us apart, I hope you understand me.

I should have kept to myself, then you would have never felt my pain.
It's so sad that you remind me of, "her..."
And I kick my own ass on the thought.
I wait and bleed, see - I have done this to me.
You my angel, I'll hold in my arms.
Not even the *Final Kiss* could bring us apart.
But I do fear that you are becoming, "her." I hear all the same talk.
I'm so afraid that you might be just the same.
"And still you ask why I go insane."
She loved me and I liked her but look where we are now!
I fight the inner me because you think I still have feelings for her.
"But I won't fuck this up with you."

The Game

I lost at the game. I fear the levels are getting harder than ever.
No reset, just Game Over.
I've lost it all, the fight between myself and the dark king.
Truth awaits me at the end.
I feel my body get weaker with every turn, I see my spirit fail.
I try to power-up but I fall ten times harder into hell.
"All kinds of things in my way."
I see the faces all around me, their eyes hold over me.
Everything I said comes back to me.
I see a child cry, so the pain will grow.
And no one knows what has become of him.

"Why do I have love?" Why do I hate?
I feel my inner demons come to a fork in the road,

I the child taking control of all, my life will fail.
Everyone around me feels hate growing within.
They fear what they do not understand.

I lose at this game, on I go insane. "As I say goodbye."
I walk into the fire and burn alive.
For what I've seen, I bleed from my eyes.
So I jump off and let free my arms.
As I fall to hell, "the wind holds me up?"
I stand alone because I will mess it up - again.
I fear that the last stand is coming, "*soon it will show itself.*"

I take all into my hands and crush this world around me.
"I can hate only me." Self-pity will never find me.
I kill this life around me. "Will you leave me?"
I stand alone in a world that can just end!
And till the game is complete I stand cold.
I'm alone in this world of hate, I let all in me die.
I try to win but still I sin.

Losing.

I'm losing my mind and nothing is mine. "I'm lost."
Understand that we are in love, I will kill for you.
"You my sweet," but do you love me?
I feel the ground come out from under me! "I'm losing."
Damn it! What could I do?
I haven't been the same since I've met you.
But I don't want to think it!
Yet still - I hear all kinds of things. I hear that you've lied to me.
Drugs and sex behind my back? I've heard that and much more.
Yet I'll always let you through the door. "Still I'm losing!"
I don't know what to do.

Look to the future, further than you've ever looked before.
"Think of what you're doing."
Even if you don't love yourself, "I do."
Not one, ten million things could keep me from you.
I'm losing, can't you see? You're so close yet so far from me.

Please give me one sign – true. *That I will lose* but not you.
I will die and try, I cry and cry.
I'll die before you feel the pain of going insane,

Look to the past - my childhood.
I feel that I've killed the one I loved.
And thought that I could never love again, yet I do.

I hear things from people. They say all kinds of shit.
This world is driving me insane! I'm losing me but I won't lose you too.
No matter what you or I do. I'll always love you.
"Funny I want to cry."

Listen to me; I try as hard as I can, I'm on a quest to help both you and me.
You are my angel sweet as can be, I've seen the light.
"It's you my love - sweet love."

Please You

All you ever wanted from me... love a soul of suffering.
Feel the walls of my mind. Just hate in me all the time.
So I pray every day. I love the way I go insane.
And all I can do is please you?

I run away every day, all I can do is sing this way.
You see what you want to and love what I do for you.
Yet you do nothing for me. All that's left to see, all I'm left to be.
And I please you - and I please you.

I'm going insane! You think it's love, happiness too and I please you.
When I look into your eyes I feel I could just die.
Kill the soul of a child in me. Pleasure is all you want from me.
Happiness is all you see and you believe what you see.
I live in my own purgatory. A world where no one lives.
A world where everything ends.

Please?! Why must I please you?
And you say I'm too much for you?
And this is all I am left to do is, "please you."
I please you, but you don't do shit for me.
Yet I love you... Can't you see?
I live in a world of hate and suffering, "and I please you?"
Someday I will feel the same, so until then I am forever insane.
And I please you...

She Untrue

In darkness I lie, as angels cry. I try to live but sin holds me down.
"I've found it..." There is nothing for me, I live to be.
"Hold out insanity!"
Or I shall stand, I am but a man lost in his own mind.
"I can't find her."
Like a child in love, as I call above, "please God save me."
As I grow weak I feel sleep come for me, it comes...

No, damn it I must stay awake for her! My love, never above am I dead?
I crawl onto hot fire glass for her. As I weep I feel her laugh at me.
It would be funny to think it was love, her so happy - free as a dove.
But behind my back I feel something begin to cultivate.
"Lust, hate, deception and wickedness of all sorts of things."

Still I crawl and fall, blood all around me.
I cannot sleep! 3:00am, lost within and I feel her sin.
Yes, I must be a fool to think I could be happy.
"No not me," I am, have and will be forever just nothing.
Because I'm just a child?
The razor soon cuts my flesh and breaks my skin.
I lick up the blood so pure. I'm lost without her but will she see?
Death to me.
No matter how hard I try, I'll never cry out loud - never!

But she laughs at me. "She hates me."
Death filled dreams, loss of blood in the sky.
I try to win, yet she sins.
To think it was true. To think it was you...
Yet I feel it's time to heal the pain.
Suicide is on my mind because, "She untrue."
Yet I have one thing left to say.

Beyond the doors of what I've felt, soon again I kill myself!
For you my love be true!
"I don't know that to do!"
Forever and a day, I love you!
But do you love me too, true?!?

Dear God Help!

Dear God help:
So I ask you please! Do you truly love me?
So I CRY! But try to live with SIN! So I end me, "sorry."

Funny to think it was true, funny to think it was you.
And yet I try, yet I die and still you ASK!?
DAMN IT - I LOVE YOU!!
On and into you I see death in me; a seed of evil into our lives.
But his knife is me, and see I die, into me, I try to be!
BUT STILL YOU HATE ME! YOU HATE ME, ME!!

Cold and alone I hurt inside, but I try to cry yet still I die!!
INSIDE I'M DEAD!!

"?"

Can't no longer feel - time to kill - demon I let you in.
Feel the sin! Of blood in hand, lost within!
And she dies?! I don't cry. Why God, why?! Time to die!

Brought upon death, loss of breath, cut the death and I die!
Within her...die...cold, blood onto hate, lust must be grand.
I forgot my land of childhood, but once I could feel.
Love so true, but who are you!?!?!

I can't feel, I live so weak and I bleed, and she laughs it at last.
I am dead to a world that doesn't give a shit!
Yet the one who sung and has done... And the girl for him - life?
Think it's right? Is it? Is it love!? Is it!? Is it love? Is it!?
IS IT!? ?

God Forgive Me

Shivers down my back, what was that!?
A ghost walking through me or just the inner me - trying to leave?
Lost in a moment in which we wish would never end.
Yet it does and it must, "love is hell to me."
I can only see evil in me, a devilish heart, a mind from hell.
A soul from heaven, "I live between."
I fall to the ground and bang my head on the floor.
I shove my arm through the door and turn the knob.
I look to God and ask for forgiveness, "lord what could I do!?"
Allow me to let it out, to free the strain.
After I do could you still forgive me? "Here it goes again!"
I burn in hell; forever in sin I fall for you.
Lost in my heart, it's my bloody death in my chest.
My last breath, I'm going to die! I forever die.
Lost in you, what could I do? BURN MY SOUL! KILL MY LIFE!
Shove another knife into my side. Why must I be alone? *Alone I cry*!
I bleed what I see; I'm left to see I am nothing, forever nothing.
Shivers to my feet and I bleed out my soul.
So cold what could I do? Lost in you, I cry myself to sleep.
Bullet-tip on my eye, out of my head - gone...
So I cry to a dark day sky and I melt to nothing. "I am nothing."
So I died for nothing! Shivers down my back, *"oh lord, what was that*!?"

Teeth will crack, I'm broke like that. So we're lost in a world.
A world where the older think so little of the young.
Lost in hell, I feel every demon fill up into me.
Kill or feel the inner me. "I must get it out!"
"Evil devil eat of our flesh, drink of our blood.
Die like the rest; devil's heart in my chest."
FORGIVE ME! God forgive me.
Bone must break through the skin. *I bleed like sin*.
I spit blood and cry dust. "I love it."
What have I become? An evil soul of hate and death.
I hold my breath, under the sea I let it out and scream!
Forever I am nothing, please God forgive me.
I've cut myself so many times to see the reason of me.
"I'm me because I'm me."
Blood to hell, I must die to see further than this world of pain.
Why must we live to die? So I let it out, as I scream to him.
Please oh God forgive me. "God forgive me,"

With my heart torn apart, God what could I do?
Love, all around me and no one stops to listen.
I said I told you so, and now you're pissed?
I don't care! Love is so crazy. It means so little to me.
It's hello and goodbye. It's all just - say sweet things.
Yet behind their back, "no one knows."
Yet when they find out, they rush so quickly.
To kill themselves over something so small - hell, it's hell.
There is no such thing as love, too many people in this world.
How could there be just one for each of us?
So you get along with this person, fine.
You think it's love, two weeks later another hand you hold.

You know I'm right, how will God forgive me?
I'm so sorry for thinking like this. "I need it out!"
God I'm sorry, I can no longer see what to be.
Hate and love - love and hate. All we ever do is forsake.
Enter the snake of something, why can't I see?!
All I think, everyone around hates me. All I see is death and insanity.
I kill the, crush the, break the, melt the soul of a child in me.
I the child have done nothing wrong but breathe.
I've done nothing wrong but be. *I see nothing in me.*
I try to see but feel nothing or something into hell.
I love no one, I love nothing and that's how it will be.
I see the fuel to all my insanity; still to be...
Will God ever forgive me? Please God forgive my sins.
I've killed myself, one to heaven, the other to hell.
Yet the fight back to me, "who will win?"
It's a tie, can't you see? I am forever me, a whole man now.
"God forgive me, please."

"So I sit down and cry. I got it out, "well, some of it."
I now see the things to be, "all I see is death in me." God forgive me.
To God I pray, every day. It's what I wake up to.
God, I love you. O forgive me, please.
I am now and forever, just me...

Homeless

Slowly but surely everything I have slips through my hands like blood.
As I lay face first in mud I lose it all. Friends, family, my love be true?
"What could I do?"
Homeless I sleep and weep to God, what have I done wrong?
I feel death upon me. "Die" - would that make you happy?
I have nothing... friends, family, love - I have nothing!
I walk in a land that I do not know. I wander out in darkness alone.
"Cry or try to win."

Sin or insanity onto you, fuck the world! And you hate me?
I have nothing, am nothing, feel nothing.
Sleep, die, cry, try, why!?
So I'm lost! I feel them all talking behind my back.
So I walk with the middle finger to the world.
I stand alone, so alone, forever alone.
I fall to my knees, I bleed and a seed of pure evil grows inside.
Evil Angel, it's time once again, time to sin! I laugh at it all.
I fall and crawl dead, oh sleep and dream of demonic things.

Homeless I walk and fuck the world!
Eyes to it all, you will never fall but I end it all.
I will wake up someday from it all.
That will be the day you fall.
As a devil in my soul, I stand and I reach out so cold.
I kill my love, friends and family? As if I ever had those things.
My house was the only thing I had, it was all.
Now I have nothing, with my home there yet not.
"I have no more shelter."
Someday I will awake from this dream called life.

Suicide

The razor, knife, blade, or pill will sure kill.
But it's the person that holds it all. I will fall but "don't help me."
You were never there, so why try now? How will I survive this?!
With nothing I try to live, so with this sharp toy I play.
I love the warm feeling of blood running thick as mud down my hand.
Suicide will kill this man. In my hand lies the razor and I don't know why...
"But I feel good;"

How many more days can I live like this?
How many more lies will you tell?
In hell I'm more alone than I ever have been.
So do now I open sin? I break my skin.
I welcome the hate to take me away.
So insane, I need the time to stop the pain.
I get rid of the faces around me.
I am bound to the fate of what I seek.
I seep to the world of knowledge and untrue-loves.
The friend I thought I had.
It's been years and nothing has changed but me.

Lay me down to sleep, open mind to the world.
Dim the light and watch it fade. Just watch me fade away.
The razor, knife, blade or pill will sure kill.
But it is in the hand of that person.
The question, why? So I die - "now I awake..."

Fallen

I have fallen upon deaf ears of what I've screamed.
And what I've seen, is death.
Six feet under I let out my breath, my chest caves in.
I'm haunted by my sins. "A devil of me?"
I hate the world around us. I eat the flesh of a good friend.
Human death is just so funny to me.
I'll hate myself and go to hell and there is nothing to stop me.

I'll kill that little punk!
"I'll laugh as he bleeds," everyone knows who I'm talking about, so do you...
He is going to die, I tried to let it slide but what could I do?
I can't change who and what I am.
I'll eat you all; dust must be all that's left of you.
The world must die. I tried to live, so I'll burn _your_ ashes and laugh at it all.
I crawl on glass for God. Must I live like a dog?
The fog covers the land and I've become the man.
No one can ever stop me. "But what is this I see?"

An angel that is fallen just like me?
Her magnificence is too much for me to endure.
Her life was heaven, I'd go to hell for her before I'd let her cry.
I swear I'll love her till death;

Why must the best be the worst and the worst be the best?
I cry only for you, you the first and the last love for me.
Only for you I die. I do love you, what could I do?
Nothing can change me! No one changes but me and you.
Deceased I cry, my angel with I... Next to me I see.
I have fallen in love, with you.

Understand Me

Understand that we are both young and crazy.
I am nuts about you and I only hope you love me too.
I may not always be there, as I stare into your eyes.
I know even though I'm lost, you will still hold me.
You're the girl of my dreams. I'll love you till the end of time.
I lost my mind, God I love you.
Understand that I've seen hell once upon a time.
I've killed my mind, I killed myself.
I don't want to see you become like the rest of the world.
I want you not to be the same.
My friends lie dead because of the same old things.
"God, my life drives me insane."

Understand that I love you too much.
To watch, hear, or know that you are the same.
I want the best for you my love, please don't be the same.
Please understand I would never hurt you.
I tried to be the best, why must I feel left behind?
You my love, I wish to be mine.
I'll work to make our future better, "this band is my life."
It's the only way out of this hell.
All our sin cities are my heavens and I wish to bring you with me.
"Understand me." I love nothing but you.
Inside I cry because I don't want to see you become a bad person.
"He," is just a waste of flesh.

I can't stop you. I could only guide you to the light.
"I love you." I want to know if you love me too, oh my God I love you.
We may not talk as much, or see each other but it's not forever.
I'm not mad at you but I am mad at what you did.
Please don't do it again. So I end this, keep this by you.
So when you feel alone, you'd know someone loves you.
"I hope you understand."

Bleed I'm Dead

As I cry, sit down and bleed, as the seed is planted.
I now dance to a song in my head, forever now I am dead.
Oh no! Now I sit down and die, forever I cry in a pain filled life.
I lick the blood off the knife. Eyes to *God*, I've forgotten the true me.
I fear the inner me because it's the only thing that can stop you...
And me.

Just follow and jump! I don't see an end.
End not the feeling cold, while blood runs warm, I dance with a smile.
The song of truth, of forever I'm told.
"Bleed I'm dead," And we're at the end.

Sin

Hate to love, love to hate.
Kill to feel, to hate in me.

Hate you, kill you, love to, kill you.
See me. Hate me.
To see the inner me.
Falling further inside.

So look into a demon's heart to see.
You hate me.
You see nothing.
You feel nothing.
You are nothing.
Like me.

You just want to kill me.
Kill me?
Oh God forgive me!

Lock us in.
I could sin.

Sorry to You

So I feel, I've got to kill, I'll hurt myself and go to hell.
Yet one more tear rolls down my face.
"God I'm a disgrace."

Sorry to all, sorry to you. I'm so sorry if I ever hurt you.
To my one true love, please forgive me, I'm so sorry...
So I sit here and pray to God, heal or kill me please!
Show me the light or strike me dead. I cut myself, bleed and cry.
Yet I try, "God help me!" A teardrop of dust, must I end my life?
God give me sight. Sorry to all, sorry to you.

I feel Angel's hands on my heart.
I feel hate rise up and down my body. Please lord forgive me.
Sorry to you, I'm sorry to all, I'll fall dead.
Growing is this symbol of me. "Help me please!"
I try to cry, yet only bleed. I laugh out loud, I hate myself!
You must open and feel the inner demons grow and grow.

God help me! Cry and cry and open my eyes.
I try to breathe, "I cannot see!" Somebody help me.
I see now everything is clear. Yet I fear I know the end.
Sorry to you, sorry you.

So I feel, I've got to kill, I'll hurt myself and go to hell.
Yet one more tear rolls down my face.
"God I'm a disgrace."

Sorry but suicide has left me. I will stand strong as I weep.
Just another song to pass the time. Sorry to you but I won't lose.
I shall win, it is you the world of sin, sorry I won't die.
So as I rise, it is you who cries, "I win."
So I feel, I've got to kill, I'll hurt myself and go to hell.
Yet one more tear rolls down my face.

"God I thank you for my strength."

Chapter 3

Six Feet Within

Crawl

Rushing back to me slowly, my mind seeps into hell.
Well, what should I do? I'm lost into you, "shit!"
I crawl and fall every day without you.
I've never been the same, I'm shit without you.
Never been the same, crawling insane.
Lost in hell, well now dead in me.

Seed of conscious, boil of hate, lost in my... Wrong and late.
Sin again, lost within and I never let you cry, why?
In my soul death is late. Crawl and fall within my hate.

Crawl to hell, understand me now! How can I live this?
I'm losing grip of you, my love what could I do? "Tell me."
Do you truly love me? Would you spend your life with me?
Would you grow old with me? Please say you love me.
Love me true, love me - love me, because I love you.

Nothing

Nothing in me, nothing in us.
Nothing in a mind where I feel hate.
Insanity in me, only to see nothing!
Nothing.

So as I cry, and even try.
To never live.
In a soul where I hate to love.
And I cry and die, in a mind...
A mind where I forever never see.
See the light of something!
Or nothing.

Nothing!
And all of you eat at me.
You eat at my soul.
Snake in my heart.
It's all a part of my soul.
My soul of nothing, Nothing.

I Turn Away

I turn my back on you, well what the hell would you want me to do?
"And what do you want from me?"
I don't even want to see you again, you're lost to me!
You don't mean a thing to me. "You're nothing."
God what the hell do you want with me?
So I turn a deaf ear to you, completely all I want is to be free.
The memories come back to me, you truly loved me?
How could you mislead me, I thought it was love?
You died for me, purgatory is the only thing left - that...
And a big grin on my face. "I'm left to be."
I'll live the rest of my life with insanity.
The razor you left to remind me of what I did. "I'll never love again."

So I've seen the light, the light of sin.
When once again I break, it feels good but kills my heart later.
No one wants to hear my past. The reason I write these, *I don't know.*
So I quit all of it! No more writings, if I write for only me.
Why should I, if I am the only one who reads?
I'll keep it in and my sin builds up because no one cares.
I'm hopeless, no hope for me, I'm lost in insanity.

Why is it if I try to stop everyone keeps me going.
Yet if I go, no one listens?
No one cares to hear what I have to say, "so I turn away."
I turn from it all, "love, hate, everything."
Only God himself lives a life of holiness.
I turn away, till the end of days. "I quit..."

I turn away from the world; I turn my back on love.
No one understands but me! I am just a misunderstood kid.
No love for me, only on Sunday may I feel grace.
Out of my eyes and into his soul, God sent his only son to save us all.
Did he fail? Maybe not, but I sure did.
Could God ever find it in his heart, to forgive such an evil mind?
I find, most likely not. *What could I do?* So I turn away from you.
No more love, because what I've done, "I've killed her!"
God will never forgive me.

I'm lost in a world of hate and death.
With my soul of cold, evil blood runs through these veins.
Love was once there, now I rip out my hair,

I turn away till I end this day, with the same razor of my friends.
Purgatory I've been twice; I am just a lost mind of darkness.
Because you call me a hellish mind.
My sweet love killed herself because of me.
I cry because I'm just a twisting soul of insanity.

The evil angel lost in me, left behind so I could go crazy.
I turn away from it all. "I quit." It's over, no more, no love.
I sit in a dark room and hear the voices telling me to hate, kill, die.
So I turn away from it all. As I fall deep as a well, I go never to hell.

So Evil angel cry out to a dark day sky, to see I will never die.
Only fade away and forever stay in purgatory.
"Farewell..."

Too Much For Me

Help this soul, a cold mind, a Nothing-Heart, a part of Hell.
Fall into a Nowhere-Mind to find me, or die to see "nothing!"
"Nothing we'll always be."
You have such a nice body. I can't help but to look.
So much heart it took to ask you, your name.
"*Oh your body, it's driving me insane!*" "So this is where the fun starts."
Hate and kill, mind twist - hits the ground.
I turn and hate myself. I can't live with myself!
No more love, swallow my tongue.
Look to the black sun sky, "or never die."
Hit my head, till I'm dead, or no more light!
Pull out the knife, bleed on the floor, bang on the door.
You're so nice to me, yet I can't help but see you are nothing...
And yet you still cry to me. You want me to be good for you.
Who could still see - the true evil in me?
If yet it were to pour out of my soul at once, "Could you take it?"
Could you take all the hatred and insanity?
Or would your Godless eyes cry?
No one can help me, all you can do is, "cry or die."
Till your eyes bleed dust, this must be.
In the ground, I have found the one thing to be.
A world for all the insanity of me, "God help me!"
Cry or die, till you see, you're too much for me.
Cry or die to see. You are too much for me...

Spinning Me to Death

Spinning, spinning way too fast. "God," let the fun last.
I fall to the ground, oh no! What is this I have found?!
No more, no - no more fun for me. Can it be, is it over?
I hope to see my friends again or never live, just never live!
"End."

Watch me fall, watch me crawl; watch me die, forever cry.
I'm living with the voices in my head!
I'm living with the voices in my head!
I'm dying with the voices in my mind!
I'm dying with the voices in my mind!
I'm killing with the voices in my soul - in my soul.
And all of this is me, "it's all me."
Too far spinning, too far gone, way too long.

No, not again - not again.
And I sin and I sin.
Lost within, "oh God I miss you."
Kill my heart, till death do us part.
I miss you, do you miss me?

Lost into a world of pain.
Losing this life of going insane.
Hurt this world, yet I stand.
I am found, I am a man.
Spinning - spinning me to death.

Bitching Lost

Bitching and twisting and turning, burning is my life.
All I have - you gave me this knife.
Sands of time, so quick I sink, sinking into my dreams.
Seemingly I am dead, "why do you..?" I beat my head.
With blood in hand, I call to you, welcome to my life.
Just know, "I hate you."

Sinking are my feet, into the ground so quick.
Why do you hate me? I try to escape all I did.
"You haunt me." See - I have no life.
In darkness I fight, an endless darkness, "my life;"

Sweet sugar, a bitter life but it doesn't matter, you are my life.
Roads I walk, still I walk. I give everything to you.
Soon is it over? It is to be.
To give out my heart, like you gave to me.

God am I forsaken? Asking is my soul.
"So what." With nothing more. Still it's shut, I've shut the door.
More you wish, pissing away these endless days.
I feel no God, devils and demons, forsaken is me?
Still I wait in my purgatory, someday I'm to see.
Streams of soldiers on blood red grass.
This war is far from over, forever it lasts.
Last I am to live or to die, last I am, I am a man, I won't cry.
So try as I do, I give all to you, forgive me my love.
"I did this for you."

You Twist Me

"Have you ever thought of what could have happened?"
"If you said or done something else."
So, as I sit here and let my life pass me by.
I seem to have the time, to look into my eyes.
I look into a dark room in which reflects my life.
A mirror of things to be, love, hate and insanity.
As I seem to be lost, always am I found.
Bound to screw it up and welcome hate into me.
It's only evil to the evil eye.

" The evil inside of me could burst out and hurt someone if to that point I am heated."
I'm hated by all and you, someday I hope to see...

Beyond the doors of what I've felt.
So soon again, I'll kill myself.
Forever my love be true.
Still I don't know what to do.
Forever and a day - I love you.

But not to see why.
But all I do is cry.
Lay me to rest inside.
I'm soon to be free.
Set aside - by you and me.

Frozen

Drop it onto the ground so sweet, and let the feeling take over me.
The pain is again onto our souls, it's so cold in my heart.

Frozen to the floor like a bastard to rum.
It's the sum of the *Never* and the dream lasts forever.
So on and on I go. Never knowing if all is lost or here.
Fearing the straight point into my neck.
Stick the blade in deeper God and laugh at all, all and you.
Because I'm none, forever now I am done.

This is my life of "shit." A load of the... "Never forgive."
I sin so joyful and sin so... Unfortunately I'm just shit.
Because that's my life, a load of nothing!

That's what I have and what I am.
So sorry but I am damned.
Damned to the floor and cannot move.
"I am frozen."

So soon is the calling to the wolf and cat.
The crying death waits for me.
The so much sorrow.
I dream of tomorrow.
But still I'm alone, alone I will always be.
Seeing untruthful things.
Like the mask called you.

Forever frozen.
Forever confused.

Crying Lost In Me

It has fallen onto me again, this life of sin.
It shall hurt at first, but soon I'll win.
I take control, of this life within.

I fall and crawl onto hot fire glass for you.
Do you feel my pain? Love forever insane.
I'll fight to death, give you my last breath.
As our child cries, I forever never die.
I love this mind of yours, I do love you.

Demon into heart, it falls apart.
Crying glass - thinking lost past - forgive what I did.
Childhood lost in hellish toys, "I'm not a child anymore."
Yet I scream out to you, the owl in my dreams.
Creeping rats, and wingless bats.
Headless dogs bark at me, and the cat claws my grave.
This is the end today.
"It Ends!"

On and into hate, lost with no one around me, I see.
I will win this life of sin, yet again, "I love what I've become."
This world of death, life - or my chest caving in, lost in sin.
I stand; I am the man I fought to be. The child has grown.
I show no light, as I fight myself, I do win, yet again, "I see."

The world hates me, you hate me.
Yet I've tried to understand, "and I do."
I fall with nothing in this soul, a soul of cold, "and I love it?"
I love what I've become, and done.
I hate us and me, see - crying lost in me!
Crying lost indeed.

Keeper

The keeper of hell's door, the keeper of this mind.
A keeper you must find or find nothing in me.
"I am the keeper of me."

Look into me and see you have no feelings for me.
You're nothing, you just have nothing!
If only you'd look into me, you could see.
The true man I am. You could find a friend or fall in love.
You could watch it end or insanity begins.
Look into me and see so much love and pain.
Mixed up, torn up, "FUCKED UP childhood!"
Don't ever look to the past because the feeling will never last.
If you don't look into me and see, "you love me."

Blood onto hand, I am but man.
The beast calls my name, angels keep me strong.
As I sing a new song, "I love her."
In this soul of cold and love. I stand alone free as a dove, "I do see."
Within me I shall find, I love her mind.
I hope she loves me too. I hope to God she loves me true.

So I weep the feelings dry, watching the candle die.
I keep a finger on the trigger, "just in case."
Indeed you must see, "I am the keeper of me."

Cry Me

Drip, drop, so I cry. As I look into your Eyes.
I see something I must have. "Love true love."
It must be only for the one person,
Who sees what he must see and feels what he must feel.
I'll never awake from this dream I call life.
I cry from my Eyes, and reach to a love that does not care.
As I rip out my hair and cry, I-cry.
Falling deep, I someday hope to see.
I wish I were free. Help me see something.
Or let me die, free me please. I need to go to the next page.
Life for me is so crazed; I have no taste, in this black heart.
I am so, so numb with only pride.

Punish The Weak

Onto the slow stream of warm blood is my love and her.
Is it not time to cry, is it not time to die, or am I dead?
So why is my path so corrupt, the past so fucked and forsaken am I?
So it is her reason to be, to make me oh so crazy.
So confusing is the screaming voices in my eyes.
This pain in my mind, so punished am I?

To call to the all and her, show no fear.
I do fear her, now is the... Why is my mind folding inside?
So cold is you... So never is my heart.
So weak is my... Far away are my dreams, so sleep does my body.

Does the monster mother-load of pain drip inside?
Why does the knife of yours drop deeper into my back?
How could you laugh at my pain? "I'm so insane!"
Punished by the angel's power.
Glued to the wall of shadow, the fire grows.
The flesh drops in sorrow.
The death will soon follow, the mind tears inside.
"Punish the weak, set them aside."

Was it not time to swim - just drown?
Was it not time to listen but to feel the sound?
I feel so weak; I am punished to the ground.
There I've found only you.

Fear All In You - Kill All In Me

I love to watch you bleed. I hold the seed of it all.
The souls of the Never are my help.
To kill a man is wrong... I'm not wrong, "you're just shit."
Only will the Gods see. Speak sweet thoughts to the wind.
I just walk more, and welcome sin.
I know all, I watch all my steps - I will not slip, I fear all, to kill all.
You just need to see. I fear all in you, to kill all in me.
Open your body and laugh. A sweet drink is you.
Enjoy your breath, for it's your last. Pass up the feeling of regret.
Only will I set in my mind. Lose time and fear it's done.
I have all and lost none. Fear all in me, to kill all in you.
"Confused?"

In Love With Darkness

All is mine, I'll crush your mind, I'll kill you dead.
I'll crush your head... No, I'm not dead, "I'm home."
Alone with hate, I feel the snake wrap around my spine.
All that time was lost. The true me is only me.
The only way is to kill the world and go home.
So now my true path is here.
Now I walk with reason and confusion.
My hate is only a bit, in this world of shit.
To the true world, "here I am!" I am found, I am a man.
So only I give myself to you, and show nothing new.

If you don't love me, then all I am is nothing.
All I need is you, a hand on my heart.
And a world to crush. Must I say sorry?
"Hell no!" All I do is hate you!
In love with darkness and I kill the world!
With my love I'll forever be!
Deep in darkness I'm set free.

ROCK MY WORLD

Chosen from all with devil eyes, falling hard into my mind.
Ripping flesh, stealing your breath, I kill you monstrous fears.
Come out for me, a bastard with no family.
With a new way to hate and love forsaken.
All I care about now is how to move on.
Held down by demons, stabbed by angels.
Tormented by voices, constricted by hate.
So all I do is, I rise and love it.
So I move on to see the end but sin is all I've found.

I sit up and rock! And give out my heart.
And that's all I do, I give my *Rock* to you.
I give my soul to you. Share all I did for you.
I give no love, for all is done and I've shown no way.
Child am I? I don't grow inside. I'm forever never-none.
So I've seen I love what I've done. I give no reason as to why I hate.
Around I go until you understand. Bound I am to walk this path I made.
I give it all to you, all I do is lose. Chosen from all with devil eyes.
To despise you all and to Rock the world.

Open Is The Light "It's God Given"

God given, salt sweet tears roll down her face.
Lord forgive me, for beating my mind and growing disgraced.
Love torn, I am out of mind and out of place.
Rough bone across my teeth, biting flesh of yours.
Drip the madness into my mind, open hell through my eyes.
Tear the skin, and welcome sin, lust is my only pain.
Sanity so forsaken within, my inner hell pit.
Defeat so great, the snake opposes you all.
Popular is the sadness that crawls through my mind.
Armed with the power of demons watching angels cry.

Lose the inner way, I say more.
To the only path I find, is the taste of human flesh.
God given is the tool; I'm still full of pain.
The box grows closer, the light dims.
Sin is within, the candy body of her.
To the north shadows and one small lie.
Love is forsaken, forgotten is my life.
The darkness grows, the light no longer shows.
So many roads I'll walk till death.
I open my breath and you take it from me.
My love, please open your eyes and see.
Open is the light, "God given is me."

Heavenly You

Lost into the skies above, I kiss her lips and feel it's done.
Life is grand; I am the man with her hand on my shoulder.
I feel the heaven soldier call my name.
I love you my angel, it is the end today.
Hate is in but the love within, you're my angel.
You are everything to me,
Your heavenly body is far too much for me to bear.

Sweet as sugar is your soul. With a kiss to kiss is this knight's dream.
You are the only one for me.
I feel mad and or sad but I just wish to be with you.
I kiss your neck and feel your chest move out and in.
On endless roads of candy toys, I feel the little child inside my chest.
I'll love you even past death.
Heavenly you, I do feel it's done. I give my heart to you,

I kiss your soul and feel heaven in reach.
I feel the forever sleep next to me, I love you.
Sweet honey drops onto your lips, I kiss your mind.
I let it out; I'll be with you till the end and even more.
The angel is you my love so true, I love you.

Heavenly you, with my eyes open yet closed I feel the snow.
I see happy times ahead, with you by my side, it could change my mind.
I love the times we've had together. "I hope it lasts forever."
Heavenly you, it's time to end, within and out I love you, "heavenly you."
I cry only for you, the angel is you, only you I love.
So see, enter my heart and sweet dreams to be.
Only to one life, so to crawl. I will fall to hell and into you I see.
"Please love me true."

So the night's knight marches to the fields of the sweet.
The rain of sugar and pure souls onto our minds.
I find I love you; I kiss your soul and feel life in us.
Our child is the one to be. I love you because you love me.
So onto the clouds I dream of you.
The sand-man is the freedom of me.
When I dream I see love in us, so lost into the sugar clouded skies.
I feel so alive. Don't you see?
I love you, as I call your name I feel sleep come for me, I kiss you true.
I do love only you, heavenly you. I do love - I love heavenly you.

Just Understand Me

Daily and daily, I feel a development inside.
Although you might not understand,
I could only say I'll love her day by day.
So I dig up and up and out in dark.
I see the light in night and the cool summer rain.
It stops the pain, I feel her near. Still I fear only me, will she?
I need her... does she need me?
I run out into fire for her, the spirits will keep me strong.
She is my angel... I love her life.
I am the knife, I cut our hearts in two. Angel I need you.
This is all a story of love I'm writing, to tell you how I feel,

So the black-burnt dove and a demonic thing flies high above head.
I sit lost in my own bed. I do wish I were dead.
I stand in a field of nothing, I feel nothing, I am the soul of nothing.
I love her, she's my angel, I'll fight even God to keep her in my arms.
"Yet I fear the end."
I'll fight again and again to keep her, yet I'm in lost-mind?
I found the something of nothing...
"Yes, I know it's crazy, but you don't understand me."
I'll love her always.

Crushed into a ball of pain, I love her every day.
Till it ends, I so need her.
So I say, lock us in and it does end.
Just understand you have helped me in every way.
I love you forever more.
Yet to be, please love me the way I love you.
"See, it's crazy."
So I'm lost, so I'm in love with an angel.
"We must stay together."
It's for the best I feel, still I love her.
I give my heart to you; I give my soul to you.
I've given myself to you, I do love you...
Please just understand me.
Not everything will be good, but that's life.
Evil and love are the two sides of all.
So all I give is me, sorry but I do love you, "so true I do."
I have nothing to give but body and soul.
"I so love you, yes I do." I need you too.

Just understand me and my ways.
The things I say might not mean a lot to you now, but...
Please just give it more time.
I'm more alive than I have ever been in a lifetime "or two."
So on we move, please just understand me...

"I love you."

Lost So Sweet

It has fallen onto me again, have I won or I sin?
So lost in myself, no life to live, nowhere to go.
So I ask for the light to show, so drop a tear onto the ground.
I have found, I love her and only her. She's my angel, and I'll fight to death.
I give to her my last breath. Forever I wish I'll never hurt you.
Forgive me; I'm so sorry, "I'm lost so sweet."
So there I sit, alone and cold, I'm forever a twisting soul.
Sorry my love, I didn't mean to hurt you and alone I sit.
Looking to the stars and moon. Soon I'll rise.

I hold you tight, my forever vice?
Forever mine, so I'm on one knee, I ask you, "please," be with me.
Lost so sweet. Sorry my love and so it rains fire and ice.
It's nice to lose it. "I'm gone so sweet."
And in the sky I'll play and it's mine to be.
I love you my sweet. Together I wish us to be.
I give you this ring and a new song I'll sing.
I give you my body, heart, mind, spirit, and soul.
So I stand, take my hand, to the heavens we fly.
Tonight I sleep and weep tears of happiness.
Good to know that you love me true, I so love you.
So I feel it's time to heal the pain of going insane.

I rise in dark, you my angel so pure, I love you forever in *Lost-Night.*
I'm so happy that I'm with you. It will last forever, I need you.
I want you, love you, must have you, "God!" be with me.
I love only you, lost so sweet in a dream of pure things.
And I wish you were here with me.
I fear only me, I'm just so sorry if I ever hurt you.
Deep in your eyes I fall, lost so sweet. "Feel the pain of me."
I'm sorry, so I weep. I never want to hurt you.
Tears like ice, on me when I'm dead.
I feel only love, hate and insanity.
So over and over and over again. I love only you - free the sin.

I fear what I could do, God I love you, and only you.
As above I see no end to this dream. I see sin in the thought that I'd win.
I must have you, forever I will love you. "Lost so sweet."
Now on one knee, I ask you, "please be with me."
I love you always and always it shall be;

When I'm all alone I know truly I'm not because I have you.
My heart is in your hands, "love me."
I'm lost so sweet, it's funny to think it could end.
But it can, yet it won't because I'll fight.
I will always be there for you, please be mine.
Till the end of time, because I'm yours to keep.
"Lost so sweet."

Within Me I See

If I were to leave you would you move on?
If you were to leave me should I move on?
I have sung this song in my head.
Would you still love me if I were dead?
I feel death is here for me. I love you, forever and free.
I creep into insanity because I know nothing else, "I fear only myself."
I fear our death, yet I'll love you to the end.
I fear your sin and again I do love you.
I fear the end will be soon, I fear the end is noon.
The break is yours and my sin; so lock us in.
I shall win this life, their sin and take all that once was and make it what is.
"For you and me."

If I were ever to leave you would you move on?
If you were to leave me, should I move on?
I have done wrong since I've been with you.
I've dreamed of us apart, my soul is in two.
I see the demon in the angel called I.
I see within me and within me I see. "I love you."
Do you see that I've never grown?
I know I will break in two without you.
I am to see, I have nothing but you.
And if you were to leave, what should I do?

In this land I have found I have no light.
I fall to the burn of hell's fire, my true fate.
Inside you deeper and deeper I see.
Within me I see, please don't leave, "please, oh please."
I do have the light inside, I fight it all.
I crawl on hot burning glass, "I love you." Here's my last...
Father shall I not be someday?
I live this life in pain, lust with whom I see;

Do you truly love me?
I do see within and within me I see. I fear what you said.
And you try to call me dead and untrue.
Ask the one for forgiveness for me too.
Within me I see... "I love you." Oh dear God please!
So to the days apart from the devil and God.
The light is all to me, it's all I need.
The seed is yours to hold, the father I shall be?
I fear the child won't love me. "I hate me."
So to dark minds of loathing or gone and forgot.
Seek out voices for the dream is lost.
I do fear that God is mad, I am sorry that I've gone mad.
The insanity is in, so I'm sorry to say. The sight is far away.
The dream of our death is too much for me.
I love you, so what should I do?
Would I move on or stay? Tell me what to do, move on?
"Would you?" Tell me, I must know.

God, I love you, so far it is to see, the forever sleep.
It seeps into my head. Would you move on if I were dead?
I must know, sorry for me. Within it all I see, within me I see.
I need you but do you need me?
It's hard to see, hard to breathe, I see within.
And within me I see.

In Darkness I Cry

Slowly I sit back in a room so cold and dark.
I try to sleep, sink into dreams... But nightmares all over again.
In shadows I see, my true fear so cold in a mind so lost.
The price was too great, too much for me to see only God.
The devil is inside and I fade to the back again, "twice it's happened..."
To all that say I'm dumb and lost, the reject I am.
So cold and insane... "Yes!" Upon the souls that are lost and forsaken.
The only way to cry is to kill it all and watch it die.
So under the sheets I scream like the child I am.
I don't know a thing, I sleep so insane.

I wake up to see; I have nothing at all, so into nights of stars I fall.
Onto the sugar sweet lips of hers but them I'll never have.
So what if you don't fully understand! I cry inside for not even me, only her!
The angel my love, of the sand in mind, only dust is left of me;

I have nothing, I'm just a freak!
See nothing but death in the endless halls of this childish mind.
I'm lost in this darkness alone... Showing nothing but hate.
"Being crushed by the devilish snake of all," all is gone now.
Seeping through the walls that lead to hell.
I welcome the pain because I know nothing else. So I just sit up and try.
Pain all around but I cannot cry, only try!
To see the light of my pain and death.
My chest grows cold, so it is time to run.
I try to hide, scream and bleed, last scenes of something or not.
So jump onto the fire so lost!
So I give up the reason, the pain inside, "in darkness I cry."

The pain so sweet, like honey it drops.
The blood so thick, this time that's it.
With no one on my side, it's hard to hide.
In the ground I weep, only six more feet.
From the light so pure, the light - my cure.
Of this curse in me, indeed - I the seed of no love for God.
Just these voices from Nod or is it hell itself?
I watch the angels weep, so much pleasure I seep.
Through the walls of this mind, "in darkness I try!"
But fallen for you, is what I choose.
To help her out, with my sinful mouth.
The demons I call, to crawl up now! "Dig me out!"
The light is gone, the song, I'm wrong! But still I'll try.
"So in darkness I cry..."

Under All - I Wait For You

Equalized - mesmerized, can't you see you're killing me?
Why can't you, why can't you see?
Crying hard, dying fast, I hope to God that it won't last.
"Confusing, I'm dooming only me."
Seeing pain, feeling life, hurt in words, I die tonight.
So under I see no God. "God I need some heart."
To the all of seeing the dead, crying none, I see no sun but I'm dead.
So creeping in shadows and the sand of my own grave.
I made for you and I, I weep and try, waiting for you.
"Under I am a man,"

"Under all, I wait for you."
Soon is my end, the pain is all sin, my being is a lie.
My point is a lie, so now I cry, screaming to the pit.
Snakes and monsters spewing from it, I–to shall–see.
Dooming only me, I call to it all; under it I wait for you.

Under I see I love you and me.
I fear it all but I won't fall. So six more feet I crawl for you.
Trying not to confuse, I'm dying hard and crying fast.
So to you I give my last breath, the past I need.
The seed is you, trying not to confuse, so under all I wait for you.
I need to cry, try to see. I love now you and me. "I'm so sorry."
So faster and harder, I fall further and further, I need to see.

Now falling further, my goal is, "I'm a father?"
I love my child, I try to teach him. I need to be with my love.
And so I cry, so I try to walk in, see your love and forget our sins.
Still I see no God. I need some heart, so I run in pain...
Understand that I love so insane.
I kill the everything I see, equal is unjust,
This pain, God I must, I need to see a goal.
Now jumping off and letting go, sorry to you.
So I sit here and wait, I feel so lost in hate, "sorry my only child."

So on I wait, feel my hate, so still I think, I sink into you.
I'm lost for you under the ground.
"Bound for none," I've sung to all, I feel so...
"God what do I do?" Under all I wait for you.
Lost in a zoo of my own demons.
My pain, I need the light I need it again. "On I sin."

I'm running in place.
I feel so disgraced, sorry my child, I didn't forget you.
Tell your mother I love her.
I will be home soon, yet I wait for you? Under all I stay.
So I wait for you, still I feel I need the all...
The fall, the light, the pain, so damn it, "yes I'm insane!"
But you say it like it's bad. So my son I wish I were a better dad.
"So wish me dead." Kill me gone. So under I wait, a life so long.
So to the world and my love, "under all I wait for you."
But still I'm alone, still on my stone.
"Waiting and waiting for nothing to come..."

Am I Right To Hate It All "Am I?"

First of all, I live my life by my rules, my job, my tools.
I take shit from nobody; everybody thinks I'm a freak.
I sink into my old world of pain, so I grab the knife by the blade.
Looking to the light, "I am dead." Running around, grabbing my head.
I wake up alone in my bed; I am alone and dead.
I try to wish it all away, I hate it all, it drives me insane!
Is it right to think these things?
This Godless world has no devil, "my mind, it hurts."
I feel I'm going to burst, "God!"
I must get it out and stop running around.
Let me out of this mind, "I hate it all."

With nothing but my hands, I dig to hell itself.
To find the inner me, still you think I'm nothing.
But I am something, a killer with a mind from hell!
Unlikely to think it's here for me.
Death is on my chest and it laughs at me.
The only thing I have is me, not a thing but me!
So, am I right to hate it all, "am I?"

Yes - I do hate it all, this world of shit.
See, I've been locked in my own mind to find it gone.
Like a child in pain, I hate it all, I hate me.
This world, I will never understand.
I'm lost in the endless sand of my heart.
I know the story won't end here.
Truly the reincarnation of it all in this body, I will see.
The thing I don't understand is me. So am I right? I hate it and me.
The quest was to find the thing that made me, Me.
I see - I hurt everybody around and me.
So I turn my back to this world and see.
I hate everything and me, so to fall, far to crawl.
I do see - I hate all and me. "See?"
It will never end, I kill the light within.
Sorry but I must die, I try to fight and I do win.
But myself, in sin again with a voice in me.
Walk in lost, fear and bleed. A seed of confusion in my heart.
I feel I'm dead and torn apart, "oh God?"
With ash to ash and dust to dust, the feeling must die.
As I bleed and cry, "oh God why?!" So am I?
Our God has forgiven, over time and time again;

The reason I don't see.
How can I believe in him - If he doesn't believe in me?
"So what if I die." My love does wish me dead.
No friends or family, just my head, "so I wish for death."
It's not that far away, the death of it all, "somebody help me!"
Oh God I'm dumb yet smart enough to see.
I hate it all because all hates me.
The call of painful heart and death.
So always to be, I hate it all because I hate me.
Am I right, "am I?"

Rise Out In Hellish Dark

As deep in the west our sun lies to rest.
And the moon rises to give forth her gravity love.
All the little stars dance and play, as the moon shines a path to a new day.
"Welcome home."

So I dig up from the deep, crawl out in snow, "the finger to God!"
So everyone can know, "I am home."
The ground caves in, six feet more I walk, so I stalk my past.
"I'm awake at last." I shake off the dust, "the truth must hurt."
And the angel cries and soon she dies.
It's time to take control, of the world I'll crush.
I must, because this I've known to be.
It's time for a showdown, so I run to the door.
I shove my arm through and turn the knob.
I look to God, "this is it," so fuck it.

The world has gone, it's all wrong and now I fight, tonight I kill the light.
So the sword I grab, by the blade at hand, I call the demons to me.
The end is now, the blood so sweet.
Death is only the beginning, and I know the end.
As my mind fills with sin, the devil weeps, so I rise out in hellish dark.
So I walk alone and I show no love to anyone, "not even you."
I am a whole man; I have the power to crush this land.
I am found – I am a man. So I creep into this land so lost.
And I see this world of hate, they don't understand my job.
To kill all that matters to me, they hate me because I'm me.
"Damn this is funny!" So I find the one who has caused all of this pain.
My curse of going insane;

Slowly he dies; I twist, pull and rip out his eyes.
I shove my arm through his chest.
Crushing his lungs, "that's his last breath."
And the Ever-Angel weeps for me.
And back I go, "so" just six more feet under I wait till I rise again.
I wait to sin, once again.
So I dig, oh so deep, six feet from death, I wait till all.
I wait and fall, fast asleep, till the next day. When the end comes again.
So lock us in, I am done, it's over - goodnight.
It's just another day I live, I hurt this world.
I found the death, it's lost to me.
"Purgatory is all!" So I never fall and now I sleep.
And let the world weep, I love this hate and the voices are all to me.
You see - this world is the foundation to my lunacy.
So I wait till once again, I rise out in hellish dark...

Regress

On and into my very own mind, I hope now it begins.
As I fall in deeper I see. I must go back, fall in sleep.
So I dream and seem to have it good, covers and sheets.
So I regress all that happened, I go back to see.
I'll have nothing, if I don't have me.

I see a light; it's the glow of hell.
So I fall deeper for you, the childhood love.
The blood, so you see. I hate all - I hate me.
I feel no light, I still fight myself.
My demons are them, my angel is dead.
I found one true but I fear I'll be used.
So sleep I do, but no rest, it's only shit!
I fear all around me, I see no God so regress I do.
I'm so afraid of losing you too. I need some time, so sleep I do.

I dream so much, I forget what's real.
I still have no way; I say I hate it, "I do."
I so fear all of you, I see so many reasons.
But in the past, I must awake from this nightmare.
I so, so fear you, I need to see.
To find myself, "God I hope," to see them again.
The voices are back, "in with sin." I see none, all - I fall, I saw it all.
I know I must sleep, I regress it all, I must find me.
I see the walls caving in. I feel the pain, a pain within,

See so much, I must know, I need, I need so many things.
I need some heart, I'm so insane.
Damn it all to hell, my childhood and me.
The world of eyes holds over me.
I need to awake from this dream, it seems I already did.
I live a dream so lost in a man.
So creep I do in sleep, I'm so fucked, she doesn't love me.
I'm just dust, I'm shit to her because I had talked and laughed.
I'm sorry but it wasn't that, so back I go.

To see the light of day, but I'm dead.
Just dead and forsaken by her, she doesn't love me.
"So it's true," not a dream.
I seem to have had it good, but now at rock bottom.
I'm so fucked! So I dig, I'll find a way out.
No this isn't the end... Yet it draws near.
So I do fear you too, I love you - I loved you!
So I sleep and wait for it to go away.
I'm just screwing it up for her.

I'm just a blur, I'm shit! I'm nothing - so sorry but I'm Not cheating!
I'll love her always.
But she'll never believe me, so I'm stuck in the middle.
So throw me away, I'll fall insane, the key will be lost.
But if I am lost in all of this? I'm shit to them.
To my family and friends, I'm nothing.
I'm just air, the reason I'm here, I don't know.
Hell must have been full.

So to earth I'm bound, maybe I'm not?!
Maybe I'm just someone's dream. I seem to have it so good.
But in the end, I'll be alone or bound for all.
So more I fall, I try to sleep, regress under six feet.
My voices do help but I'm just a child in sin.
I need to sleep, sleep again. It's time to leave my mind.

I regress.

These Voices Bring Me Back

Keeping me grounded to all that is lost - killing time, this I must.
Must I see the light? The pain is you, get away! "I run from you."
So try I do, to see some light, still I feel, "I must fight."
I know I need some heart; voices in me, I see no clearing.
I'm so fearing these vast pits of hell - the hell is you. So do you see?
You bring me back in deed, in the childhood memory.
I do feel neglect and fear; cold is my tears I give to the world.
The calling to God and the devil too. Angel of evil - the demon is you.
So jump out I do but rock bottom I've found. "Bound to hell."
Well that's my "cue," the time is now, the end so sweet.
The taste of blood, the death of me. The dig down six more feet.
The next might work, I'm just a rebirth of evil - the evil I am.
"These voices bring me back."

Back to human, the master I am. To see the God of the forsaken few.
I've forsaken you, with lost souls I hate. "Yes I do."
I see no God - God I know I must go far but the world is against me.
It hates me, so all to fall in my eyes so pure. What a blur, I killed her.
Mind and soul, so I do feel true pain. On and on and on again.
I see so many truths and lies; why do I see these things?
These voices bring me back to feel the hate - I've forsaken all and me.
Forgive the things to be, I fear so many things; see I need to be with her.
Please don't take her away! God I say I need some heart.
These voices bring me back, back apart from the truth.
The truth that which you gave to me on that day.
The lie you spoke and the heart you took away.

The day that I said no more, the cure of me and my sickness that I call life.
And all I need to do, is give you a reason to think something else.
And all I'll have in the end is what I had at the start. "Nothing."
And nothing I am, "oh well!" That's my fate and I feel it calling.
Coming for the reason and being of my way. I say, "Take it!"
And leave me be to Rock the lives of so many people.
And move on is all that's left to be, see - I have no way.
Running lost every day; saying so many things.
Things that bring them back to me and they bring me back to hell.
With the fall, I give away my life to the voices, the land of hand and head.
The toys and games, the playing and showing of my childhood.
"The all is to be." These voices bring me back to my purgatory.
My land, stuck here within my mind. Sorry! Grounded to all but all I see.
I have nothing and nothing has me and I'd like to keep it this way.

Six Feet Under I Wait For Death

Step into a land of *Nowhere* to see. I have nothing and nothing has me.
So I see within me, I do feel, I have killed. "Yet I've killed only me."
Blood in the sky as my pain rains onto her.
The ground moves from under me. So I fall six more feet.
Under the earth I sleep, waiting for my demons to creep.
With teeth like fire, it burns through my flesh.
I cry out blood, I bleed like sin and I scream! Only six feet from life.
So I scream to the moonless night. I feel my soul, the source I've lost.
I feel so alone, into the ground. So I dig deeper and hope never to be found.
I am lost in an endless hive of hallways, "what a maze."
Doors to somewhere, nowhere, everywhere.
So I wait, running in place, I can't see.
I'm running in my mind, so six more feet.
Death is only the start. I feel the light fall apart.

I feel so sick, this is it! I see the devil cry, I feel so alive, yet I'm dead.
I cannot weep, so I sleep all my fears away.
I try to forget myself. I do fall deeper to hell.
It's so good to know, that no one knows me.
It's fate, call it destiny, call it shit! "I'm not shit!"
So I sit here and think, forever I wait for death, yet I'm dead.
Meant to cry, I can't weep. I'm so alone in this world, I have nothing.
No friends, no family of my own, the one I love has been untrue.
"They must think I'm blind."
They're nothing! "or is it just me?"

So I step away, sorry to all.
I'll let go and forever fall, asleep I see the voices.
They are back. I can't feel a thing! I love the love of going insane.
So up I dig, harder and faster. The light is gone, the love is dead.
The pain is here, the end is near. The song was sung, the world is done.
"With me."
I wait in purgatory, so I sleep and six more feet I fall a day.
"Funny that I love the love of going insane."
Forever I wait for nothing...

And on I wait.

Crawling Madness

Like 100 bricks falling, my eyes seem to close.
The darkness comes for me. "So to God please help me."
As I fall 1,000 harder into sadness.
Forgive my madness, crawling in our souls.
A cold heart, a life of death, a hopeless act and the crawling death.

"Spin in joyful mindless hate, within a pit - monsters, snakes...
So to mother, I am sorry. To my brother, forgive me.
To my sisters, I'm the saddest. Forgive my sadness, in crawling madness."

The sea of falling, with legless crawling.
Forgive my sadness, forever that's it.
See my sorrow as I wish for tomorrow.
"The king of something," the God of nothing.
A child in pain, love so insane.
The burning of my flesh, a heartless chest.
The God of forgiven, the man within sin, my life is broken.
So here I soak in, tears of sadness. In my crawling madness.
"Oh, God, that's it!"
With voices in my mind, I am soon to find the light in dark.
So I got this, the demon must - an angel's lust.
My soul of sorrow, "yes, you know."
With God in hand, the devil I fight, the blood in night. *The Knight I am.*

Lost I am in your soul, so I am him.
I have the tool, to the moonless night, the forever fight.
Of a child in me, the seed is this, the world is gone.
So to my father, I am sorry but you were wrong, "I must fall."
Onto night, I see the sand pour out of my eyes and the Gods do cry.
The demon dies, our life does break, and soon I'll awake in my life.
I see no light and I must cry, but "I will not please you all."
Never to you, to my friends I am nothing.
Soon to kill them all and make me something!

To my one true love, *"Always & Forever."*
So to all, never - never I die. You won't cry - not for me, just for him.
I'm not loved, I'm just a sin.
To the world, forgive my sadness, I am the saddest.
"In crawling madness."
A forsaken child am I not? The nothing I've got in my hands.
The fire of hell, within this man, the power is lost to my feet in midair,

The fall to crawl into despair; the truth is there, my family is dead.
My love and friends are gone. I wish I could stop, stop this song.
The air is bad, I've gone mad, the forever madness, "Oh God that's it!"
It took sometime but now I'm found.
It's over and I see crawling inside of nothing but me.
I hate my life I had made for me! I hate it all, crawling in me.
The madness! I love the madness.
Forgive my sadness, in lost madness.
"God!" Into a soul of insanity and pain.
Crawling, singing to a world so insane.
Sane I am not, so soon to scream, to a friend, "I love her and me."
Crawling indeed, to see nothing but me.

So to mother I am sorry, to my brother, forgive me.
To my sisters, I'm the saddest; forgive my sadness in crawling madness.
Of our souls so cold yet sweet - Sorry.

"It's Just Insanity Mom"

"It has fallen onto me again, this life of sin.
It shall hurt at first but soon I'll win, I take control of this life within."

And the pain does rise up into the air so I kill the light in wind.
So it's time to say, the blood shall rain.
In my heart but soon to crack, I'm broke like that and I love it.
Like liquid fire onto heavenly snow.
The knight does scream to God, forgiveness we wish.
Yet again, I pissed it away, I say, "I hate it."
Onto vast lands of hell, I drop to my knees and see.
I have nothing but me, stuck in this sinking boat with my enemy, "I hate me."

I try to understand these things, I try to see.
I hate everything because I hate me.
And my life seems to get shorter, the light it burns out.
The pain is again the reason of my living.
The lie I call my life, because I am a freak to them and her.
Insanity in my mind and the pain in those Eyes.
Left broken and alone since I was a child, the dark-clouds grow in my dreams.
I seem to hate it all, "I do." Sorry mom "am I killing you;"

The world and she be dead to me.
In a sea of nothing but my mind, I find it's dead.
The days have passed in hellish past.
I see no love; I love no love but the one.
She pisses me off, I try to rise but fall again.
I hate this world, "world of sin."
But still I walk alone, in death filled dreams.
Shooting at bottles, I see something -"me."
With faces all around, I am bound to kill it all.
Over and over again I fight myself.
But no one cares, I feel no air.
In nothing I creep, in hate filled dreams.
I see only hells light.

I'm sorry to say, I give my soul away.
Freely it's my loves to keep. I ask her to be nice.
I hold her tight, I look into her eyes.
"But don't worry your little head off mom."
It's okay, so what if I die.
I feel death every day; "as if you would cry!" I think not.
Sorry to all but the world is dead; my life is gone, lost in head.

I'm running in sand up to my neck, six more feet.
I see my death in my hands.
I fall apart, in a *Nowhere* land.
The icy frost covers my heart, this is all I have.
It's mine to crush. Not yours to break.
The time has come, I ask if I'm too late.
The world is lost; the end so soon, the night is noon.
The fight in mind, "is it time?"
To kill it all, the world I call, to kill my soul.
I see the devil in the Gods of me?
But don't worry - "it's just insanity mom."

"See?"

And Only Death Will Show

It was the child, I was a man. I killed demons but now I am.
The glass did break, the pit of snakes.
The call to hate because the endless time.
The pain filled mind, the mind is mine.
The roads I've walked in times of pain.
The world is lost so insane, "the pain is you."
The memories in my dreams.
They seem to bring be back to the darkness.
The light fades away, the world is mine to...
"Great burns the fire!" My childhood love.
She hurt me, but nothing I've done.
So cry and whine as I do, bitching about my loss.
I get nothing from you.

Only pity and rejection; you're so confusing my mind.
With the demons, the angel is me.
The evil is all, the fall is grand. My dream of being human.
And I have nothing more to hold.
The sands of time cover me like a sheet of paper so thick.
"Oh God, this is it!"
So a twist of fate brought me to see the hate in you.
"The world so..." you cannot be.
No, not with me, you're just a monster of hate.
And how could this ever be?
No! I do see the wall of the mind is mine.
It's my soul and heart. I am so far apart from the truth.

I know you, and I'm shit. So this is all - all is my reason to be.
To see only hate, to feel only cold.
The tears I've given to her mean shit now today.
How was I then? I'm now just so confused.
The soon end of life, the knife is her, damn me.
So I cry and try to see, I hate all, because all hates me.
And now it shows, to the crawling madness in my soul.
The soul is mine, the time is mine. The way is - I would say "Wrong."

The song I sing of life, my life is shit, so now this is it.
The call to God, to see some path.
The path was fucked; I hear it every day.
Sorry but I pissed it away. So I say - "forsake it."
And move on to see I'll have nothing if I don't have me;

So on and on I move to see something and none.
The sun will not shine in this mind because I hate it.
And so it shuts off and down, down to the ground.
The seeping clowns are dead and fun is dead; God my soul is lost.
Because of the cost and curse, that is what I've given to myself.
I have no way and the day is almost over.
The heavenly soldier is calling me.
The fight is inside, and now it's time.
Because all I've ever said and done was the truth.
I killed her and do hate you.
Because of my ways, the days have passed in hellish past.
"And I am dead."

So I lied, I am alive, my - my soul is gone.
It's time but not to end this song, "no, I'll move on and on."
Over time and time because I'm not lying, but it shows.
Truth is all, the death of me.
I show to you - I kill me and the seed of all is dead...

"I am dead."

Chapter 4

Deep in the Knight

Now Time to Kill
It's Time Again - So sin I do.

Ghosts of the calling, legless you're crawling away from me.
Consideration with a dedication to the awe.
Still I wish I could live again, without sin.
I'm dead again, so call to hell I do, I am nothing without you.
Grim is the seeing of myself and beating my head today.
Creeping and crawling, you're so much about killing me.
So joyful is the ripping of my flesh and decay of my bones, with the murder of angels.
The call to the slipping and gripping; blood filled eyes of the dead.
I'm not a zombie, but I'm still the dead-walking and killing you, "yes I do."
So now the turning wood, the killing would, the cat could but not for me.
Sorry, I'm not doomed - as are you. I'm just dead, to the world in my head.
It's time again, to see the world through my eyes.
The blood is flooding my mind, crying and dying are your ways.
"Are they trying to give you away?"
So just run from your fears and hide, time will catch-up with you soon.
Slow murder of the nothing but us.
Must I grow and regress? Why did I piss away my life?
Now nothing on my side and only voices inside.
I so need to awake from this pain, I feel so, so unsane - break me!
Dark mother open my skin. Time to kill, it's time again.
The twist of the broken world is so used.
I use the power that was given to me, I need only help.
Your death drops into my mouth. I taste the decaying death of you.
The constriction of the world will bring me to hell.
"Well," that's my fate. I hate this world of blood.
The blood running down my face, my neck twists and breaks.
The hair turns and rips, the skin - the sin - the nothing I am.
Open the door - jump to hell - swim to the abyss! "I know that this is not it."
The cross I'm nailed to, next to the son of God.
Did I to ask for forgiveness? Sorry I killed and sinned.
Begin the decay of my body, I ask this of you my Lord.
"You may forgive me, but I do not."
Ghosts of the calling, bring me to life.
The light is gone yet I still see nothing but pain.
Only insane, human is not what I am, human is what I'm not.
Now we see, set down the fire and let me free!
Open body next to hell, look to God and fall deeper to hell because of her.
It's time to kill, it's time again - so sin I do.

It Hurts

Questions have been asked, bringing back the past and it hurts.
The roaring flames in my mind burning through my eyes and the pain must be heard.
"I must be heard." It hurts - as I hold her in my arms so tight.
I wish I could hold her all night. "And it hurts inside."
The pain of my life, into her eyes I stare - walking lost, "somewhere..."
Into heaven or hell I do fall for you.
It hurts to think you don't love me true but still I love you? "Yes I do."
So always onto the roads I walk insane, to the cloud I crawl for the pain of loss.
I'm so lost and alone, but the reasons I ask these things I don't know.
But when I'm with you, I wish for more, so much more.
Yet I'm stuck with nothing. Am I nothing to her?
Does she love me too? Who am I to ask these things? Who am I to you?
Am I your love so true? - Am I? - Are you?
It hurts so dear. Wishing for an endless nothing, "I do."
It hurts when I'm not with you. God it hurts! I feel I'm gonna burst.
With hate and love - love and hate - I feel no love, only will I see...
I hate this world! "It hurts me." And why does she drive me insane?
She kills my heart, tearing me apart again.
Into ash and dust, dirt is I... *I kill all love and it hurts inside.*
The world is running lost indeed. I am running lost so deep.
Deep is the pit, deep is our minds, it hurts when I'm not at your side.
I'm jumping off the ledge to my death.
Wishing, dreaming, thinking, what we could have had. "And it hurts."
To God I call but I get no reply, to God I'll call till I die, asking for forgiveness.
To God I pray, "Sorry if I hurt you."
You were my friend, now I most likely lost everything.
When we held each other and kissed I felt so sane.
But now I'm losing, "everything!"
Losing and crawling, crying in every way.
"I'm lost in these endless fields of pain. Lost is alone am I?"
I'm trying to see; within my childhood-self is the love in me.
So to the all of the world and my pain. I've felt only hurt in my life.
In a mind so sweet, sweet is my love for her. "And I hurt inside."
The world is so lost in my mind or the other way around.
Crying, find me dead in the back room. It hurts, Oh the pain!
The questions have been brought back to me, "*she is crying seas of tears.*"
The fears are coming out in a pain so lost, the pain is my loss.
"And it hurts - it hurts." I the king of pain and loss.
I hurt because I know nothing else. I know only pain and it hurts.

Pain of Lust

As been onto hateful death, I feel my chest caving in.
I still love her, *my life of sin.* Sorry but I can't tell you everything I do.
As if I were, it would kill you and I the child bleeds.
I'm in love with an angel so sweet.
Yet a demon calls out to me. I do feel the fiery-death.
I feel it in my hand, still I'm found, I'm a man.
The man who sees his new death to be.

I fear the next in me; I've sold my soul to the devil.
My heart and mind I give to God. "This is what I've fought."
Slowly I fall and fall; I hit and crawl, screaming out to him and me.
The two of me, I fear and love the inner us. *I see an angel with demon wings.*
It sings to a soul so cold and I've never wept over my loss, "or have I?"
I love this evil angel. I am a man and I do love the evil in our soul.
But the angel cries and my soul dies, or is it the other way around.

I found I am done, I've sung a song to her and she lives on in my mind.
I do find no other way, I can't win - this heart and sanity; "anarchy is I."
I see hate in me, I feel Nothing but drip it into a glass of wine, I find I love her.
I the child and I the man. Within this hand lies life and death.
I give her my last breath but she laughs at me. I feel her lust behind me.
I feel voices near; I feel the monster creep into my spine.

I love the fact that I'm not the one - nor number two, I do feel...
"Time to kill." Or I feel purgatory is my fate.
I love the girl, my new knife. My pain, "me insane."
Yet lust is lost to me, feel and love the burnt black dove.
I do feel, "she untrue." Yet I love you, so razor onto me.
See - I do, you do hate me. See "I'm fucking crazy!"
Yet I'll be with you till the end, I feel my heart, a heart of sin.
I can't hate you because I am so much worse, do you see? "*I hate me.*"
You say you love me, "so I say okay," I love you too.
So I'll laugh as I give my last breath to you.

No More For All

I can't - no more! As I run in, jump - fall - let out my arms.
Twist turn and hit the floor. I look to the sky and know what I've done.
I've sung this before, "and no more."
So screaming, playing and lots of toys, my childhood; "*myself as a boy...*"
These days have passed in hellish past and I know you don't care.
I'm just talking to air, but it was always there for me.
No matter who I am, it held me.
My love is no more, not for you, "sorry but I kill you."
You're dead to me, just shit - that's it.
No more for you and all, so I wish you to fall.
I hate you because of what you did to me.
I hate you because you hate me. *So all will fall, I know it to be.*
I know I hate you. So know you hate me.
You were never - always talking shit to me.
You're nothing to me, sorry but it's over.
It's over to me, "I so need to watch you die." So cry to me as if I cared.
Your blood I'd taste but I won't kill you yet you fucking disgrace!
Consider the fact that you left me, confusing all these Goddamn things.
You're losing me in this endless hive, "sorry but I care even less."
I don't want you to cry, I just want you to die!
Die because you made me dead... "I'm dead to you."
No, I'm not a child - yes I hate you! I want you to scream and bleed so much.
"The death is mine to give."
The sin of my old love, the time has come. Sorry but no "*no more for all.*"
You are my pain in the world, *the world* - the sin is you.
I know I hate you, I see all the truths. *The truth is all, all I have is none.*
"*No I don't.*" I won't understand you, I know I - no way! "You hate me."
I know - no more for you, everything you do to me, see so much...
Because I hate it all "yes I do." And no more, no more for all.
All is lost to me, seeing nothing but fear in me, that's all I see.
The seed of confusion in death filled dreams, it seems I'm lost, God I'm lost, so lost.
So cutting the - stabbing the - eating the flesh of a loved one.
I've sung this before and no more for all.
Seeing the call to the dead, seeing the dead so clear; I fear only me!
I hate all of you, "*yes I do.*" *I do see none but you; I'll kill all of you till I die.*
I will die every day, fell so insane. With blood so warm, the fire is you.
The pain is all - kill and fall, no more for all. All I do is hate all of you.
Seeing demons and voices so - no, no more for all - fall, I wish to do!
So till the end I'll kill, I kill all of you... *All is lost.*

Inside Grounded Lost

Grounded to the bottom of the sea, I know within me and inside I know nothing.
The knowledge of reborn and the storm in night.
I feel the fight inside my dream. I seem to know everything of nothing.
I'm moved by an angel, in a dark town - "*Nothing.*"
I do believe in something, "as if I could win within my sin."
I know I'm a man of God, yet the devil too. *I'm just a man, inside lost-you.*
Grounded to nothing but sugar sweet love. Inside lost-me.
In death-no dreams, the knife into my back.
The ghost cries and laughs - the spirit of us... "*And it must fall.*"
Yet me to crawl onto... And fall and laugh it all...
The pain of lust must be lost to me, *inside grounded lost and I scream!*
As the blood oozes onto the ground of God, the light burns out.
And so I am lost, I do know the show is now, the fight is now.
The fight is NOW! I jump into the sky so high and the... "I love her!"
All I can think, I sink to the ground, I look up at God, *then let out the air.*
The road is broke and I see the ice on my hands.
I am the man, "lock us in, I could sin." I hate this world, I could feel no love.
Yet the sun, it must cry like the child in pain.
The life so insane and I do love her!
The angels weep as I sleep. The demon-dog barks at the moon.
Soon I'll rise in dark, I fear only me.
I must see something or I'll have nothing; *I am nothing or just lost in me!*
I do have nothing but love for her.
The power is lost but I'll find the light again.
I have sinned but not again, never more.
I do love you; the air is rising into me. The air is falling!
Inside grounded lost, must I die to prove myself to you?
My dear Angel, I do love you and only for the time alone will it show.
I hate me and insanity so into EuQiNu and unique is me.
Or I'm to see purgatory is to be, I love you and me.
Grounded lost in me and I love you so deep.
As my soul seeps into a mind so cold, the pain is calling me.
The seed of evil is growing large; so far I am, inside grounded lost must I cry?
I cannot cry, only die, "sorry."
As waiting for nothing but her, I see God and the devil.
My own reflection kills my heart.
So still I fall apart because I'm inside grounded lost.
Sorry but I'll take it, whatever the cost.

This World is Lost

This world is lost, "*to me.*" I can only see the pain, I'll live this lie again.

So I stand alone, *I have love for no one, "this I show. I feel in this life only pain.*

Sorry I did it again. I'll crush this world, a world within.

"*WHY DO I HATE?*" My life of going insane, "tonight," lost within.

I fight no more, no more, NO!

This world is lost, "*to me,*" I stand alone so free.

Lost in deep, "*I see,*" it's done - it won...

So I sung, "*to her,*" but she never understands my pain.

I've lost this world again.

Forever sleep, "I creep," onto dreams so sweet.

This world is lost to me, "to me." Why can't she see, I fear only me.

"I see," runaway - run away - run - done - gone.

So I've sung this life to all, sing it till I fall "again!"

This world is lost, "this world within..." So crush my heart, you do.

I am lost inside of you, "the pain is YOU!" The light I've got.

It's hellish loss of the world so...

System loss, the cost is grand. To kill a man is wrong?

So why am I dead? This world is lost, alone I am.

Into the crawling of the damned.

Running into life so dead, this world is lost, this world is dead - alone I am.

I'm just a child, a man or demon of all.

The fall was great - to this world of hate because I am a little strange.

I sing in this weird way – I just tell it how it is.

I'm hated every day by the world of all.

The light I call, to the night I fight, "I must win."

I kill this world, "a world within."

Sin of lust must die; all must crumble and find a way to heal.

It's killing my heart because I must die or all is lost. Inside of you, inside of me.

Killing all, to watch them fall because of, "you."

Lost is all, lost is you, lost is this world.

Running, screaming; dreaming of the past! Wishing God on Angel's lust.

Within the demon, "God." What have they done?

It's screaming loud through the cloud, the world does cry.

This world should die - the pain is all, so soon is noon.

The endless moon or soon to see. Lost is this world, it's lost to me.

Found is the memory of all or to fall to the endless night.

Trying to fight myself, trying to kill the world of what I've seen.

The seeing of the dead tormented is my soul - cold endless nothing is my heart.

A come together is my wish but all the world did was piss me away.

"*I hate it all.*" Lost is this world, lost is all. The end so soon, so - so soon.

<u>*I Hate You All*</u>

Upon the tree - a sea of death, *hold your breath as you die*, angels cry.
Have you ever once taken the time to look inside to see what's around you?
Angels die, as I cry, trying to live, seen the sin, "I hate you all."
You will fall, all to death inside my chest, *your last breath and you're dead.*
In my head you will see, enter voices... Death filled dreams.
"It seems to be only me and my love."

You're all mud, blood of you, "cry so soon?"
And I hate you all, fall to death.
Feel my chest caving in, a life of sin, let it begin or it all ends!
"See my sin?" It all ends inside my mind!
Find me now, how shall you die? I let you cry.
Because I hate you all, *Eye will twitch*! I am pissed, crying dust.
"Must it be only me and my love?"

I plan to kill, feel me now, how will I survive this?
You're all shit! Death to me! Do you see?
You all hate me, cry upon a seed...
You hate me for nothing, do you see?
YOU ARE NOTHING..!
And still I walk in the path of carnage and hate filled minds.
"I hate you all."

All my time I give, to love hating you and should you see.
I hate you because you hate me.
So why do you act like you don't understand?
I'll kill all that stands in my way.
I say I hate it, "I do!" Hey do you know what?
"I hate you too," so wish me dead.
And wish me gone, kill you all - I kill the sun and move on in life.
I pull the knife out from my back.
I turn my head and laugh at the way you try to beat me.
I'll always win. So I move on - on with sin and "I hate you all."

Death is Open

Death is but a door and life is but a hall.
You walk in every day and fear you're gonna fall.
Into dreams I crawl, "with eyeless sight." Enter her mind and find I'm dead.
Or her soul in ice so cold, the water is rising, "no point in fighting."
In depth with my death, "I see no God."
But with a single thought I say naught, the finger to him and leave my sin.
"It's now or never!" To live forever in hell or heaven, earth is lost, cold in frost.
I love my death, so I open it to you.

Up tight is our father, "the one to save," *my soul is gone, so I live this song.*
After day after day, I spill the blood onto the heaven's ground, *"it's dead."*
The grounded dead with open death within my love.
So to her my life is gone, so I see... I fear nothing but me!
I see death in us, so I fear my heart, it's growing inside.
The ball shall grow, the pain I've shown, *in my soul so lost, the frost in me.*
"So cold inside," I fear it crawling in me, "I see death!"
So I open it to her... And on angel wings I sing to myself.
"In a ball of pain we go insane," to myself I am dead.

To God I wish me dead, or just gone.
Lost in the land of Nod, just my mind lost in the sands of time.
I sink to see my childhood has me late.
Blood and dust of man, the sin is again my life.
So the light is my knife, a heart of dust.
The goal is lost, into the pit so far - crawling in a mind so far.
I find the way to live, only there's no life left in me, so God I kill, kill it all.
So the spinning reaction of lost child in head.
Spit up blood, dust in us, the pain I open to all.
"I'm soon to crawl," but I'm not done, I'm not finished!
The light is gone, so to all I crawl and fall.

Into the pit so sweet, with demons in mind I won't find.
The thing I seek - the child in me.
Or to all in... do you feel the sin or just all of me?
Voices in mind, "the door - it's dead." The cut, burn and feast of flesh.
The God is dead, my mind so full of pain and lust of child thoughts.
The rising of him into my hand, the tool I hold - the gift I control *"or not."*
I don't care about the world I've fought, the war I win.
The control all sin or your love so true. *Death is open, "I open it to you..."*
So through endless halls I walk, in a mind so lost - I have nothing but you.
So now it's open, open for you....

Under My Skin

You fight about the littlest of things; all I do is drive you insane.
Eating and ripping away, tearing at my brain, you get under my skin.
All I do is confuse by doing nothing at all.
All I do is hate it all, "I wish to fall and die."
But it's not that time; it's only time to scream!
Seeming to never end, "I wish it would." It could but no - *all I know...*
So to stop - stop it all, these voices keep me going.
On I move to this hell.

Well that's my life, that's my knife. I've seen no God and I feel no devil.
The world is trouble, so all I need is trust, must I be alone? "*I hope not.*"
But I will not give it up, I won't shut up, "*and I'll try to win.*"
"Oh God, why do you get under my skin - seeming to never end?"
I walk so alone, alone in a mind so lost.
Darkness of the world is crushing onto me.
Well that's my life, so I give you my knife.
I hope to end this life. "Well, not that much."
Such a hard day it will be when I do.
I will see the dark shadow called love, am I done, "No!"

On I go to let it fall; the nerves do crack into a numb heart.
I feel I have no hope, "God give me some heart," so I can move on.
I must not give up so soon. Soon it will be, to see some God.
But I feel the devil is on my track.
Standing behind my back, so I'll never return, "*well, try not to.*"
Under my skin you are - truth is shown - bring out the unknown.
"I see all." You will fall, "you're dead." As walking more every day.
I see the light that you're insane. Unsane to think that I'm that dumb.
"Because of what you said and what you've done."
I've shown the light onto you, "you lost," I'm done - it's over!

Under my skin no more, we fight so insane; it hurts.
I hurt, the never is our forever-ever and I won't go on.
I'm calling to, show no new... Screaming dead, losing our heads.
I fall through you, horror and pain, lust so insane; forgotten am I?
Darkness I've tried! The lost so sweet, the calling of the beast.
Enemies I kill, still I show no way, I say - I am alone.
Because of you, alone in my mind, calling it to show the light so true.
"Under my skin I find you."

This World Is All To See
<u>And I See You Are Nothing</u>

Why do I have so many names?
Voices and faces eating at my brain!
Sources and uncalled dreams.
It seems I'm dead, "or am I?"

Well, the dream does seem to have so many demons.
And all I have is you, so on I go without a breath.
My chest caves in, so sin I do, on in life without you.
Honestly, I didn't know what to do if I lost you, "*but I did.*"

I have nothing but a twisting fate, on the ground so pure.
In a snake's eyes lies the truth of my universe and tool.
The carnage and slaughter of the little children in the house.
Why! Why do I see these things?
So on I move in a hellish path.

On my way more, more I wish to leave, *"God what is happening to me?!"*
As if you would care, where are you going?! "No, don't run from me!"
I don't run from you, I thought you were my friend? "And now I sin."
On into a world of hate, in a soul so cold and lost, "I don't care!"

No, not about you! You don't care about me.
Dead and decaying, "I am gone."
My ways are lost and forgot, I did move on and on and more.
I wish I could feel some light, but I fight my heart and soul.
It's hard to win when your enemy is yourself, "God!"

So no self-pity I give to me.
I move on, so move away from me.
Get away, I don't care. I wish it in darkness and hate.
I move on with my life because I fear all to be, "I see."
So must I say to the all inside of me?

"God forgive me..."

Why Are You Crying My Love?

Creeping slowly, the door opens and reveals her with her hands on her face.
She's crying slow, trying not but it shows. Why is she crying? "I don't know."
She sounds so alone, she's lost and alone; that is what she's shown.

Like a million bricks falling, she won't stop sobbing.
Did I say or do something wrong? She's lost, grabbing her head.
Tossing and turning, she acts like I'm not there.
I try to speak but only air. I want to hold her but I might hurt her more.
I try to ask her why, watching her makes me want to... "Why?!"
Is she crying because of me? Oh please say something, why can't I see?
Why is she crying, because of me?
It's my fault right? Was it a fight? What did I say?
Please stop crying, it's driving me insane.

As I sit next to her, she lies down to sleep. Why - is she mad at me?
She's sobbing and dreaming, so I sit next to her.
"Always & forever," is what she whispered in her sleep.
She told me goodbye and farewell, she said she'll miss me...
"What did she mean, *farewell?*" I'm not going anywhere, I'm right here.
I'm right by her side, what did she mean goodbye?
She's crying more in her sleep, what did I miss?
I glance back at the door closed tight.
"But I left it open, I opened it wide."
No my love don't cry, here I am, I'll hold you tight.
The closer I got the colder she became, oh God my love, oh my fear.
As I moved closer, she opened her eyes to see me.
So I whispered softly to her...
"That's not it, it's not over yet, goodbye is not forever."
"I will always love you." "You are free now, I free you my love."

She asked if she was dreaming - I said yes.
I kissed her goodnight, said I'll always hold her tight.
She looked at me, she was so happy; I looked at her and said.
"Good night." She stopped me but before she could speak.
I placed a finger over her lips and said.
"Why are you crying me love? I'm only dead."

Good night...

The Knight I Am

I fight it in my mind; I'll fight to death every time... Lost in fields of pain.
Hurt this world in my dreams. It seems I have no light, in darkness I fight.
Over time and time, it is my life, to win or to die but by the sword I live.
Within sin the world does fall, sorry. I'd fall but I must win...
In the darkness I fight. The moonless night, the blood so warm, on the ground.
"It's sweet;" to see death so fun. "It's my mind." I'm not done.
I run in and hit, the skull does crack, I laugh at last.
With blood in eyes I see it's time - the war I win but battle after battle I lose.
The light I crush, "am I confused?" Should I save our queen or watch her die?
Should I risk it all, should I waste my time? The land is lost, the land is mine.
Forget my soul, lose my mind. With flesh dropped onto the sand.
The demons feast upon the body of this man; I kill it again. "The knight I am."
With no love - just blood, I've said kill them all, leave the dead.
I must kill the world I hate - to God I say, "Please help me," no light I see.
Only fire in death, so my heart is gone, the day turns to night, forever I fight.
Creep in night, the devil I see in my eyes so sweet, watch them die, "I laugh."
The pain is theirs at last and so I fight, no one on my side, "God I cry!"
Only in dreams, to be - it is dead. Onto the land so sweet, the blood is nice, the war in me.
So to the God of us, in this light I am the knight; lost again.

So into the pit I fall...

After the fight, no one crawls, I must win, so always sin, the demon I am.
To the land in which I die, sorry to all, sorry... "I fight!"
So is it not the king I seek or is it the true end? I must fight, I fight all sin.
The world is in my hands, the knight I am... "So I fight evil with evil."
Fire to fire - hell in me - seed of nothing I am. Armor of flesh, cut it again.
"Laugh and love," scream and die. Kill our king and watch the angels cry.
So life is only to live, in my heart so blue. True, I am a knight.
Fight in night, for this world so sad. "Am I mad?" Or just done.
Finished with the world of sin. "I try to die," but I live again.
Just the darkness of my soul to guide my way, I jump and fall.
I give it away, so I see God in me, Devil in you; so now I choose the path.
Of hell and love in my Eyes. So fight my ways, cry and try till I end this day.
With love so true, only God will know.
I show no love, only hate, myself I kill but always I live, the war I win.
So I kill you all, I kill all sin, the world is in my hands.

"The knight I am."

Shouldn't Have Said That
So Cut Out My Tongue...

Over me... do I - I should see? "Saying things that make no sense."
Crying hard, yes I do see. I look in her eyes and feel so sorry.
"But that doesn't change a thing." With faces turned, I feel like crying.
I hope to God that our loves is not dying.
"Should I have told her the truth from the start that my games will tear us apart?"
Mazes of riddles have brought me down, "I feel like shit."
Just a heartless clown, my love I hope you forgive me.
It's been hard times, "because of me."
Sorry, I should have told you but now you want me to die.
Sorry my love, I don't want you to cry.
So I should just shut up, keep my jaw closed.
I didn't mean to hurt you but I did. The past is back and I'm just a sin.
"Teardrops hit this paper because I lied only to see if you would love me."
I said things, you got pissed! So lost are you?
I'm just so sorry, so I give my tongue to you.
When I joke and play, it drives you insane.
So I quit for you, I will not breath without you.
"I will not speak without your consent." I fucked up, I'm just shit.
I don't know what to say, so I stay quiet - quietly insane.
I shouldn't have said that to her. "I'M SORRY!"
So I kill myself for you, now with blood running like a waterfall onto the floor.
I give you my tongue, I'll speak no more. I meant good but messed up.
I know shit - shit I am. I'll let you decide what to do.
I'll let you think it over but remember, "I love you."
But you probably don't believe me and I don't blame you.
Blind is I - I see only you...
Hate myself more I do, because I fucked everything up for you.
"I didn't mean to hurt you too." Should I have said that?
Damn it, I ruined it for you! I'm sorry I love you.
I need you, I must have you. Please, please forgive me, I'm sorry.
I shouldn't have spoken and never will I.
I spill blood for you; I know you don't believe me when I say I love you.
I need you but you said you didn't believe me.
So I quit for you, I cut my tongue out for you.
"I know you don't love me, so I give my life to you. Forgive me but I do love you."
So I stop writing this to you. I speak naught to you.
I'm sorry but I have to say one last thing.
Before I go, there's one thing left. "I love you..."
I shouldn't have said that so I cut out my tongue - *Sorry.*

That Hurt.

It's funny how when all I do is try but in the end, I still cry.
No matter how much blood I shed.
No matter if I'm alive or dead, you'll hate me the same.
I'm the same either way around, I've found, "it's over."
I was right, I fight the world and now, "you too."
Another slap in my face, thank you for hating me.

No! I'm sorry for loving you.
I was right; the truth would bring hell, "well?" Sorry!
Questions to myself, on should I leave or stay.
No, I stopped running from you. You the world I hate true.
So what if you "THINK!" you saw what you saw, but no!

You still ran and hit and hit and hit me.
So now I'm pissed, I'll let you decide where we go from here.
Because I don't give a shit! I love you but that was it!
All we have is shit, "think about it!"
I don't care about anything right now!
How could you say you love me, when all we do is fight?
I loved you, but you treated me like shit!
"No, fuck it!" I don't care anymore.
I don't care if you think something's wrong. "It's not!!!"
But just know that, "that hurt" a lot.
I loved you and that's all I've got?

"I love you too..."

Inner Death Show

Step to step - foot to foot, the light is dim, the show of sin "so I speak."
Seek out all and fall to hell the world does, but who am I to try and help?
To help the world, I seek voices and demons.
Call out to me, in dream or streams of blood.
I walk in and feel so loved yet hate is all I get from the world for yes war is my life.
"Just sit back and enjoy the show."
I'll let it go, welcome - to the Inner Death Show.
On dark roads with blood red skies.
With red moon light, I move in to fight.
Fight the world, feel and kill and I steal the devil's thoughts.
So I stalk my dreams, it seems grand.
To kill a man, even if it's me. To watch you fall - I seep it all.
Inner Death Show is me. Inner death Show is we...
"Don't forget to tune in next week."

I Am Nothing - Like You Said

"It's true... You learn something new every day; I found a new way to go insane."
I know now that I am nothing, like you said.
So here I am, blood in hand and a new reason.
An evil pointless mind, endless times I've wished to die.
I scream out loud, in the cloud I hear God.
He tells me to die, he takes away my time. "I'm nothing."
Dastardly deeds I give to God, giving away myself.
It's true - there is a new way to be, "see?"
I have no light, all I do is fight. Fighting time - *the time I don't have.*
Lost inside, in quick endless lives. "I'm nothing."
Like you said, I wish I were dead but soon I will be.
Inside I hide to give away my pain, to show you, "who?" *It's over...*
On I go with no sense, on I move and it is nonsense!
Told I'm nothing by the one I love, so I die forever inside.
Given no way, shown no light, so here I fight. "Are you happy?"
I hope to understand because you never will, still I wait to see.
And I know you don't love me. "Encouragement" I've had none...
So sung to you all day but here I am, still insane, are you happy?!
"I'm nothing!" So move on I do, to prove to you that I'm something.
I am something, "nothing!" I'm just shit! So I quit, all of it, it's over. "Are you happy?"
I give up my life because that's what you want.
So I give it away and go insane, "I love it."
I am dumb but I still know what you said and what you do.
"It's over."

I'm The Bad Guy Again

So here I sit and wish for life.
Endless knives I find in my back.
Cast out by the world.
I've lost good friends, over and over again.
I'm so alone; I try to seek but must be blind.
I seek the world, I'm so small, "I'm but a blur."
Just a freak, beating my head.
So I'm the bad guy again.

Out of control, they stole my life.
I lost the fight, "I'm dead."
God I'm so numb, I am dumb, "God I'm dead."
Dead inside, dead in my mind, just alone, "am I right?"
To hate it all, "I think so."
But you don't, they don't listen!
Must I run further and deeper into hell?

Well, I'm lost, the cost so grand.
Me - a soulless man.
"I'm nothing!" just me.
Hated by all, tormented by you.
So I sit back and lose.
I choose the pit, this is it.
With nothing to love.
Well, I guess I'm bad again.
"I'm the bad guy again?"

I'm just me.

She Untrue? #2

"It" as I've once said to the walls.

I wish I could fall dead, stop running lost inside my head.

The voices are too much for me. Please God, *SOMEBODY KILL ME!*

I'm lost in my own mind. *To the one I love.* Help find the light with me.

"Please damn it help me see!"

Unlike my soul, my heart does break in two still I feel, "She untrue?"

What could I do? Feeling lost inside of you. Only my heart is lost.

Inside I try to hide but I'm found to all, I'm lost to me.

Feeling nothing but hate in me, losing track of all but them.

Finding reasons to hate the world, lost in nothing but all.

Finding time, time to fall; falling into nightmares or memories of the past.

Questions and demons bring me back.

And still she acts like there's nothing wrong.

"Must I repeat this song of reason and law?"

My road is gone, I'm lost in all. So to the nothing of my mind.

Finding angels and Gods, finding nothing but me lost.

"I'm dead to all." So running fast on hot fire glass for her.

All I do is cry blood to you. Hold my life to the vast mind of hers.

Holding the truth so tight, holding her tight - so tight.

Hitting and screaming with nothing but hate.

The hate is yours, the life is gone, I'm gone. Oh so alone am I.

On nothing but the awe of my sheet, paper doesn't lie.

Only the writer his mouth, his mind.

Untrue is the world. Untrue is my life.

Only to the endless of the forever I have no way.

Crying, seeping the things of my being.

Seeing only untruthful lies. The lie is you.

Screaming low, so slow I don't see.

Demons, voices within you or me?

Streaming tears, I'm so alone.

Pushing and shoving I see no way. Faces and faces so insane.

Untrue is the world, she confuses me. "She untrue?" Untrue to me?

Losing slowly, crying, showing, slowing is my heart.

Soon so torn apart. Forgiving her? I'm killing them.

I'm wanting more; shut the doors of my mind.

Mine is yours, our soul is lost. Screaming lost.

So on no reasons or much more, cells of my own jail; my mind is my own hell.

Locked and so cold, so lost in a maze.

I am oh so crazed and confused, "She untrue?"

Not to me, only I see the dripping and growing shadow of God;

Showing no walk way, only just rock. Must I rock my mind to let it free?
"Rock you all?" Welcome to purgatory.
I the child in pain. Is her love no more?
With faces all around I can't see. Seeping slowly I won't see.
You must tell me, but untrue is she?
And only she would know; no way will I try.
Never to all, only I die. God, will she cry?
Lost on love and I loathe them all. Wrong are my voices? So should I die?
Neither my head nor hand, questions are screaming out to me.
"She untrue?" Is she untrue to me?
Reasons to think this I have. Reasons to die I do have.
The reason I try is for her, trying and crying is she? "I must be nothing."
So onto the words I screamed.
The worlds untruthful lies. How could I forget my suicide?
To live with her is my heaven, alone is my hell.
"Crying is she now?" How will I live?
I'm losing my drive, and she untrue is all I fear.
Now with none, have I done it right? Or am I wrong?
It's not over; I'm far from done with this song of law.
The end I fear, but I feel it so near... "I'm sorry my love."

In Painful Pleasure
"With Only I?"

Over and over and never again. Upon pointless lies - lifeless sins.
So do you see, the truth in me? The way to go, "I do love you."
But you don't see, that you hate me, "yes you do."
In my mind I know you lie. I'm not the one, "no - you lie."
"In painful pleasure with only I?" Don't think so, no not me.
Don't lie, "don't fucking lie to me!"
People think I sink away, "I seep the hate."
I know I have the way, but you confuse me.
And try to make me think something more.
I'm not selfish you fucking whore.
I know you lie, flat out in my face.
Well so, am I the disgrace? "I think not."
No, you show me only wrongs and hate. I see through your fake.
Drop me not into sadness but into madness, where I wish to stay.
I feel alone, I know you lie. "In painful pleasure with only I?"
Why don't you love me?

114

<u>*Walk in Rain*</u>

Along a wide road I walk, alone I stalk my childhood and God.
Alone I walk, gone and forgot. In cold-hot blood like water, it rains onto me.
I try to see, the true me, or "God I feel nothing."
Alone I'm lost inside. I walk, run but cannot hide.
Upon faces and faces of pointless lives. Endless tries and a lonely walk.
But wind, hail and dust in mind and the rain turns to snow.
So cold in heart, sleep I must but cannot dream, "or am I now?"
Please somebody wake me. Blood red skies, a moonless night.
And the creeping shadow in my face - kill my world, "feel the hate."
The disgrace I am, so I walk again and again.
The road is turning and the light is burning-out.
The blood does pour from my mouth.
So the angel cries, I forever try, to live my sin.
The lie, my life, my point is lost and "so are you."
I'm just a child grounded in you. Only a life's breath.
So drop does my body onto the ground.
Looking to the sky, so I scream out loud, the light I see.
A tunnel in deep, yet it's hell's true glow.
I wake up and know the point I don't - won't have.
So I just laugh, the God and devil.
The angel demon of me; to kill a God is no way indeed.
So seeds of the un-forgiven have the way.
But the voices have the right, a fight of day and dusk.
The dust is rolling over me, I must stand.
"I'm still walking in me," so the light over my head.
Into a land I don't know, "still I walk," I walk alone.
Showing no one love, I see no light. It's the inner demons I fight.
The world is only a step away, I'm just a child gone insane.
The pain is dripping onto her.
The reason I sin in a world of hell and heaven, the angel's demon is calling.
Forsaken lives and pointless lies, so I try.
The God I've forgiven, but a tool in me, to crush this light.
This light of my true love, the reason to choose the road.
"I'm done." Or onto this land I seep.
Into your mind or mine, to find the clue.
I've lost the reason I walk, to find it all. "So soon I'll fall."
But only for her, so alone I am, and will always be.
In conscious I wait for day, only to the road shall it know my only fear?
To be alone, "yet I am." To see no light, but in darkness I lie.
So along the road and her, or God or the devil's angel in me.
Shining twinkling razors fall from the sky. *The blood will run from her eyes;*

In a godless mind I find the walk is growing, the pain is showing.
I must end it all, cut this wrist or lose my mind, even if I already did.
Only in dreams I find, though I don't in a land I walk.
So I will stalk our God or devil in a rain of pain.
I walk alone, forever alone - "I walk in rain."

"Swimming Lost" In Cold Blood

Swimming alone, in my own, the night is forever.
The dead is my never of seeing the Gods of the all.
Creeping in sorrow - the dream called tomorrow.
The sadness is mine, destroy all mind in a frost-lust.
So to a demon or angel of crawling within sin.
Calling to Angel, blood of my own, swimming alone.
I show no love, crying are the eyes around and over me.
Creeping into torment I see the God of the never.
Crying or forever am I lost? Cold in mine, losing all time or just lost.
Dreaming on the crying is my soul. Dreaming is my heart.
"Swimming lost in cold blood."
Only the side to side is the turning and twisting.
And I know I will win; jumping into nothing is the king and end.
The end is my soul of confusion.
My blood runs cold, harder and faster does it stream.
Seeming to stop, yet only goes faster, the sky is dead.
These skies are gone, the sung is my song.
The light is done, the end is my way; swimming lost insane.

Pain and sadness are my ways.
Godless tears do they shed, cold blood is a reason to go away.
Screaming is the dead or just the voices in my head.
Growing is my hate, constricting does the snake.
My cells are gone. Kill - dead, wrong are your ways.
In sky-dead on toy-less child cries, the fun of neglect.
That's my forever, the never is my cold.
That's my rock to the world. To my heart it's a loss.
The "all I know" is all I show. I love only my never.
No way, I know I will never have a hand to hold.
I must see, yet only I creep. Only I dream and seem to have no light.
Only I fight myself. I have no self.

No self-consideration only a dedication to an angel.
I'm dead to all. "Swimming lost in cold blood."
I do not, I must find a God. I have no grip and see no light;

"Lost?" Only I kill God, hurting and bursting hate.
Killing and killing my hate, I do see a loss.
My childhood was lost to me. Seeing no light, every day I fight.
No love only pain, reactions are late and no matter what I do or say.
You'll laugh at my pain, that's my fate.
I HAVE NO WAY TO LIVE AGAIN! I KILLED MYSELF!
I LET EVIL IN! SORRY FOR THIS SIN, I CANT TAKE IT!

I know I was right, I should have fought back.
A love and friends so untrue. Swimming lost in you.
I should kill all thoughts of the matter but the voices did so much for me.
I would but I'm not sorry.
So swimming again, lost in blood so warm yet growing cold.
Lost in sorrow and so I scream.
Seeming to call it to the never, so I scream forever and I see no God.
But maybe that's the way it should be.
So cold and lost, hurt and the point is my reason.
My life is cold, cold is my heart and you never cared.
And my rock is a world stuck between.
The seeing is my all; the system is controlling our minds.
The world is a lie, "a lie am I?" So in my own I've shown no love.
I have my own ways to hold.

My head, the tool of knowledge, lawless is my world.
So alone is a walk or jump and some do swim.
So of my own blood I drink, the blood is my way.
So insane, so to the God of the never, Nod is my home.
"Swimming lost in cold blood," so my God is a fall.
I fall to pits and dreams, seeming-less things I see.
A sane of none, this is what I've said; this is what I've done.
So great is the cost, on I dream oh so lost.

Lost.

Running Water On The Roads of Pain

What are you... commanded to?
Control my life, our burning life, it's no more to them.
It's calling me, the sea of sorrow, the dream "tomorrow."
And forsaken minds, endless times or running dead, twisting death.
A puzzle, "my head." It's caving into dust, most was this.
With my compassion I feel the random stab of pain, my soul so insane.
The crumble of tormented lives. The lives are over, *the pain...*
It's covering my mind of loathing. So here I am showing, tears of madness!
Fears and sadness, the vast minds of crawling dead.
Envisions of metallic shines, the rip of human flesh.
I'm not holding my breath because I don't care, in running there.
The land of lost, the pain is lost. With fears and madness.
The cold shadow of time. The calling of crying in my mind. Recourses are lost!
The forever frost covers my mind, the game controlled by time.
Our soul is divine to them, "or not." Bleeding and seeing these roads you forgot.
You must seek out the demons of winged Gods.
Seeping into your heart, I see not or so no one can know.
"The hypnotic way you convince the world that you're from heaven."
The lies are too great for them. "No one can understand,"
My point and reason. "*The reason is you.*" So I stand wishing for goodness.
In the sins of calling the light, tonight in memory of the dead...
So crawling six feet under lost.
Digging up or down in this loss, sorry but she is dead to me.
In memory of the forsaken "8" the time is late.
Of running dead or calling the death of God or devil.
The price is great; the snake is constricting my soul.
Cold is the rain, the pain rushes down onto my dreams.
Staring into my fears and hell, the heaven light is lost.
In depth with all that matters to her, I must consider it all, or I'd fall.
Her love holds me tight in her arms. The reason is her, the angel, my love.
So the freedom Dove is the God of all. The pain rains in so many ways.
Faster I fall with speed like God. The life I forgot.
So the interactive ways the demons play with my mind. The Gods life is a lie.
The way it falls onto the roads of pain, so many souls insane.
The way it convinces the wrong, the way I live this song.
The blackened-sun rises onto her, the blood in my dreams, the stream of tears in mind.
The way I never cry, as it pours onto the road. The blood rains the pain.
Only to see the dream is me. The light is gone, the soul was wrong.
On the roads of pain this light is away, the soul is forever, "*just like me.*"
The running water on the roads, so sweet the pain grows onto me.
Soulless minds it calls for me, but I'm not sorry.

Speed Slows Me Down

Faster as I hit the turn, wait for the light then let the tires burn.
Combustions and a source of right. Now it's green, "the time it right!"
Metal is all I wish, with my fist griped tight to the wheel.
Still I fight and hold control of my life, so how do I say these things to you?
I love all and hate too. So running down my demons with my head.
Holding confusion and wishing death. Death to the world and me.
The speed is in my hands, "lost again, lost within."
So many roads, so very little time, insanity and lost abilities with you.
So I run away I run from you, faster I go as I sleep and creep into madness.
The wheel is jerked, "so sorry for sadness."
My one and only, have I not been true?
So lost and confused are we? A path I give to the finger tips and now this is it.
So the time to back out has past.
The fast death I await, 109MPH and still I accelerate, "No!"
Faster and more I need, I love it all, I need the speed.
Am I not man enough to do these things?!
Or rejection and neglect are your ways, "I say yes."
And this is it - over the top, the needle is gone.
The time to begin the song, with monster sound.
Vibrations through my body, the bridge is up.
So welcome to my hobby and the time is, "now...!"
"In mid-air I scream out loud."
So I hit, sparks fly with the windows down.
The cool air in my - "wow!" it's mine. To give it time and rush the fate onto me.
Speed and insanity are my family and friends.
Sin, and all was left behind, just one more time, I wish it more.
With no self-consideration and all my *deadication* to the road.
The show is forever and never will I back out.
The rush of death in my grips, I feel the angel's lips.
A kiss from above, I know what I've done.
I'm flirting with death and my sanity. "Well," aren't we all?
Maybe not, but I am true. So on I go, on I move.
Should I turn left or hit the runway?
I let the road decide where I live and when I'll die.
So upon my loss of nations and my source of friction. I give my heart to the car.
The Gods of the forgiven and the seed of the given.
And I'll never stop my drug and love.
Jet black and smooth finish, upon the roads of choice.
I give it all, slowing down in my mind and feeling the speed in my *Eyes*.
"Am I not right, am I?" So time to fly and kiss my sanity goodbye.
On my own wings of pure. "Speed - I'm yours."

You Don't Understand

I understand what I am, and why I'm me.
Because of the world, it's what created me.
A world of rules and a life of hate. Stuck in this inner mind state.
"A drug that has fried my brain." Ruled to take it twice a day.
It is you the world that drove me insane.
My mother and father broke apart. So is that too my fate, that's just a bit of it all.
Growing and never knowing what it would be like to have a _family of my own._
"Watching and hearing others happy."
And lying to myself, saying it's all right.
Growing and never knowing to fight.
Never standing up for myself, having no one stand up for me.
All the kids beat me up. Laughing at me - but they were my friends...
Never knowing and still don't - what a true friend is.
Bitches and assholes surround me now but that's not the - whole story.
Sure I had and have no friends and will never have a family of my own.
Was beat up, I am FUCKED! But there is more, I've tried so hard to be seen.
To be seen by the one person who should love me.
Hold me when I cry, she was never there and it breaks my mind!
I met a girl, "and then some."
They all said one thing that I grew to hate, "love."
But I tried, from the age of six to 13.
I never knew love and one day came to know - I never will.
That dumb bitch tried to kill herself. "What the fuck?!"
But you still don't understand, it's not over yet that's not the end.
There is more, "shit!" When I was six I was put on a pill.
A pill for something I did not have.
My father disagreed and tired, but "Our _society_ - look what it has done to me."
A depressed kid forced to take those fucking pills!
Well you do the math, then look inside and see.
I understand, the world did this to me.
Dumb teachers that think I didn't pay attention.
"I had problems at home!"
But did anyone stop to think what that pill could do to me? _No_!
And now look, stuck in a state of mind with a loss of time.
Always sleepy and dreaming of the truth.
And truth I'll never have, surrounded by all these jackasses.
Stuck inside - it's been years since I last took that pill. But still!
The aftereffects are and must be here, 8 years of straight sadness.
Now stuck with forever madness! "Okay." I understand.
All around me and everyone I know, everyone is untrue.
"You don't understand;"

Nobody could know what it's like in my mind.
To be sad for all of their life.
Those bastards have money, a family and friends. In their pictures I see only smiles.
I see and hear their happiness. None of them are sad for a reason.
They make it bad so they can get some pity, "not from me."
If I had half of what they have. No, fuck them!
Spoiled rotten little punks. Screw them all, still you don't understand.
Unless you've felt one day of the pain I live. You don't understand.

<u>On I Go - Into Unknown</u>

On I go, into the unknown. Seeing no life, ending my life.
I wish for death, yet I'm dead. On I go, beating me dead.
Shoved under the earth - stuck in between this life and you.
The God of man I feel in hand. "I'm so crazy!"
I feel the unreal and still I'm alone. Stone and dust are all that's left of me.
So wait as I do to show something new, a heart I do wish.
I pissed away my life, in dark moonless nights - I sleep so unjust.
Nights of demons, kill I must. So wait I do, on I go on no truth.
Truth of wishes and endless lies. So crush my soul and I see fear in your eyes.
So on I die, kill my mind endless times and endless more.
I shut the door to let it free, I try to crawl and walk to run.
Stunted by the light of heaven's true glow.
I feel things that no man knows.
So I move no more, more I wish this is it - I'm stuck inside.
In my mind - sanity so insane! "To think me sane?" Loss of brain.
Eat human flesh, I hold my breath. To the blood in sky.
I wish to die, I want more but you give me none.
I'm stuck in none. "*Fearing I'm done.*"
In this world of pain, still so insane, I eat your brain.
I cut your flesh and tear your heart from your chest.
I love what I've done, "sun gone," night here. So I die, with endless fear.
Fearing of nothing but endless space.
I'm out of place, I am a demon stuck in a man.
Angels call to watch me fall and they laugh at my mistakes.
Who is evil, who has hate? Reasons of hating the world, I have.
But I shall not just hand you the truth.
Give to me a reason to let you live. "*Time's up*, welcome to the end!"
Sleep my dear child, awake in hell, a destiny of - a fate of nothing, just pain.
Why go insane? When the trip is here and looking for us.
Is the world on top of me or do I stand on it?
Should I move on or just quit? As a lifetime I have not;

Finding time to decide to live or choose to die.
Jump or turn, spill or fill the glass of life.
Open and see, "time has run out." End your life, run and jump.
Land six feet under like me. Or wait for death? "*You wait for me.*"
On I go inside your mind.
Stuck in a place with an unknown face, even if it's mine.
The time is right. So decide now how you go!
Now I go, into the unknown of death.

It's Not Over till I Cry
<u>*"Not till I die."*</u>

That's not it! Feeling nothing, feeling pissed.
Screaming hard, dying fast, killing God, I live in Nod.
"I'm so cold," cold I am - kill I do, so lost in you.
I fear I am - lost and dead - die I will - still I want to cry.
"Cry I do, only with you."
In crawling skin, clawing sin - sin I do, "I do" I love you.
I see I've tried but more pain I find, finding the way, feeling insane.
My descent to you, I fall for you and see only us.
I love only us but you still act like I don't.
"You know I do." I love you and only you, why can't you see?!
It's not time, not till you try - until I die.
I want to cry - so time for me to choose, I won't lose. "Not again!"
I love my love, her bliss, her sins. So run I do, so killing and confused.
Forgiving none - I've lived my sung song.
I'm feeling only pain, so why do I stay?
Maybe so I would no longer have to fight.
So why should I go? To show the world I'm a man.
To give out myself because this I can.
Let's say I don't and kill I do. Still I'm lost, still lost in you.
Should I try or just say goodbye. Try to win and let in sin. "Sin I do."
Now I know you won't let me in, I try to love but still I sin.
I hate and kill, so the evil I am, the hate I am.
The God I need - the seed is lost - the lost is you - the fire so "you."
I need a new light to shine but the darkness is all.
The fall so grand, the love to kill a man.
"To watch him die makes me alive."
When I see the final spark in his eye fade - *oh I kill just to watch them die.*
"At least I can feel something."
I feel the sum of the none. I need to choose, I need some heart.
"Something like God." Something like you;

I need to choose, I chose hell because I need to sail past this all.
I need to fall to see the goal. My hell is heaven and so I descend down to you.
I need to see - I see only you, I go and show no love.
I part with me to see something - I am nothing.
I fear only me - I see no God - I feel no love - I kill only me.
To see it die, I try to grow - grow I do.
I'm a man yet an adolescent too, so I need some time - time to choose.
I walk in this field of pain - alone - and I'll keep it that way.
It's not that insane, "So I need some help," I help only you.
It's not over till I cry, "*Not till I die.*"
Yet I'm already dead - so no more from you - *Not you...*

DreamInsane

Into shadows I run away, trying to hide from the pain.
Seeing none "fear" it's done and I walk away, "I walk away!"
See the God and killing it all - so now I scream... "DreamInsane!"
Demons calling - the evil clawing - "clawing at my grave."
An angel must - I turn to dust - so I drift away "I go insane."
So I am in pain "DreamInsane" crying hard - I'm torn apart.
"Apart from all your ways."
It's insane, dropping hard and trying fast, losing heart, "*I wish for death.*"
So I go insane - "I wish to be sane."
Going to, I show nothing new - God I am insane "eating my own brain."
Telling God to give it up, "I am so insane."
Stabbing myself - crawling to hell - so now I am on my way.
Silence of the forever madness, drowning deep in my sadness.
So God now! I am the darkness, God I hate this day "*and I'm away.*"
All I have is hate, so I sit in my mind.
Waiting for the time to awake, "I'm awake."
"Well?" On and on I go again to see some light and feel some sin.
The questions and demons all bring me back "*At last - I'm here.*"
The darkness I've brought onto me.
To see something and nothing or just God.
So on and on I go, showing no path because I make my own.
And sorry but it's all my fault - the killing of her.
And forsaken is I? "*DreamInsane*" lose my mind.
Darkness is growing, the shadow is telling me to awake.
I know not why I cry - why I die - inside I have no way.
So I dream insane, open my eyes and see the voices growing in me.
I need to go and find the light "I fight" running from the day.
Running from the sane - I need to go away;

The question why, in my mind - I go insane "DreamInsane!"
Evil points - evil lies - twisted dreams - only in my mind.
I need to go, I need to know, so many more tears I have.
The darkness grows and no light shows, I need to awake.
I seek to know - so I grow and go away "DreamInsane."

I Love You But
You Can't Take Away My Life

Why do we fight? Why is it every time you see me you want to die?
Why do you want to take away my life and change the way I am?
"Well, I think." I know I've already changed a lot for you.
A whole lifestyle I gave away for you.
Now you want me to change "sorry" *but hell no*!
I gave it all to you but still you want more. "*So I show you the door.*"
No matter what I say or do no one cares - not even you.
Why should I move on?
If I try and try and cry and cry, it doesn't matter, it's pointless.
"Well - shit." I do wish I were smart.
I wish I would not fall apart when I'm put on the spot.
But you want me to change again, you're insane you stupid bitch!
"Everything I seem to know, I never knew... Everyone has been untrue.
Everyone has been untrue, even you."
It was all you - so did you think you were going to get away with it?
You crazy bitch, yes I love you but you can't take away my life.
As if life could be good, as if I could even have a life.
Only pain is what I see. You drive me so, so over the edge.
I need to get away - away from all of this.
You try to take away my life, why do you want me to change?
"No fucking way!"
You won't get me to change; we're over, "I'm done."
"I can't take all this shit!"
I do need to be alone and alone I'll always be.
I do love you but you can't change me.
I love you but you can't take away my life.

"Damn it - it's over..."

Hold Over Me Again

It's funny how when you see the devil...
And or God within your love - there is nothing to do but stare.
Looking at her golden blond hair.
I can't help but tell there's no future there - "in my Eyes!"
Lost with voices all around, I'm bound to see that the eyes have left me.
Forever I'm just me, so is this the beginning or end of this world of sin?
I see it within lost eyes, in hell I fall through a love so true.
I see there is nothing in you. So I sit and rock my dreams.
It seems the Eyes are dead. "So I've said."
The time is now to rise back from the land in witch I've fallen.
It's time now to crawl back within me.
It's time for a back beat - it's time for you to let me be...
The one true thing to make you love me. "*Dead.*"
Inside of my head, inside of these 2 Eyes!
These Godless Eyes have always been, the world of sin is.
The forgotten Eyes are and will be forever stuck in insanity.
So die Eyes die! Forever in my mind.
Yet hold over me - Eyes hold over me again "*It's my sin.*"
So I cry and die - Angels Eyes cry only for me.
I see it's time for a back beat "No!" Flip it around...
Into hell I'm bound for 100 spiders. In my grave I'm awake.
This rotten flesh has grown back to life, I pull out the knife and it's time.
To destroy a mind or three, inside of me.
Forever I love the love of sin. So I burn in hell, deep I fall in love.
I see myself in a room in which reflects my life.
I hold her tight and let love in. Once again, oh sweet love.
I feel I must stand, I am a man and I know the show won't end.
What a sin, I forever live in purgatory.
Maybe it's hell - "Maybe I'm death himself."
Or sent from God - the time is now - so Eyes hold over me again.
Here it goes again! It won't get out, just get it out!
The voices in my head - I'm burning in hell - forever in hell.
It's time for a back beat. It's time for you to let me go.
"God those Eyes..."

Angle I ask you to hold over me again.
I so love this love of sin.

She's Dead - Get Over It

A nice... A nice is the way to say a God of the all and me.
Because a way or a naught of the all...
"I'm the all," I need something of the war.
More is my wish. I wish it dead and gone.
"She's dead get over it!"
So to the none I've sung to my life and the days I wish it away.
The times I've cried and the pain I've shown.
With her razor I wish I could play.
The time has come today, "I say I have no goal."
My goal is lost in her "I fear no death."
I see no breath - death is lost in me so cold in my heart I fall asleep.
Creeping in my heart, death is a part of me.
My mind finding time to cry, I try to win - I try to live with sin.
Call - call my world to the pit, I'm just spiting in the wind.
Send the demons to my soul, cool is the call to call the fire in my sleep.
Seeping into the ground, the razor is my game.
I love the love of living in pain.

"But get over it! She's dead."
She left us, "Great - now I'm talking to myself?"
The girl is alive yet dead to us.
Three in one - not so fun. "But get over it!"
That's it! She was flat-lined because of me.
"Forget it man!" She forgot me.
So what do I do? This song I've sung, it's time I got over it all!
It's done. "She's dead, get over it!"
I need to forget it all; all will fall if I just can't open my eyes.
"Don't worry about the past - that love will never last."
You need to move on.

"Forget it man it's past, leave it in the dirt.
"STOP!" you're gonna burst!"
"Slow down and take a breath, "damn, take two."
"Stop it! You are going to lose."
"Just forget her, she forgot you."
"You're neglecting the ones around you."
"She's dead, what are you trying to do?
"Miles away, years past and not a word."
"She said forget it, leave it gone."
"You say you loved her well, just a bit;"

"You think it was love.... MAN IT WAS JUST SHIT!"
"Forget the life you had, you have love now."
"Why are you mad? Forget it now!"

So onto the walls I paint, a symbol in blood.
I sleep face first in mud.
Calling to the none of my mind to find the time to see.
The life I live is because of me.
I see no way, I feel on goal, I have a love but I neglect.
"I'm so wrong." I should forget - forget it all.
Forget it now or I will fall. I must forget it - I need help.

I the king of the some - the God of none.
This song I've sung - so I forget it all.
I need to move on and forget that life, forget that lie.
You died because of me Angel. You walk now so happy.
Damn I need to see - I forget you because you've forgotten me.

I love a girl now so sweet.
I must forget the past. The feeling must pass.
I know I need to forget.
So Angel sorry but once again and forever goodbye.

"Good-bye."

Chapter 5

Blanketed Fear

Call Them Up
From The Ground So Sweet

Time to call the un-forgiven, dim the light now it's beginning.
The candles lit - this is it - wait for a sign.
Pull it together, drain our mind.
Its positive-negatives draw the line.
A symbol under my feet and the power rages up into me.
So I cut my arm - spit out blood - cry out dust, "this it must."
And the power rages on, the ground seems to tremble.
The light pours from my eyes, "call them up," the loss is right.
As my feet rise and no longer touch the ground.
In my heart I have found... "In midair - I scream out loud."

As I fall in deeper to sleep, far away my soul does creep.
So I feel my pain - the power calls out to me.
The candles drain, so the pain does rain.
Losing my mind - I'm loving it again, so cut it down - this world of sin.
Spin in air and once again, lock us in - into the earth so sweet.
The wind does thrash, up and down.
I have found the angel or demon inside my body.
Hurt my life - it's a new hobby - I lost the light.
I cannot feel, I need the voices!
Faces, my friends, "lock us in, time to sin."
So the teardrop of dust turns to blood and I laugh out loud.
To the skies and cloud, to scream to God.
"Why have you forgiven me?!"
Such an evil mind, "oh lord!"
It's time...

There here! There here!
Oh my God I fear - I fear - the ground - it's gone!
The song - it's wrong - "the light" - it's gone...!

It's over, nothing happened, they're gone, was I wrong?
Or am I even here!? The room is dark "the quiet I fear," No.
They're here...
SPIN – RUN - TURN AND JUMP.
LOST AGAIN - WHAT HAVE I DONE?!
Somebody save me!!!

"UNSEEN"

Was the river of fire not my life? Was the death in water not my fight?
When the world turns and the light dims. Sin will grow onto the child.
Sands of time have grown to rock; stone covers me as I sleep under six feet.
Dark-sun rises, *the noon is onto me*; the cover of shadow is only "unseen."
Join the dark - rise in the night - flesh is the only truth.
"The truth is forgotten."
Signs from demons, from the house of the damned.
The only truth is, "unseen."
Children cry, the years die-out.
The pain is growing; I see no light showing, please God!
Grow to the point where no soul cares.
I feel my fear die-out, the words die-out in me.
I'm nailed down next to the son of God, I'm hated for no reason, I see the season of lust.
Grand is the feeling I have when I'm alone in the house of the damned.
The land is so corrupt, I see only the cup.
A cup of blood, I'm bleeding dead.
Lord! Let me free - free this soul - I wish to not exist and *yet I do.*
Unseen is all that has been; all I did was enjoy the lust of sin.
Call the dreams to surface and grow so unseen, so unknown, "why?!"
Open your body and bleed, open your eyes and bleed.
Look inside and die, "just bleed."
Just see, just move away from me and die, "just bleed."
I cry for me, I'll die only to see nothing in this soul, "God I'm cold."
Cold with the question why! Why do I hurt inside so, so unseen?
In a Godless mind, in Godless eyes, within this soul of hate.
In this life with the snake, spiders all around,
I feel my soul crack; I feel my heart so cold.
Free my soul of nothing, forever untold.
Or cry for the death of a true friend, "Please God don't let it end."
Not here - not now - how do you expect me to move on in life?
Kill it all - I'll kill all in me, free this soul of insanity.
Unseen, un-free, I die for nothing, I must move this stone.
I live in a life to be, I now see insanity is all you left for me.
Truth - forever a lie, unseen by me, I move on with no light.
I'm just another little child who wishes his life could be better.
Could my life get better or worse? Yes it is and forever it will be.
Little child start to cry because soon I will die freeing this soul and mind.
Unseen by even me - I wish I could move - the stone does grow.
The river of fire washes me away - so I stay "unseen."

Noon Rising

Carnage and a hateful mind of death - hold my heart, let out my breath.
This is the end, "lock us in" _this is the end of sin and lust;_ it ends "it must."
Noon is rising onto me. I can't take it, "hold over me."
Walk to something forever lost and dead.
Bleed and run within my head, "it's dead."
How could you tell me what to do?
The end is soon, the end is noon rising onto me.
To see the sun gone - the sung song and my life is done.
It all comes to me again; I'll kill the child, my life within.

This is it, "oh God!" It ends.
So I turn, run and hit my head and laugh out loud, "I wish for death."
So to God, here's my last breath.
So now it's time, now it ends. Soon I cry - soon I die.
But still I'll rise, so my soul does die. It's soon, it's noon onto us.
The dust covers our eyes, the fire burns the light.
Sin - I ask you to help me. Please, I call the king, so now it ends.
So I ask the one I fear, myself as God or devil.
It is trouble so now I run away, till I end this day with my own two hands.
Kill it all, and never love again.

So to the all of the hate and me.
See the end, it's rising onto me. The song is my reason to kill.
Into noon of soon to all, the reason I fall because I see the awe of God.
The demon is to see the dead. It's my reason to live, my sin "it ends."
So to the lost and forgotten of him and her.
Sorry, the razor is my cure to love for her.
With no way out, you scream out loud, to me.
I was your friend, "you left me."
Her tears of sadness are my fuel of madness.
So now it's my turn, the razor and hell burns.
"Ode to the voices of hate and death," her love for me is ending at last.
So soon, it's noon onto them.
The God is calling to all. Soon the razor... And soon I'll fall.
Noon is all, the wait I see.
The time to see - time to bleed - on growing does our child.
But soon I'll end life and sin.
Noon is rising onto me, Lord I must see, something or nothing of me.

Justice I wish to ask.
Of burning up the past of mine and hers, the end is soon;

The end is noon rising onto me, the light is gone.
Your song is forever to be. I'm so alone, sleeping under six feet.
The reason you died is no good for me.
Should you have died, is it the same way with me?
So I do see something or nothing of it all?
Fall on paper, the shadow's dream.
The seeing of all to death is God and us. "It ends, it must."
So to the Never of the dead and me.
Noon is rising upon us all, "So now I see."

My Bloody Prize

Fingernails cutting through the skin, tear off flesh and eat of skin.
Tear off body and the finger to God. *I stand in rejoice of the freshly dead.*
Well now it's time, of the shallow pool.
The blood is running, white bone crunching beneath my teeth "yes."
Hunger of wishing human blood.
Murder has befallen your only daughter.
Daughters and mothers are my only feast.
The beast is calling me to show, now is the time, I'll let it go.
"Cannibalistic ways of life," now here is something, my forever life.
Twist of joints, break of bones, I kiss your lips and hold you tight.
"It's going to be a very long night."
I lay you down, in my bed - lick your ear - kiss your neck.
I say sweet things and you hold your breath; "I sit you up."
And I eat your heart from your chest.
Scream while you can, you're going to die. Shut up bitch, "time to die!"
I hold you up, my new found prize.
A gift from God, because he didn't care.
I've seen no hell and found no heaven.
Countless names I've torn apart, families and families I've yet to choose.
You know what - I like you...
So kiss of you to me and carnage from me to you.
I do love you, my new found food. By the moon is your blood drained out.
And in the sun it dries away, stained with pure red.
I sit up and ask out loud, "well, are you happy God?"
I didn't sin, you could have stopped me.
So I just sit here and wait for the next to cross my path.
Once I start there will be nothing left, so I sit here and you ask me why.
Why do I sit there and watch you cry?
Screaming and begging for your life.
"Just sit down and swallow this knife;"

It's fine little girl, the pain won't last forever.
But ask yourself one thing, do you love God?
Have you ever confessed your sins? Well if so, *then let the pain begin.*
Slowly with a razor I push down on your neck.
Drowning in your own blood, "well," heaven or hell - life or death.
I am evil with a heartless chest, "cold is your soul in a life of pain."
Dripping with the insane, over your shoulders you stare.
I won't even try - you will come to me.
Come to die, so on I wait to let it fly, your death is mine.
Your life is over, I'm done. You're forever none, it's over.
You, my bloody prize - my sweet prize, my only love.
To watch you bleed, I love to watch you die, my bloody prize.
"You're mine."

Maybe So

Maybe I was alive, maybe I could try.
Maybe I have love - maybe so *"but I think - No."*
All I give and hate, maybe I should wait but no, "God?" *Maybe so.*
God should I give me a better reason to move on?
Should I give it the time or am I just wasting my mind?
God let me free, free this mind, endless times.
I try so hard, feeling so lost.
I give it time, I give in mind but you don't care.
"Maybe so."

Maybe I could know, but I don't.
And I won't - till the end - I shall sin.
Could I die - try to hide - maybe so *"but I don't know."*
And on I move into life, maybe death "well, that's my destiny."
Maybe I could know, maybe so "but I think - No."

I know I don't and never will, still insane and I do love it.
Well, on I hate and hate some more.
Loss of path, you've locked the door.
On I bang and go insane. I want inside, I try to die, lie and bleed.
With seeds of evil in my chest, ice cold blood and nothing left.
Maybe I could cry, *"And maybe,"* I should die, maybe so...

"Well - I still move;"

I drop to hell and still I'm stuck - in the never.
My forever death - pain of love - heartless chest.
So I'm done with this world and maybe I wish to be free...
God I hate you because you hate me.
So do we and I want to be alone, demons are inside, *I do wish to die.*
Maybe be alone, stone and dust covering me.
Over the years, these years of nothing.
Nothing but forsaken truth, youth has left me and maybe I could die.

No, just forever, forever just stuck in my own hell.
Maybe in mind and maybe I could just stop. "Maybe not."
So on I go, to show you some way out, I wish to find out why.
Why am I here? To put fear in the souls of all? So now call it up.
Let me free, seeds of evil planted into you.
God is gone, I've lived too long.
"And I fear only me."

Well, maybe I'm fine, and maybe I'm dying?
Just maybe it's over.
So I haven't stopped yet.
Maybe it's all just a dream - No.
On I go into hell, "well - I love it."
Crawl in shadows - creeping in death.
Well, maybe I'm all that's left? Maybe so, "still I think - No."

In joyful bliss of hating you, on I go - I kill you.
In death is my question, in life is the answer.
"Or the other way around."
Bound to the fiery pit of my mind.
And now I have found the time.
And I choose never to quit, so this is it, maybe so.
Still I think no, yes I know, maybe.

"Maybe so..."

"Six More Feet I Die"

Slowly creeping onto more, free my mind and feel no more.
All I have is nothing and you - destination I await.
I feel the hate pull me down - I am done with all of you.
A world of voices and the eyes in my mind.
So all I do is die and wish for more - I need more.
I'd wait forever, I wait to die - six feet under I ask why.
All I need is time, and time is all I have.
So underground I look for light, fighting my own demons and God.
Looking for a better reason than the one I have.
I am dead inside, killing my mind.
That's all I do - wish for more - then kill you.
With pain of razors and other sharp toys, my childhood lost, I kill more.
Rip and cut, tear off flesh - grab my heart from my chest.
I cry out dust, I feel no lust, "hold up God!"
I've gone too far, it's my life - yet I'm dead.
Still I'm lost, inside my head. I wait in between two worlds, *Shit* & *Pain*.
So here I sit, I go insane because of her and her and him and me.
On I go in my purgatory. Death is inevitable but the awe is lost and me.
So give me a new death or God take my breath.
Just let me die, as no Angel cries, I laugh and scream in a joyful breath.
So all I have is all I want is nothing. I step back and I don't know what to do.
I can't remember this face - even if it's mine. Here I am, lost inside.
And I see no way out, only through these words from my mouth.
I don't remember this face; I'm so out of place.
I'm so fucked and I am far too late. To try and stop it all.
So here I am, I wish to fall, I wish to die - yet I'm dead.
Kill my mind, leave my head.
Why am I so - so lost inside?
Find not the light for me my love - I move on in the shadows.
We move on with no hallow - so I slow the flow of time.
I lose my mind. "So I lose the light to win the fight,"
Call me down dark lord - call me to the show.
With darkness so - so cold. I wish her warmth, I want no more.
So unjust - I must be gone - so far gone.
Alone inside, I die yet cry, "oh God why?!"
I am and will always be so alone; I say this is the end.
So alone in this world, I am lost, why? I can't see!
You're nothing, just shit!
"God! Cold! Cry! Lost! Why?!"

Forsaken You

I find the only thing I need... is to see.
To be in a joyful mind state but that's just a dream.
The world around me is... the things around me are...
The face in the mirror is still here.
And I don't understand its ways.
I the child - I the man - I'm so insane.

So on I go, making no sense - no way to sense the things to be.
I the God - I the devil - I'm a demon - I'm an angel.
I so need some heart, to fill this pit.
The shit I've seen in dreams, just seeming to never end.
The night will never end, I'm just dead.
"And forsaken."

So on I walk in a mindless state, so killing me is your hate.
The hate is new to me, to see the... all of nothing.
Well it is something! And I know I'll win.
Or maybe die - I'll never cry for this world so unjust.
The fight is calling me to trust the cat on my path.
And the dog in my way.

The owl is screaming - screaming to God, to let him free.
See - I know nothing and I need to see.
The glass is broken, the tears I soak in.
The hobby is to sleep and let the demons creep into place.

I don't know this face, even if it's mine.
My mind is caving into itself. The walls will soon fall.
I must call to someone – something - or forsaken am I more.
I know I'm nothing but what if I could change?
No! *Never change* - the evil in my mind - the evil in these Eyes.

To see the blood is mine.
The time is right, to kill it all or just fall again.
In sinful love for none...

My Little Friend

You my friend, I love how you don't fight back. You are neither a dog nor a bird or cat.
You're always there but hard to find. I always hold you tight.
I love you, "my one true," I love you - you. So you my friend with me.
I want you to be, I need you around when no one's there.
I need you always, because you're always there.
I know I know nothing but with you I am something, "a man."
You don't care if I'm tall, small, fat or thin.
Dumb or smart, I know we'll never be apart. *Never apart...*
I know I love you and you'll never be "number two" even if you are #2.
I so need to be alone, I will always be alone.
Alone I am, "*I'm so forgotten.*" I need to sort out my demons.
So to unlock but with you I'm someone.
Even if I'm no one, I'll find someone like you. No, you're not just #2.
My little friend, I want to play, come out today. Where could you be?
Oh, here you are; "stick with me and we'll go far." Far as my mind can take us.
I show so many things; loves, hates and pains. *More bad than good.*
But you don't care; I know you'll always be there, so we play.
I'll never throw you away, because you've felt my pain and loves.
You're always there, behind this dumb kid, I know I neglect them all.
Fuck it! They're just jealous that I have you all to myself, it doesn't matter.
They don't love me! I see so many things, I feel so insane, so far in pain.
But you don't give a flying fuck because your half me, I love my little friend.
Because it loves me.
What would it matter if all is lost? Free we are, yes; I know the cost.
But I know I won't leave you, no! I do need you.
So on and on and a little more. My friend I need you more.
Always there, fear and hate, love and loath.
I do not forsake you; I need you, so stay with me my little friend.
I'll always be there with you till the end. I so need you, I'll never let you go.
I always show you warmth, I'm yours and you're mine.
I'm sorry if I neglected you at times. I'm sorry but I lose my mind.
But you don't care, do you? No, you don't care at all.
Not if I fall, or call for death, if I'm alive, just not if I'm dead.
You want me, and need me too.
No you're not "number two," even if you are, #2.
My pencil, my little friend, I'll keep you with me till the end.
With me here you feel alive, pencil and paper are my life.
I write all that happens, the good and the bad.
I keep you with me my little friend.
I keep you, I need you, so love me, don't leave me.
Even if I don't have a friend that is true, at least I still have you.

Must I Awake?

Endless nights I toss and turn. I try to awake but feel my soul burn.
Crushing this world is - onto my chest. Should I try or wait for death?
I scream no sound, to the night in mind. Must I go on, must I try?
I step on broken glass for the all in my life.
I crawl on my knees, I bleed for you. Must I live, *must I choose*?
All I do is lose my path, with a loss of breath. "I am awake…"
Nightmares of demons with angels stabbing.
Stabbing me inside, so I awake to find.
This is my life, this is my knife. Stuck in my soul, stuck in my heart.
I am to find, it's all a part of me.
Stuck in dreams of insanity, while I'm awake.
I am constricted by the snake of my soul.
Cold I am, I'm a lost man. "Must I awake..?"

Light

I feel like I'm walking on the clouds.
On the morning dew, a mist of harmony.
A smell I soon won't forget, with a glow from heaven, *I am to witness.*
Should I be here, or away? It's too heavenly, this early day.
Brightness running through the land.
Like a million horses of a fire glow.
Pure God-light, spread on the world.
My eyes are struck by the heavens light.
I've awoke to the birth of the world, on the edge of this cliff.
I sit here and seem to dream. If only I could be a part of it.
The dew dries away, and then grows the sound of this day…
It rings in my ear, I fear it's gone but I know I'm not alone.
The early day never forgotten. I've seen heaven but I'm alive.
It just takes time, heart and mind.
Its light will warm your soul.
A sun rise in the sky - with an ocean of light.
But you all - could never feel this love.
Have you ever walked on the clouds and awoke with the sun?
Maybe so but you don't know a blind man's sight.
I can see, only God's light…

Inside

So to all! I see inside. I won't fall! I'll be alive.
I do now see! The path for me. So I choose! And I won't lose.
I am alive! I see inside...
In my mind, I see no cloud. So in my heart, I am so loud.
Load my heart, with her true love. So I know, I'll live above.
Free my soul, I'm not done. Here I fight, to make it right.
I'm now so tall, because I see inside. I just call, to the all I fight.
I won't fall, I am so tall.
Above you all, I'll just fight. Fight the world, I try to stop me.
I'll make it fall, because I have it. Without a fist, I fight with words.
From my mouth, to your ears. Ear of all, I won't fall.
I'm inside, I am alive.
Jump inside, in my eyes. Dream the dream, I seem to win.
Win I do, I fight for you. To make it right, I will fight.
Inside my mind, I know I'm right.
So on I walk to forever, "just." Justice of none, is what I've sung.
But you won't win; I'll beat your sin. "I win."

Backwards Eyes

"One more time."
Seeping through this child's Eyes - seeping into his mind.
With a demon on the wings of God.
Evil love is running through the halls.
Halls of this mind - end my time - I wish it gone!
"One more time."
1, 2, see 8. Lost in mind with love for hate.
9, 9, 9 more times yet look at me upside down.
Evil is calling me to kill - spill the blood of God. "It's done..."
Wishing - beating - cutting - death. Crying, trying, *loss of breath.*
One more time, I lose my mind. To this world, I hate it all.
"One last time!"
God is ripping me down, tearing my flesh apart.
Reaching in, taking my heart. Killing my soul, in my mind.
One last time! With the voices in my - "Eyes!"
Spill it more. Let it go - go - go - Oh!

"God those Eyes."

Blanket Me

Blanket me, cover my pain. Blanket me, cover me please.
Watch over me, see me bleed. Watch over me, don't let it be.
Cover me, don't let me go. Cover me, I'm so cold.
Mommy please, please don't go. Mommy please, don't let me go.
Daddy please, awake from your pain. Daddy please, forgive my pain.

Cover me, don't let me go. Cover me, I'm so cold.
Blanket me, don't let me dream. Blanket me, it's more than it seems.
Watch over me, while I dream. Watch over me as I bleed.
Mommy please, don't walk away. Mommy please, *don't drive me insane.*
Daddy please, forgive my pain. Daddy please, don't go away.
Sorry love, I'm insane. Sorry love, I'm going away.
Blanket me, cover me please *"I'm so cold..."*

"8 "

Hate - eat your body.
8 times - I love this diversion of murder.
Your love is calling, I love this show.
Wars of the mind, "end my time."
Six feet under I wait for death...

8 more losses - 8 more minds.
All I wish, to crush your mind.
8 more disappointments, 8 more lies.
Stuck with her, kill my mind.
No more reason, no more lies.
I've dealt with this world and I've wasted my time.

You are nothing, just a lie.
You're just forever out of my mind.
Demon wings, God is a lie. Am I wrong, did I lie?
Thoughtless minds, running inside.
I'm just nothing so crush this mind.
8 more something's, I am nothing.
Lost in mind, "loss of time."
8 more somethings - 8 more nothings.

"This whole world is a lie."

Faster

Harder faster, I want to die. Harder faster, I lose my mind.
Harder faster, I fall inside. Harder faster, "oh God why?"
Falling faster, into hell. Falling faster, oh God, well?
Running deeper, in my heart. Running deeper, I fall apart.
Killing faster, "oh God why?" Killing faster, killing my mind.
Killing faster, all the time. Lose you bastard, lose your mind.
Harder faster, I ask God why. Harder faster, free the pain inside.
Kill it faster, kill my mind. Kill you bastard, killing time.
Running deeper, in my soul. Running deeper, through the cold.
Running deeper, into love. Look in deeper, "what have I done?"
Falling faster, "oh God why?" Falling faster, in my mind...

I Fall

"Get ready, now fall!"

Speed to the ground. Faster than God.
Speed of the unseen, I am gone.
Hold my breath, six feet from death.
I stop, *"in midair I weep."*
Asking God why, "should I die?"
With no life to flash before my eyes.
Only pain and regret. I feel hate and neglect.
I'm sorry but I can't take it!

No one listens. No ear to hear my pain.
Nobody cares, I'm so in pain.

"Insane?" Maybe so.
But nobody cares, nobody cares.
In midair I stay, "no breath, no way."
Should I die, just wait and bleed?
With nothing but regret.
"I fall."

Still I steal the light from heaven.
I feel I've done so wrong.
So six feet under I fall.

Down

Fast, let to the ground. Bound to the walls of hell.
Stuck in my mind, hating the times I'm alone.
Stone and dust are me. I must be nothing.
Nothing I am, I'm just a lost man. God is the reason I cry.
Kill the thought of winning, lose the light.
Storms of crying, I hear the children dying, "*please God save me.*"

On I move, showing no heart. Apart I wish me to be.
So I scream and wait to die. Let the world bleed.
I love to watch you cry.
So I'd love to see you die! *Blood spilt onto the ground of heaven.*
So I watch the hate grow and I know it's gone...

My Documents:

My documents of life.
I store in the back of my mind.
I wish to let the world know.
No, I don't know why I'm here.
Her only reason to be.
Is to make me forever nothing!

Blood, spit, tears and sweat.
Have all been put into my work.
But nobody cares to listen to my world.
I'm alone in this world, a world in my own mind.
I find nothing but me. In a sea of my own blood.
"God I wish I were done."

So I'm an evil person to the world.
And the one girl I love doesn't talk to me.
She's scared of who I am.
"I'm NOTHING!"
So I document my life and tell the world of my pain.
I know what it's like to be alone and alone I wish to stay.

"Turn the page."

My Web

Like a spider crawling, I awake to see. My web has covered *everything*.
I feed upon the small and weak, until they grow old and strong.
Enough to crush me gone.
I hide in darkness and regret. I hate the world, as I spin my web.
Small red eyes, glowing in the abyss. I know I'll miss the end.
I'm left alone, with only sin.
Blood is my wish, just a drop or two.
Open yourself, I'm inside of you. Small but strong, I wish I were gone.

Lost in my head. Stuck in my web. I'm alone in hell.
Crushing gone, killing all, so I fall.
In my web.

Counting Sheep

1, 2, 3, 4. The more sheep I count the more I'm awake.
5, 6, 7, 8. Please wipe clean the slate, please let me dream.
9, 10, 11, 12. As time moves on, I drift to hell.
13, 14, 15, 16. The more years that pass, I hate my past.
17, 18, 19, 20. Sunny days will never shine for me.
"No," all alone I weep. Set aside, I count sheep.

All of the things I've seen, of all the ways I've been.
Open the shutter and feel the wind.
Close the eyes and forget all the time you've spent.
Lie down, breathe in and out. Breathe in, breathe out.
Stop spending time, stop wasting mind.
Stop running inside, just free my mind.

1, 2, 3, 4. The more I wait, the more I hate.
5, 6, 7, 8. Why do I wait? Just clean the slate.
9, 10, 11, 12. Just stand up - and I walk away from hell.
13, 14, 15, 16, 17, 18, 19, 20.

"Funny; I'm asleep."

Too Far Gone

I'm too far gone, I've lived too long, I'll sing this song, till I die.
In my mind, I am dead. Forever dead, in my head.
Running far, trying hard. Wishing more, finding more.
Lost in none, from what I've done. "Killing me."

Don't let me see, don't let me breathe.
Watch me die, let me cry.
Don't help me, "you won't help me!"
Can't you see? Inside me?
I'm too far gone.
No way out, of my own jail.
No way out, of my own hell.
All I'm left to do is, "scream!"
Bleed this body, "don't let me be!"

Can't you see? I'm too far gone. I've lived too long.
I end this song, "today!" I wish I were not insane.
I'm too far gone, "I am away."

FEAR

Tongue-less screaming, crying no tears.
Legless crawling, finding new fears.
Look inside! Look in deep!
Killing you all, like pointless sheep.
Your just living meat!
Finding no point. Finding no reason.
Seasons of blood. Seas of mud.
Am I mad, am I dead?!

Living this life. Finding new knives.
Crawling and calling. To your own God.
Here I stay. Forever insane!
Loss of mind. Loss of time.
Finding no reason.
Just fear and lust.
Must I die?
I wish to be dust.

Running

Well, time to fall! Run to the peak and see!
Always running, trying hard! Crying dust, bleeding hard!
I wish to be alone. Stone covers me.
Six feet under I wish to see. Don't let me be.
Kill me while you have the chance, our love will not last.
Run into the past. The love will never last!

Jump into hell, wish for pain. Still I'm here, still insane.
I wish to rip my body apart. Deep inside, deep in mind.
Tearing and tearing away my skin.
I kill it all. And welcome sin!
Fall!

I Stand

So I stand, rise up to the world. I will win, without sin.
Only my past is corrupt but with my mind, *I'll find some luck...*
Stuck inside, I'll find some light.
The roads I've walked "*but I'll take it,*" this life is mine.
With all my time, I'll make it right. I stand now, I'll win this fight.
"Life."

Life is just a sugarcoating of the truth.
Reason and understanding is the truth.
So many things in my way but still I'll move on to show.
That a child like me, can grow.
Grow into a man, and make his own life.
I stand now, to make it right.
I fight not with my fists.
There is another way, to fight with more.
"Your heart and soul," that's all you need.
I fight with rage, insanity, truth, hate, and love.
I stand to make you know. The truth will always be hidden.
You have to fight to know. Truth is only the beginning.
The pain is all we see. I stand to fight this insanity.
I grow to know the truth.

"*I have it,* now time for you."

Alone With Her

Hearing no sound! Screaming out loud!
Fighting and fighting my inner-self!
I welcome it all, I love this hell!
Still inside, a demons mind! And Angel's eyes, "*it dies.*"

I look at her golden blond hair, she doesn't care, she never cared.
Still I am trying. Still I am dying - inside.
"I run away, run away," creep in the darkness of hate and regret.
I cut out my heart and give her my last breath!
Feel the neglect, cutting and fearing.
Ripping and biting, spilling blood. I watch children weep.
A teardrop from heaven - I've killed my mind! But...
She doesn't care, she never cared, *yet still I'm here*!?

Life Is

Life is only to live - and I've seen what you've never - sin.
And I've did what you never did - and I've been where you'll never be.
And -I-see-you-are-nothing! Yet...
Life is only to feel - and I've seen what you've never killed.
And I feel this inner pain. "*I love this life of going insane*!" But...
Life is only to live - I've sinned inside my mind. *Running lost, all the time.*
So I try - sit here and bleed, with seeds of evil inside of me, and still.

God is only truth, true to the likes of you – and the voices inside my mind.
Controlling me, all the time. And...
Time is only a stream - of the river of life, so I fall, ending this life.
Strong is the world - with one weak point. "*To be shown the truth.*"
Free my youth from this mind. But...
Life is only to live - and I've seen what you've never sin.
I am what you'll never be.
"And I know you are nothing!"

Dig Me To Sleep

Must I go on and on and on and on?
Leave me to fall, watch me dream.
I seep through these paper sheets and seek the reason why.
Why do all these things happen to me?
Broken truth, still I've had no youth.
On I run, deeper I dig. Dig myself to a better place.
Other than my mind. Help find a new reason for me to be.
Hold my hand dear Angel, guide me to something I need, "*please*!"
Please let me find a new reason to see.
Deeper I dig, dig me to sleep.
All I want, all I need is, "Nothing!"
I am a twisting soul of confusion, I need a helping hand.
In my chest - feel my breath - only the truth will fade.
Watch me fade away. Dig me deeper to sleep.
I need to seek the question why?
The deeper I dig. The more I hide.
Dig me to sleep. Watch me fade away.
Must I go on and on and on and on some more?
You opened the door. Now I dig myself to sleep.

Tie Me To You

Tie me to the bed post - the most I ever wanted was you.
Lock my hands together, I'm waiting for you. "Faster!"
Sweet sadness, with crawling madness.
I watch your body become mine.
Drive me deeper into sorrow.
The pain fills - you're hollow.
All I need is you, "*I want you.*"
All we need is us, "*we must go on.*"
On I breathe and see no light, hold me tight and scream.
Bite my neck and watch me bleed.
See the darkness - feel so sick, *I die with love for you.*
Apart with madness, tie us together - I bleed.
You bleed so true. Only for you do I die.
Open your body and let me inside.
Watch us untie. "*I die...*"

Gift Me

Good God - just leave me to die! Oh lord, let me cry.
Open my body to free the sin. Please God forgive me again.
Good God - free this pain! Oh lord, let me stay.
Open my soul to free myself. God I wish her - never to hell.
Was I the only person alive, or was I asleep inside?
Was I the only person that cared? Let me up, give me air...
"GOOD GOD!"

Watch me fall. I see the nothing.
On the moon I dream - Gift me with the life of death.
Hold my chest - watch me laugh - Good God - it's past.

Oh lord - Gift me.

Dusk

Hell dropped through my mind.
Heaven's tears, they're all lies.
Through the inner pit without you.
Could I go on in my life so used?

Drop me deep into your arms.
Knife point through my heart.
Behind my back, I feel you laugh.
I weep dust till dusk.
Forever clouded inside.

Till dusk do us part.
Apart from you, still so used.
Crying tears only inside.
Crawling away, away from my mind.
Dark death brought to me.
Sorry, so sorry.

Have I never loved? "No."
Have I ever been loved? "No."
Well, without you - I'm broken.
So break me - well - break me - just break me.
Dusk brought so soon.

Chapter 6

Love Torn

Only Time Will Tell

Running lost, to find the reason.
Hitting hard, running far. Into hell "*well*" dead in me.
A sea of nothing but hate in me. So all I do, is lose my time.
Finding lies, this is my life. So what to do? I hate you.
"More!"
The tree of life, a seed of evil. I take the light and turn to Nod.
It's all I have, forgiven God... All I need is heart, "please."
Give me some time, God! Please free my mind, God!
God give me the time; please, to let free my mind.
"More!"
God, I so need the time. My mind is crushing hard.
The light is rushing out. I need the mind to see.
I need the time to tell me. I need the time to set me free.
"More!"
Only the mind. Only the time. Only my heart.
I'm so torn apart and I so need some heart.
Well, I know something, out of all - only time will tell.
"*Just give it time.*"

New Pain

It falls - I stand. Loss of breath, blood in hand.
It feels so good, to eat your body.
She steps up to me without a care in the world.
Her world will soon be mine. I taste her flesh and consume her mind.
You try to run away. I love your new pain.
Eating your heart, taking your soul but still I wish more.

Lie down my love in warmth, the hour is drawing near.
With every breath you take, every wish you make.
Every evil thought will be mine.
I love your new pain, from deep inside.

Hunger and pleasure are my true friends, the carnage is only yours.
The pain is new. The sin won't lose.
I chose you over all.
So I laugh, as I eat you whole.

Wait No More

No longer will I wait for death - and I wait no more.
I seek to find it, I want it more.
I seek and quest to see, please Death - find me!
I call to you and wish it more.
Stone and dust - I'll die some more.
I wait no more...

Running in fast - forehead to the gravestone.
Bleed I'm dead, with a rush to my head.
I forever love what the world has made me.
The demonic monster I was born to be.
I see - God truly hates me - I see.
A joke and a laugh - funny to think it was me.
On I go, into insanity.

Jump in - let death find me.
I wait no more, I quest to see.
Where is my eternity?
Where will I sleep away the pain?
Let me die, free my soul.
I ask you to care no more.
I wait no more...

Fresh death must be set aside for me.
I wish I would die - "please!"
I wish I could see through the pain.
Still I rock back and forth.
Singing to myself - in my head.
"Wish I were gone - wish I were dead."

Rock me to sleep, as I cry.
I wait no more... I want to die.

Open

On paper is my life - twisting and turning is my life.
The burning and hating, "Oh God, the time is right!"
To let it all fall and call to hell.
Hell is all I have, I have no way.
God and the world drive me insane.
On my last breath, I cut open my chest to let the blood free.
All I need is none. Onto this paper I try to write.
I'm lost but I won't quit without a fight.
No, I must go on and on I move.
To show some heart - rip out my heart you do.
To show some - new and kill is all I do.
No, never is my life for you.
And I am free, openly crying – my body is dying.
To God I scream out loud.
"Wow!?"

Love Torn

Torn - born to destroy the world, I cry and laugh.
Torn - blood rains onto me, *"Good God, it's more than it seems."*
Warm - with a hate-sheet over me, I live so cold.
Dying - with only myself, inner voices untold.
Torn away from all your ways, falling fast.
Seeping my mind deeper to hell, unjust I fall so fast.
How far do I have to fall? Good hell drawing near.
How deep do I need to dig? The world growing queer.
Pick me up on fine comfort, lay me down to sleep.
Dream away my demons, "father help me!"
I struggle under this red sheet, I have no air.
Bloom the hate, above will it grow?
Bone to dust, tears to ice - torn from love, torn from mind.
Torn from my soul, I fall away.
As falling deeper into madness - forever that's it.
Never forgiving my soul. Lost torments, sins in joyfulness.
You are the one true love I lost.
It cost me much more in the eyes of evil. So all I need is all I have.
Torn away from peace, I see nothing but the awe.
Torn - born to lose it all.

Away I Cry

I am too small, the world too tall, *in the Sea of Dead*, wishing for death.
Getting nothing, feeling the something but all I am is dead, "*I am dead.*"
Bringing me down, nothing I've found, so away I cry "why?"
The open flesh, a loss of breath, the question why, the deepness *"Eyes."*
The faraway sleep, in creeping death.
My calling death, so I guess I'm dead.
Here's my life, my never ending knife. I fear the sleep *"so away I creep."*
Bringing me down, nothing I've found, so away I cry "why?"
Slowing time, eating my mind, all I give is time and my soul so small.
God I wish for more, so to demons, I've opened the door, *"it's over."*
And still you want more, "so I show more."
Wanting more, God is all and all I have is you.
Bringing me down, nothing I've found, so away I cry, "why?"
God in hand, devil in "Eyes," so now it's time.
It's done, sung to you, that's all I do.
I let it fall, away I crawl, "God?"
To be a man, insane and dead.
I still wish for none, black out the sun.
Let it be over, forgive me now, Oh how will I die?
So far away, away I cry.
My pain is over, it's all over. Rain of blood, a fear of flood.
The light is forgotten, I am forgotten.
I'm dead, to you and the world.
My war is not over, I'm not finished.
So here I stay, forever done. "I'm done."
Bringing me down, nothing I've found, so away I cry "why?"
Forever madness and lost sadness. Here's my life, on this line.
In no trouble, I'm in trouble, for what I've said, *forever dead.*
The world is over - done with me, see - I'm dead.
Giving me sadness and I guess that's it.
I'm over and hidden, away from you.
Hidden from love, I'm hiding from you.
You bring me down, still nothing I have found, as sleeping away my fears.
Sleeping away these tears - love is not here.
I'm done with this life.
God - I've lost the light and so far away - away I cry.

"Why?"

Rest

Lay to rest my head, upon the endless gray.
Seep all my dreams - streams of life.
I wait for life, in darkness I try, to see a reason - a reason to cry.
Still I'm here, still I fight...
Lay to rest my children, the end is here.
We're going to fall. Deep away, seep all the pain.
"Weep my love," I'm going to die.
Weep my children, to the endless night.
Cover me with a sheet of sadness. Sorrow will come tomorrow.
The dream will forever be.
Me under the bed - me inside my head. Me... *I wish I were gone.*
I've gone too far. Stuck inside my own world.
A time of pain, I've left the sane. I'm so ready to sleep.
So I count the sheep. Lay to rest my body, into this world between.
I seem to go on and on.
Lay me to rest. The time has passed.
Lay to rest my head, and I dream...

To You Once More:

Forever I wish us never apart. Deep inside, deep in heart.
Falling away as dreams cover shadows.
Sweet teardrops roll down her face.
I open up, the light so pure. Pouring out from me.
These rivers of life – "Night" I ask you to set me free.
Let free this internal battle. "*Eternal struggle...*"
Slide, cover, blanket, shelter, filter my mind.
Time wasting, draining like a burnt match.
Nothing can match the love I have for you.
Insane how unsane I could be.
"*Free as life.*" Water running through streams of eternity.

Funny... Second after second. Breath after breath.
Life is not forever. Never forever is life.
Light is burning out, I'm not forever.
And forever will we never be apart.
Farewell.

INNER MOON TEARS

The moon's tears drip. Vast-Death floods the land.
Corruption and corrosion, it breaks me down.
I'm crumbling at your feet. With this one finger to God.
Did time stop for only I? I know not what to do.
Deep in your eyes, forever I'm confused.
Abusing the power that was given to me.
"Great Angel set me free."
Darkness is growing, with no light showing - I scream!
I hear children crying, I feel my soul dying.
"What the hell is happening to me?!"
This seed is growing; the fear is holding me down.
Crush this world onto my body, with hobbies of unfaithful lies.
I turn, eyelids open. My breath is taken from me.
Possessed by an awesome gift. *This is what I've longed to be.*
Squeeze my neck tighter God! Stab me deep and leave me to bleed.
It's time for the world to know my pain.
These walls now fall. Unfortunately, this time has already passed.
So, *No more wishes - Only fighting - Reach in deep - See no lighting.*
Falling hard - Killing fast - Vast pits grow unseen - Seemingly I'm dead.
"*I am.*" But not to worry; I have enough hatred for you all...

No

Shoot me in the wrist. To bleed me dead.
I wish I were alone. No knowledge of this.
To love is to hate the world.
I've sinned again. Within my inner pit.
I wish I could see. The gravity is crushing me.
I grow every day - I grow, grow away. Away from the ones I love.
Was it something I've done?
I'm done with this pain. I wish I would not DreamInsane.
Ideal is the feel. The wash of our mother earth.
Drop me under the sea. Shooting at my troubles - shooting at me.
Bleed me my loved ones, I have nowhere to go.
Must I relay on stuff I do not know? No!
I won't go - I wish only to sleep - weep away the insane.
I drop under this sheet.
No..! I know.

Help

So, don't you think I'm alone?
Still I walk in dark. I feel so torn apart, with no eyes to see.
I'm blind in my mind. "Please somebody help me!"
Drop to the pit inside. My mind is crushed by time.
I wish for love. I find only hate. So alone in my ways.
"Please save me."
God, I wish I were known. I wish I were not so alone.
But I'm only here for time. The time is running out.
Somebody let me out.
Skin is torn off bone. The tear of flesh. The crack of teeth
The blood runs free. Only death is inside.
"I only give it time."
So alone inside, I was once alive.
But now dead inside, "*I need only the truth*!" I just need to see.
"Somebody help me."

I'm Drowning

Scream bleeding, calling pain. Die trying, seeping pain.
Feel killing, only you. Under water, will I lose?
FALL! To you. WHY! Would you? HOW! Deep am I?
Call me more, you little whore. Find the sands of time have all-run-out.
Free the pain, through my mouth.
Speak the truth, because of you. Under water, will I lose?
STILL! I lose. WILL! I ever choose? HOW! Far have I drifted away?
Say you stay, running far inside. Drift me deep, away I will hide.
Calling me, will I never ever see?
Please somebody call me to-the-light.
Drift away, "what to choose?" Under water, will I lose?
CRAWL! Because I fall. FALL! Because of you.
UNDER! This water, will I lose?
WHY! Can't I choose? NO! I won't wait for you.
WHY! Won't you wait for me?

"Someday, I hope to see."

Bleed Me

"Shoot me in the wrist, to bleed me dead."
"A soul with no wits, a body with no breath."
Sluggish crawling, I slump into my grave.
Time is but a sloth, with no heart to illuminate.
I stand on the horizon, only needles in my brain.
"Shoot me in the wrist, to watch me die."
Just heartless constrictions of my mind.
"Shoot me in the soul, shoot me in the eye."
So alone with the demon on my back.
Festering bodies, the flesh is no longer sweet.
Stab me in the heart, watch the loss of life.
Rich is the minds, that hate me good.
I wish I were more evil or just gone.
Sink into the endless sand. The sands of time, run down my mind.
I have no friends, only the wish for death.
So shoot me in the wrist, "just end this!"
Should I write this in blood? Should I even let this end?
Shoot me inside, or rip the life from my chest.
I'm so lonely, God I am only at the end.
So I'm alone, I wish the world would end.
"Shoot me in the wrist, to bleed me dead."
I am only at the end. The end I've wished for, now I am dead...
"So - just bleed me."

In Her Mind

Did I never see the light? Did I ever stand and fight?
Am I still alone? Will I never know the truth?
Did I never fight with God? Did I ever try to be gone?
Am I still alone? Will I never be known?
Was it that hard to go? Was it that hard to know?
Will I ever be loved by her? Will I ever be done and burned?
Should I jump into death? Should I cut my heart from my own chest?
Could I go to the next page? Should I ever see the next level?
Would I never go to the forever? I do fall inside her eyes.
I've always loved her mind. I just need to go on some more.
I need to crawl off of the floor, "I need God."
Forever stay in her heart, I wish to stay in her mind.
Could I never find the light?
I should just go on. I will move on and fight.

Lost In You

Enter my head, I'm wishing for death, "I'm broke."
Stuck in my mind, wasting my time, "I am dead."
Looking for God, finding me lost, "in my head."
Wanting no more, killing me more, "I am gone."
Lost in her eyes, a new loss of mind, "it's you."

"Cut me, cut me, just cut me off."

No more, I'm just a bore, "I'm gone."
Here I stay, walk along, "with my song."
Enter death; enter God, "I am gone."
Lost inside, lost in mind, "it's you."
I'm forever, enter the never, "you all."
All I need, all I see, "is death."

"Rip out my mind, a true loss of time, it's you."

Endless lies, I wish to cry, "But I won't."
Loss of truth, kill I must, "but you."
I walk alone; I'm just thrown "away." Forever now I am insane!
Forever madness, years of sadness, "I am lost."
Must I beat, beat my head? "I am dead."
Dead inside, loss of mind, "kill me now." *"God let me out."*
So I fight and wish for reason, "something to believe in."
All I find, is a lost mind, "it's mine."
Yet you help, help me to see, "I am nothing."
Nothing for you, nothing for all, "I wish to fall."
So I do, because of you.
"Lost in you."

"Cut me off - I am dead."

Fighting Time

With the lifting of my eyes. Time I'll always fight.
Trying to get ahead in this world. I try to stand, but so weak I am.
Crawling out, above the sand. With a black sun, and red sky.
The child inside, he calls to me. To take control of life, control of time.
So on and on, on I fight. Why do these faces confuse me?
Trying and crying, I feel so alone.
Stone and grass, road and passing on to the shadow.
Fighting my dreams, time is against me. The world is crushing "*I see.*"
Demons and angels call me to the fight.
I fight time, I try to cry. I whine and whine.
In my time I don't have. This is the half of me.
To take control. I control me, "see?"
Fighting time is all I have. That half of us is over.
"*Just give it time.*"

SPIT BLOOD

Blood spit into the sky. I see pain and I feel fear.
Still it's here, the only truth. You stole my youth but I do love you.
I fall with the memory of us.
Must I die? Must I... "Why!?" Why do these tears run cold?
Why do I cry only dust?
I stab myself with broken glass. The past must be mine.
My toes are on the edge. That's all I have.
The cries are on the edge... So I fly!
"I spit blood."
I fall, so small I feel. I fall and that's all.
I scream, I bleed the only love I have.
I spit blood into the sky. I sit here and wish to die.
I fall asleep and feel so numb.
I drift away. I feel so unsane.
Blood and mud, damn you! I wish for new.
I bleed - we die.

Dim

Dim the light and open the skin. Rip open your chest and welcome sin.
Knives and pens stuck under the skin. Soon it fades, trapped in black.
The back of our minds are torn away.
So it dims and I love sin. The taste of blood on my lips.
A kiss of death to you. Well, so it's right and the fire dims out.
Speak the word of pain, nails shot through your mouth.
And so you try and so you cry and wish to die.
Would you have ever loved me? Could I *escape* this war?
Could I find the light in dark? Why am I so scared?
The crow spoke my name. Am I dead or insane?
Death finds me on dark wings.
Shadow in mirrors, crying all my fears.
Sleep dark pain. Scream so low insane.
Unsane is the mind that reflects me, I'm sorry but the light is gone.
The song was wrong. The light did dim. "I let in sin."
We all see things in the shadow.
Memories or things to be but for me, it's dim.

Fight

Fight the day, lose my way. Trying to cry, crushing the sky.
I just need to pray for the end today. Screaming so hard, crying so hard.
Hiding so far, running away. Jumping in deep, seeping the hate.
Constricting of the snake, am I dead?
On I move to see some light. Enter darkness and I fight.
All I do is pray. Fighting all your ways.
I choose to grow away. Enter darkness, go insane.
Seep the tears of the dead. Fight the world, till my death.
Fall deep inside, lose the only light. God given is the pain.
The world under the sane. The pain will grow with time.
Soon is the turn of mind.
I'm sorry that this is the only way. I must fight! Fight the day.
Or this is the end today. So I fight the sane, I scream so hard.
Jump in deep, fall apart.
So I pray...

Dry Courage

When courage has run dry and the night falls from the sky.
We look to the east to see the end. So the razor is my only salvation.
Her love has driven me over the edge. Now I feel so small.
All I've ever had was pain. Still I'm running away.
So far gone, have I lived too long? Long away from sane.
Box me true under you. Courage dropped onto the table.

Stained red walls of my home. It's all I've ever known.
Dried out in the sun. My body wastes away. "Will I be saved?"
Flash me *hope* - in your eyes. Brought by voices up so high.
Night come soon. The north rests aside.
When courage has run dry. Happiness... forever a lie.
I reach in deep to find the end. Please sweet razor find me soon.
"I'm so cold."

Her Hair

Swimming in her hair, lost and cannot see.
Endless backstrokes in pools of LSD.
We're running through the mountains, *drowning in pools of LSD.*
To touch her face, to touch her skin.
Smooth milky flesh, without a drop of sin.
Swimming through her hair and I touch her fingers.
She sets me free, now I see... Swimming in endless pools of LSD.
"Orange rainbows with a hint of blue. Yellow rainbows with a cloud for a noose."
Hang me in the hallway, hang me above the stairs.
Leave me in the shadow. I'm swimming through her hair.
Heaven is a reach away. The cloud is now turning gray.
She kills me inside, because she loves someone else.
Now I sit here and wish for hell but she's got me there.
She's got me there... Still I'm swimming through her hair.
Let me die, please end my life. Somebody just take my air.
Swimming through her hair, lost and cannot see.
So here I wait, in my purgatory.
Still I'm here, swimming through her hair, *drowning in pools of LSD.*
I swim through her hair.
And she moves on without me...

Heartless You

A million stabs in my heart. So I'm sick and torn apart.
Her only wish, is to kill my heart.
She watches me cry, it kills my mind. To see her hold another hand.
Aim for my chest, rip out my heart.
Tie me to the train tracks. You tear me apart.
I wish I never met you but I'm happy I did.

Still I sit here and love you, you heartless bitch.
Tear inside, kill my mind! Sorry but I love you.
You want me dead. I wish it all done.
See, if I ever love again. I don't want to, I just want you.
But you just wish me dead. So I lose my head.
Heartless cries, so many times. I wish I could just die.
I sit here and weep. So no more because of you.
So heartless - heartless you.
Consumed by hate. I die inside but "why!?"
Because of you, "Heartless you."

Damned

I was a child, and still may be. But I am a man, I'm bold indeed.
Still I crawl, and still I fall "yet." You see nothing but "shit."
So is that it, am I only that? Maybe to you, maybe you too.
Who could ever care about the *damned*?

I rise in the dark, to eat your flesh. I rise in the shadow, seeking rest.
I am a child, evil with pain. I am a man, I've grown insane.
I am the damned, I love only pain. I live in darkness with only hate.

Fall I do, every day. Sleep I do, away the pain.
Inside I fall, a million feet. I wish to see, I see only pain.
I am damned so unjust. Must I always be a freak?
I'm forever damned. I feel so weak.
Drop the weapon from my mind. Drip the blood from the vines.
Bleed me so unsane. Drop me in the shadow. Just to end the pain.

I was a child, and still may be but I am a man, bold indeed.
I am damned. Forever un-free.

Truth is Lost

It's funny how when you know something but you can't speak a single word.
The truth is right there and all these faces eat at my brain.
The truth is straight in front of my face and I trust nobody.
Voices and faces all around, must I be bound to the hell fire?
I wish I were dead to the world "I am." *I wish the world were dead like me.*
I could see only hate, because of that I wipe clean the slate.
I am hated because I'm me. I wish the world could just see.
I'm alone and alone I'll always be.
Even if she holds me tight, I'll never sleep good at night.
Cover the past I should. Would I even have been loved if she knew the truth?
So what, I could know the truth but she doesn't care. And no one will!
She covers her eyes, to hide the truth. I do wish I were alone.
Darkness is but a shadow but only God knows "why."
Why I wish to kill the world - so please set me free.
"I'm dead."

Deep Loss

Well, let's see. How many papers will I fill in one life time?
How many times can one man lose his mind?
How far do I have to run? And how deep do I need to dig?
I must run from the pain. I must stop running insane.

I never did think that I'd get this far. I'm stuck so deep in my heart.
I so need some light, to show a path. I must find - my lost past.
Well, let's see. Did you ever think I was insane?
Did you ever look at me in a different way? Did I ever look not so evil?
Why does the world think I'm evil?

Everybody tries to make me out to be the bad guy.
If they think I'm so evil, maybe I'll try.
I'll try to just let it go. Forget the world.
Kill it all. Pain to you.
I love my loss.
Is it a loss or gain?
Am I here? Am I insane? And forgotten?
Well - let's see...

Deep Darkness

Well, on the roads I bleed, and see the light fade.
I walk some more, and run from the day.
In the fields I hide, I hide in my own mind.
No one on my side so I try, try to kill this pain.

So it floods my soul, am I really that cold?
I wish I would just die, cry myself to sleep.
Fall in deep, to her *Never-Side.*
I wish I would just leave.
Please put me to sleep.

Onto dreams I crawl, to watch the world fade.
Dim the world within, sin for the joy of it.
Run in darkness, hide from myself.
Deep *within-side* my own hell, well I'm still here.
Fearing my own self, deep within my... "Well?"
Darkness in the darkest hour, we'll see.
Alone with hatred, with only the evil to seep.
So I walk these roads a little more.
Look to the sky, I'm nailed to the floor.

I jump into darkness and hide from the day.
Sit back and watch as the world fades.
I need to see more than that which is in front of my eyes.
Inside the deep darkness, I'll find my mind.

Too far gone, I weep only dust.
Kill the pain within, enjoy the death within.
To the deepest shadow I crawl.
Sit back my children, watch me fall.
To the deepest darkness I call...
Watch me fall.

Sweet Dove

So, on the roads I've walked in my life.
Looking for reason, the reason I'll find.
Stopped by the sound of a song singing, so soft.
A beautiful Goddess with a voice like an angel's tune.
A sound that should only be heard by Gods.
I stopped to listen and my pains were forgotten.
Lost in her blue eyes - I swim.
An ocean of dreams and wishes for love.
With a long white dress, pure as a beautiful dove.

I closed my eyes and nodded my head.
She was so beautiful; I wish it wouldn't have to end.
A song I'll never forget, a song of love.
I just stopped to listen, to the *beautiful white dove.*
"She seems so happy," I do wish to know.
Is she unavailable, "should I move?"

She was singing on the steps of her home.
I wished to speak, but felt so weak.
"Should I have asked or turn away?"
I would have asked but her voice just took me away.
With wings I fly, into the skies of *Mind.*
"I *don't even know her name.*"
But I felt so relaxed as if I've known her for ages, from way far back.

She stopped and looked into my eyes.
I just spoke the first thing that came to mind.
"Please, sing that song once more, I wish not to take any of your time."
"I will leave you be but please sing your song once more, for me."
"I don't know you, you don't know me but I'd love to hear your song again."

She just stared at me, I felt so weak.
I wished to run and hide.
But then she started to sing...

"Her beautiful voice, it frees my mind."

Alone I Die

So cold in my body, blood is unknown.
I bleed only dust, because I've forsaken you.
"You broke the trust." God watch me cry alone. Watch me die alone.
You don't love me true but in all, I still love you.
"You kill me." Good sweet death, alone my chest crushes.
I breathe no more.
More pain every moment. I die because of you.
We all see me as the unjust - justice is unseen.
We are all forgiven, all but me. "Please somebody free me."
So I die alone. Lonely drops of blood, this age is forgotten.
Among all I've ever seen. I see nothing in me.
So I die alone, I won't go on. I feel so wrong but I'm gone.
"I die alone."

Evil Eyes

Cry through the eyes of the devil and God.
Fight the world, win at any cost.
Here I fight, in the eyes of the forsaken. I'm hating all your sick ways.
And all is still forever dead, it's dead. Running in so fast, losing my past.
Killing our God, I've killed your God.
It's evil through these Eyes, evil in my mind.
All I did was kill, still I am lost. Still I fight, an endless fight.
My soul of hate, life of hate. I'm always and forever, the king.
"I stand still and bleed."

Evil minds, evil Eyes. Evil souls, evil cries.
Did the demon come for you? Did you get the chance to choose?
Did you win? Because I just lose.

Seep through the walls, cry only pain. Crush all the walls, kill the insane.
I grow only with hate, forsaking the truth. Forsaken you, endless times.
Lose your mind, steal your soul and kill the world.

Evil minds, evil times. Evil cries, evil tries to enter me.
Evil minds, evil lies. I so need to be wished away.
Evil in me, "forever insane."

"God these Eyes."

Away

Away and I'm alone, stone dead, I cannot sleep.
Wanting to know why but all I do is cry.
Why do you... all I see is nothing.

I'll go on forever and never see God.
I'll always be alone, forever apart.
"I say," I've grown away.
I've grown with *pain*.
I'm so insane and I love you.
Drop fast, hope it to last, I hope I'm not last.
I need to see the light, forever move on and fight.
So I go away!

I turn to the mirror and see a face of nothing.
So away I hide, to be alone.
Running from the day, hiding from my face.
I don't know where I am but I know it's home.

How far away must I be?
Just to see the sight?
Lay me down to sleep, just to end the fight.
Why am I here?
Here is where I fear...

Chapter 7

Faceless Youth

Faceless

Through the chambers in this cube, I'm running to my shelter.
Transformations, and the room shifts out of place.
"So I'm stuck faceless."
Fall under the water, as I cry. Feel the world crumble.
I'm welcomed to hell. Will I die, will I fight?
In the mirror, I am faceless.
Unknown with a life of the unjust. Must I go on and cry only dust?
I call to the darkness and wish I were known. Unseen by even me.
"I am faceless."
Faced with the taste of blood from you. Moon-tears fall and drift to me.
The sweet razor shines warm with red. The end is in my hand.
Faceless by the words of the *Just*. Must we all enjoy the pain?
So, unsane the insane is by me. I fall to the shadow and open arms free.
Deep into my shelter, we're welcomed to hell.
United by hatred. I wish me to the abyss.

"Faceless I face the world."

Evil Angel

I wish I were not here anymore. *Blocked by the walls, the halls I walk inside.*
Loss of mind because of her, she stole my heart.
Boxed in myself, I wish I were somewhere else.
Put me in hell, it's better than my mind.
Drained by her love, a blackened soul is all that's left for me.
"SHE KILLS ME!"
In my mind I see the darkness, her love tears me apart.
She's an evil angel, to God I wish me apart.
Better than my home, no heart. Better than my soul, it's my heart.
"SHE TEARS ME APART!"
Am I blind anymore? So much more pain!
Stuck in my soul, so unsane. Insane with the pain she gave to me.
"LOVE!?"
Should I die, say it's done? Should I cry, till it's done?
Could I ever have a home? Could I ever be known?
"NO!"
Why does the Angel make me dead? Why did the gravestone stop my head?
Did I ever see the truth? Did I never have a youth?
So cold inside, I cry. So alone inside, I cry.

THINK ABOUT US

I do love you, more than he ever could. I do need you, to end my sin.
I've never felt true love, until I met you.
How could you stand there, while I wish to die?
I love you my angel, open your eyes. So deep in pain, you've put me.
Just sit there and think, think of me. Please don't cry, just open your eyes.
I love you my sweet. I have not much to give you.
Just my life, "PLEASE MY LOVE!" Don't be another knife in my mind.
You make me a whole person when I'm with you.
Can you say he feels the same? Can you?
I'll give you my heart, I'll tear myself apart.
The only reason I'm alive is, "for you."
Open your eyes and think of us.
Please, all I'm asking is for you to stop and think.
If you could ever love me, please don't hate me for loving you.
When I see you with him, I die inside.
He gives nothing; I'll give you my life.
Please my sweet angel, think about us.
"I love you."

Show Me

There wasn't time, to free my mind.
I can't control, it takes my soul. Please somebody save me.

I wish for light, I wish for sight.
I need some guidance from this endless pain.
On the way from grace, sweet death is your taste.
O what a waste - I feel I'm gonna die.
In my mind, I'm already dead.

To the left shadow, to the right darkness. *I fall apart inside.*
To the never, is my forever-ever. *I need the path to shine.*
"God I am so alone inside."

I feel so small, the world so tall, the question why.
In my mind, I am dead...

CREEP INSIDE

Creeping through the back alleys in my mind.
Reaping through the shadow in my soul.
Ripping away the insane, calling the darkness to show.
Did God intend for us to grow? Did the snow turn warm as blood?
Flooding my mind with hate. Consuming my spirit within.

Did I ever live - did I never sin?
Grow now my evil children. Grow to show the world our pain.
Soon the soul will die out. The moon seems closer.
The gravity is crushing me down. Pull out the knife of the universe.
With gold slinking into the mind. The power does take control.
The pull of earth takes me.

In midair I seem, I scream out to my children, dark-water finds us all.
Creeping through the halls of our minds.
Seeping through the walls of my mind.
I find that hope is lost. "I am lost."

FATE?

It grows deep in the back of the abyss.
I seem to piss away the days I've known.
I know nothing and nothing knows me.
Drown me deep into insanity.
I'm growing into sleek madness, I'm finding that the hour is past.
The time did pass, I know only hate.
I see the snake, wrap around my soul.
I see voices in me. I fear the time I lie in darkness.
The shadow does encrypt me - I find myself stabbing God.
The blade shines red through the sky. I see the angels weep and die.
I grow in madness. Forever that's it!
I, the evil son of a bitch - I am forever and forever that's it.
I've grown only in hate. I see now that I'm too late.
The slate was clean but now I've seen.
I am the forever death of the world.
I see the placid fires grow, in flame I see fame.
I see the shatter, scatter me across the land.
I am forever the one. 9 times I've been to hell - well, that's my fate.

To The North

Slip into madness, consumed by sadness.
The question God gives to me, my fate is still unseen.
Being told what to do, day by day. Demons within, see a rush of pain.
So slip deeply into sound sorrow with a dream of tomorrow.
The bell rings numb.
Was she not there while I died? Did the angel weep as I cried?
I try to get out, stop running around but the madness grows within.
Dream sweet my love, I only wish to die.
Sleep slipping slimy demons crawling up my grave.
My spine does crack in two, drowning forever in this river of blood.
Mud, blood, tears of dust, the candles drain as the child grows insane.
Forever I see that you're unjust
To the north, where the water grows. To the south, where no man knows.
Inside we wish to die; God set me free, free my mind.
To the north, where the light dies. To the east, where the children cry.
Why do we lose our minds?
Please, you unseen freak! Give me back my mind!
Untrue did the reflection seem. The mirror told me to kill.
To the north where the child still loves her. Blue roses I hand to you.
Under my skin, I warm you. Razor toys, knives for boys.
"I seem to lose it."

TO ALL NONE

Sleek sorrow, a dream called tomorrow, I see God question his fate.
Faith on the face if a coin, the wine will grow into poison.
Sweet death consumed by the human soul. We are all cold in our own ways.
Drip and slumber while I see the Gods weep. The conspiracy grows.
The light flickers and dims. The ground trembles and...
I welcome in sin.
The only truth of life is fake. We're all freaks, psycho bastards.
We are all just sheep to the slaughter. We're meat to be fed on.
I know not why God lets us die. He'll let his children feel pain.
Of all who be insane I choose him as one.
Ruling the world by doing nothing.
I find something, that life is a lie - time to die, time to try and see.
I hate all because all hates me. I see life so unjust.
The dust covers us all. We all fall because we're nothing.
We're nothing to him and he's nothing to me.

Death Drops

Death drops from my teeth. Life pours from my grave.
The end is too soon to hide. The love will soon die.
Voices so sweet, tell me how to live.
I cry, and only death drops into my mind.
We all grow apart, life is a bitch. I die a million times, I wish to end this.
Death drops onto me; I see the voices are true. I never knew the truth.
But it's too late for me. Death Drops grow insanity.
The seed of evil I plant into you. I knew the truth, you - so untrue.
I ask God to end it. Drop me dead, in my head. I wish to die but I only cry.
We are only alone, when we are alone inside. I hide the truth.
As your death drops onto me, I see the only truth.
I'm only alone - when I'm not with you.

BLOOM

Love - I was there love. Under the sky, the light should grow.
Light - fight as I do, I wish to keep you.
Tight - I'll hold you tight, forever night.
Me - me alone with only hate, "smile please."
Sorry, sorry to him, not to me.
Love - see the forever, our never-never, "yet..."
Still, still I fight an endless fight.
But you are there, do you care, "please!?"
Love - I was there love.
I bloom the rose blue. I wish I could give this to you.
More, more in life you should have, "and have you will."
Happy, I'm happy when you're happy. Inside I die when you cry.
I so see something in you. Yes I do. I bloom the rose blue, just for you.
You're my angel, but you need to see.
I give you my heart to keep you happy.
So should you cry, inside I'll die. I want you to be happy.
Love - I was there love. Under the sky the light should grow.
I bloom the rose blue, I give myself to you. I see you give yourself to me.
You're my angel, forever true. Me and you, forever love shall bloom.
My friend, my love, I see. I'm happy when you're happy.
Me and you, my love is forever true. I hope you can see it too.
Love - I was there for you.

Life For Her

We open - the door - it's hard - but more.
More is the wish I give to her.
Life is the dream, the dream I wish for her.
Love is so hard, life is so short. Breath after breath, I wish more.
Cool air rises up and down my body. People grow and die.
With this girl, I wish to spend my life. Life for her, to see you happy.
I give life to you, it makes me happy.

Death drops from the razor. Your love holds me true.
Life is so short. I wish I were with you.
From start to end. We all live and we all sin.
I see now, the only truth. In all I see in life, "I need you."
I give life to her. Death to me.
Life is not forever. Forever is the dream.

You Make Me Alone

"Fine," drop me so hard.
This inner love for you has torn me apart.
You would never love, even if I do love you.
You'll never love, yet I still love you.

You break me, twist my soul. You break me, "forever I'm cold."
Cold and alone, I hurt inside. Asking you why.
Why will I die alone? And alone I will always be.

Reach in deep, within my soul. Tear out my heart, leave me cold.
You don't understand, "you never will."
Because you love him, "I sit alone and welcome sin."
Death brought to me soon. Why will I die alone?
I wish I could have been with you. Thanks to you, I'd never know.

We are only friends, I feel only sin.
I die inside, you kill my mind. You make me alone, only I cry.
I die inside, with my love for you.
"I still love you."

I'll Die Alone

It's only fate, I know it's true.
You are there, but not there for me.
I know I'll die alone. I know I am not loved.
I see that you're untrue. I'm sorry but I'm too confused.

Alone in my soul, I watch you laugh. I see you happy.
This feeling won't pass. I feel hate rise up my spine.
I feel hate grow in my mind. I am away, I've gone insane.
I am a lie, time to end this life.

You only lie, I wish to die. You watch me cry, and inside I die.
I know I'll die alone with only me. I know I'll die alone with hate in me.
It's too late for me, sorry. It's too late for me, sorry.
I have nothing but me. Please save me, oh God save me.

Truth

We fall and we - SCREAM!
Bleed the Gods and watch them fall from the sky.
Truth has been forsaken. They call me to the show.
Grow in evil pits of loathing the world. I love her the same.
I love the love of going insane. We are apart, I wish us together.
Whether or not we are on the same page. Still I love you the same.
But your love for me must be forsaken, "or."
Why do you always just... why do I die inside?
I love you more every day. The truth must be told.
I must have you in my arms. I'll keep you warm, when it's cold.
I need you to love me but for now, "I'm cold."
We fall, now we - SCREAM!
Bleed the Gods and watch them fall from the sky.
Truth has been forsaken. You call me to the show.
I grow in evil pits of loathing the world.
But forever I'll love you the same.
"I love the love of going insane."
I so need to go, I wish I were with you.
I must grow on; I wish to grow with you.
I do - I love you - forget him - forget the world.
You my world, I love you the same.
I love this love of growing in pain.

179

Me to Death

Because you want me no more. I wish I were - dead on the floor.
You make me just die. You make me just cry.
I wish we were, forever just one. I do not want to die alone.
You are the reason. The season of hate, it's growing in deep.
I love you, but you don't want me.
We need to see. We need to be. Be with me forever.
"Because I love you."
So we grow apart. With love between.
It seems you could never show the truth. I do love you.
I cry and die. Deep in my hate filled life.
Hold me up to the light. You see right through me. You must hate me.
Please somebody put me to death. I love you but you just don't see.
Because you want me no more. I wish I were - dead on the floor.
Please someone put me to death.
Because I have no one...

Need You To Need Me

In my time of need, you were never there for me.
I had to live alone; I will die alone and cry my soul to sleep.
Weep angels for the unforgiving; the light is dead...
You crushed my world, "I am done."
In my time of need, you were never there for me.
I dream as demons grow inside. Cry for the death of love.
Her ways driving me insane. I'm over the edge and love to see the end.
You dropped me before you even held me.
Why am I not good enough for you? Could I ever have what he has?
In the end I'll just lose.
I need you, but you need me gone.
Out of the minds of the world. I fall into my own hell.
Could the pain grow from the time we had?
No, I so need you to need me but I'm alone, cold in my heart.
Apart from the world, inside I die.
You were never there for me.

Youth

She was my angel - I wish to speak.
The light so bright - when she's near me.
But all I am is, confused - all I have, is the truth.
It was stolen, stolen by you - I never had a youth.
Now I'm old and gray - still the pain, it feels the same.
So here I wait to die - I wish I had a life...
From my back I pull your knife.
In this darkness, I find no light - with inner darkness, I do fight.
God, I am so crazed - it is your blood I crave.
You're pushing me, away from you - God I am, so confused.
Wait I do, for the end - I open up and let in sin.
God was never there for me - all I seem to do is weep.
Am I nothing, just a freak? God I wish to sleep.
Now here I go insane - lost while you, eat at my brain.
God I wish I knew the truth - but all you did was steal my youth.

Push Me To Pleasure

It's not that easy anymore!
The darkness is growing - I see no light showing.
Please somebody let me out! Free these words, from my mouth.
Push me over the edge, just to watch me fall.
Call the devil to take my soul.
Would it be so cold, if I knew where to go?
I'm so alone with nothing but me and the thought of going away.
The wish that I was not insane. I'm sorry but that's my ways.
Drop sweet madness, mixed up with sadness.
The only truth was given to me. Dark angel I love to bleed indeed.
Push me one last time. Drive me out of mind.
Not so easy any more. With hate nailed to the floor.
More was the wish but my love, you pissed me away.
Push me to pleasure. Drive me into pain.
Cut me open to watch me bleed.
"Dear God set me free."

Stone

Stone dead, in my head. Wishing for God, wishing for death.
Stone dead, in my head. I'm wishing for God and wishing for death.
It's funny when you're known, you want to me alone.
And funny when you're alone, you want to be known.
"I'm," stone dead, in my head. Wishing for God, wishing for death.

Forgiveness is the wish, the thing the angel pissed away.
Insane is the soul. The soul is mine. With a loss of time.
I give you none, "I am done."
"Because I'm..."
Stone dead in my head. Wishing for God, wishing for death. "I'm dead."

Stone dead, wishing for death.
"I'm gone."

<u>HER OR ME</u>

Do you see what God gave to me? Would you ever take it onto you?
Could she ever forgive me? "Sorry."
Driving me over the edge, shoving me under the ground.
Am I still bound to this only hell, well?
She gave me the tool, she acted so cool.
But now we're both dead, "well," just her.
She acted so cool, she made me a fool. So I schooled her in the ways of pain.
She gave me the tool, of true hate and some love.
Did she act so cool when I drained her of blood, "well?"
STUCK INSIDE, WITHIN MY MIND!
Do you see what God gave to me? Would you ever take it onto you?
Could you ever forgive me? "Sorry."
So we're dead, a whole head of pain.
She made me so insane, but I'm dead - inside.
Should I take my life or give it to her?
Should I even care, would she ever care?
So I'm over the edge, beating my head.
I so need to die, so I give her my life. Did she ever die or only in my mind?
So I just weep, wait for the sleep, bleed to set free the pain, "it's done."
She acted so cool, she made me a fool.
To give me the tool, of true hate and some love.
Well now it's done, "I'm dead." Did she ever die, or just I?

FORSAKEN TRUTH

Open, open is my chest, my breath is gone.
Songs of time, to nobody cares.
This is my own story, a story in my head.
The truth is, that truth is forsaken.
We go on day by day. We go on and have nothing to say.
We call and scream! It seems we have nothing.
Truth is forsaken!
Flesh drops and tears rain, the pain is ours; the time has come.
What ever could I do? Whatever have I done? "I'm done."
Truth is gone, the song will forever last. In my mind I seep to the past.
I wish for nothing, only truth! I have nothing, I had no youth.
Forsake my ways, forsake my mind. Forsake my truth, you're full of lies.
Forsake the love, forsake my cries.
You've forsaken truth. And I'm left with no light.

Untrue You

Drink... let the blood flow. Spit... enter death unknown.
Cry... tears of dust inside. Only I see through you.
Hold me tight, my love untrue. Do nothing but laugh in my face.

Cut... tear the flesh off bone. Cold... and alone I ask God why.
Why – why does it hurt inside? This world of pain is so fucking insane!
And it's untrue, it's untrue. So untrue, not true - not you.
Why - why God - why? Not true?

God! Why! No! Please! Help me somebody! Why?
Not true, not you. Untrue! No! No! Not true, untrue you!
Well? The night is young and I'm alone inside.
So here I sit, on my own stone.
I rock the world, with my true hate. "I quit!"
This is it, no more for you. I moved on, so should you.
God I move, no not you! So untrue, untrue you.
And still I have much more to say.
"Damn..."

Scream For You

Watch me scream for you, watch me bleed for you.
See me stand alone, and now I die inside.
I need to watch you all fall inside.
Inside I die, inside we call to the endless push.
The drive I find and give to you.
Scream for madness, with a mind of sadness.
Drop me a million miles inside. Let me scream, watch me die.
Feel the inward pain of us. The power of the never is gone.
I drop to my knees and pray for light.
Wishing with words I could end this fight.
I scream to God, "Let me die!" I scream to all and I cry.
Watch me scream and lose. You were never there for me.
I need the time, to set me free; I need to go.
Watch me scream - scream for you - for you...

Six Feet

Cut me down to size - Am I too strong? I fear that I am right.
Brought so true, under you. Six feet I am from light.
The anger and regret of feeling too numb.
Nerves are going to war on me.
Medieval lies, I try to lie under this sheet.
Was it you, so untrue? I fear that the angel did grow unjust.
Must the anger slump out onto the ground? Bound we are to this fate.
Brought so true, under you. Six feet I am from life.
Knives and tipped shadow. The all of everything inside.
Why does my body grow so weak? Mind toys and a feeling of the *Just.*
Must we all go on to see? Six feet from being me.
Fall down the rabbit hole, the path of sacred belief.
The return of the child, the dying of my mind.
Show no way out of this maze - I am growing so confused.
Abused by the everything inside; the fate is a lie.
Brought so true, under you. Six feet I am from right.

NoD

Is it trust? Yes I must. See some God, but I fall to Nod.
Thrown away - I'm insane - it's my fault - I want to fall.
Nod is mine, all I have is time. So wait I don't... no I won't!!
Turn to hate, confused by snakes. Demons from hell, is all I have!
Thrown away - I'm insane - it's my life - I want it all.
Fall apart, is all I do. Who gives a shit, no not you!
I'm so dark, misunderstood. So God doesn't care, I've forsaken you.
8 to death and more to fall, it doesn't matter; I always fall and fall.
Thrown away - I'm insane - it's my fault - I need it all.
I need some heart; I fall apart because I have none, *so I've sung.*

On and On

On the way - lose my way! All to be - still I see!
God I'm dead, beating my head! Still I fight, an endless fight!
It's my life, so on I FIGHT!
Killing God, feel so lost! Forsake my life, so pull out the knife!
"FUCK!"

On I go - I'm so alone. But you don't care - no one cares!
All I need, the seed of light! On and on, on I fight.
Killing God, feel so lost! Forsake my life, so pull out the knife!
"God!"

Demons inside, stealing my life! God is dead, so now I'm dead!
Or just gone, my life - my song! My sin so cold, cold like mud!
My blood is thin, and thick like all! So I fall, I fall to death!
"Now I'm dead."
Killing God, feel so lost! Forsake my life, so pull out the knife.
So on and on - on I fight!

Push Me Six Feet

Push me to the last step and watch me fall.
Reach into my chest, I'll crush you all.
To the deepest pit I call, "I watch me fall!"
Crying tears of dust, much more inside.
Crawling under six feet, and I hide. To the north shadow, deeper I sink.
Seek to seep the hate from you. I need all, I'm going to lose!
Drop me under six feet, push me to the edge.
I wish I were not here, no knowledge of this.
I'm alone in darkness, in my own box.
Filed away from the world, "forever lost."
Untrue is the insane of you. All I need is to be free.
Set me free, let me go, push me six feet, I wish I were not known.
Hide me under these sheets.
Rock me till it bleeds. Kiss me forever true.
Push me six feet, six feet from you.
"I'm ready now."

I'm Right

Faces and faces all around. Cast into the pit because of words from my mouth.
Sorry, "I'm right."
Falling and falling and falling more hard.
Running in deep, running in far. Crushing the world, killing your God.
Still I am the same, forever insane.
Judging and constricting my pain. Stuck in this world, eating my brain.
Finding the time, to crush your mind and I will kill you all.
Faces and faces all around. Cast into the pit because of words from my mouth.
Sorry, "I'm right."
Jumping into death, the fire all around.
Bound to the fate, in which I have found.
Must it be, must I see? "God help me!"
God I walk, stalking my past. Finding time but time will never last.
Faces that try to win. Voices filled with sin.
Locked inside, in my mind. I find it dead, "I wish it dead."
In my soul, death is late. I crawl and fall, within my hate.
Sorry, "I'm right."

Dark Moon Love

It was to be - confusing me - seeming dead - lose my head.
She hates me good - yes she would - all I did - oh God this is it!
"God to that place in my mind, losing my sight, losing my mind."
"It's all just dark moon love."

In nowhere I find the time to see, souls and ghosts of the forsaken 3.
A flood of voices in my head, so now...
Out of my mouth and through the air.
Into the ear of her, so I show no... why did she die!
Why did I lie? Why?!
"God to that place in my mind, losing my sight, losing my mind."
"It's all just dark moon love."

Rain of hammers onto me, the God of love has forgotten me.
I give it time, the twist of mind.
But no one cares; you don't care, so now...
The sun and moon, into one and it's done!
Advice from hell and that's all I have...
The call to the all inside my head.
So time to grow and show my life, you won't know.
Welcome to my life...
"God to that place in my mind, losing my sight, losing my mind."
"It's all just dark moon love."

Alone we see, not even me, just the forever, the never never.
Love is over, I am over and it's done. This as I've said and this as I've done.
Pits of nothing, seas of blood. All I have is a dark moon love.
Sleep and dreaming, seeping death. Time to fall, away with my breath.
So here I sit, blood in fist. Crying dust, forever dust.
All I did and all I see. Time to quit and kill the light in me.
It's done, I'm done.
Done with this dark moon love.

Sleep

I feel I'm falling, under this sheet I scream.
I have no way out.
I need to stop!
Stop running around.

The darkness is growing.
I see no light showing.
"Please God help me!"

I cry as I sleep away the demons.
I try to hide.
I wish to die.
"Please somebody save me!"

The light is dim.
And I feel only sin.
I wish I could grow.
I wish I could know.
Nobody on my side.
I wish to hide.
Stop running and see.

"Please somebody save me."
I have no guide.
I have only me.

"So I sleep..."

Chapter 8

Numb Nerves

Loss of Light

Loss of time, loss of mind, I find only pain.
Drip the blood off my flesh. Feel the only truth, of life.
See within, the loss of light.
My teeth crack on your bones. The pain grows unknown.
I see the question why. So I try to end the light.
Darkness of dim dreams. It will go on unseen.
I could be only for you. With the pain, pain of the truth.
Loss of mind, loss if light. Loss of body, with an endless fight.
Loss of happy, the end is here. We're all left in the dark.
I wish I would not fall apart. I could go on no forgiveness of us.
Loss if time, lost in my mind. Loss of heart, I fall apart.
Lose the fight, with a loss of light.

Soon

Look to the shadow, "north" while the darkness grows.
The wings show guidance. The forever will never go.

Why stand when drams fly? Why cry when hope dies?
Should she move on? Should I go on to see?
This life of Death will forever be.

Stand tall my children. The pain is not yours.
Wars will come and go in this mind. The edge tip is in me.
The break is mine. The death is yours.
I go - I know - I see.
Could I never be? Please God set me free.

"I know I'm not alone inside."

Kill

Kill the world and kill it dead. Still I fight, I beat my head.
But inside I wish, I wish to die. I will kill, I kill you all.
On I fall into hate, still I hate but I just have you down.
The world is mine in hand. Kill you all, watch you fall.
God I'm ready to die, so here I am. I'll kill you all and kill again.
So time to take over the world. Time to steal your soul and take control.
Kill you all, kill them dead. I love to hate you till death.
I'll kill you all, till my last breath. I'll take you all, watch you fall.
Then I'll jump and enjoy the awe. All I need is your death.
To watch you cry. And lose your breath.
Kill the world and watch it burn. Still I fight and watch you hurt.
Lust of pain and blood, I so need to kill you all.
Watch the world crush under me. Time to free the feeling of loss.
The reason is gone, I'll kill you all - and you're mine, you're all mine.

Friend

Just like that - just like this...
You're my friend forever, so what is this I see?
"Who is this that dwells within-side me...?"
Friend oh friend - will it never end?
Never stop my friend, let's see it to the very end of time.
"Sit here, and tell me it will always be."
You're a great friend and so much more.
Friend oh friend - friends till the end.
Be with me till the end of time.
So much in life, see you are my friend, see it in my eyes.
Evil – evil... you stop the evil that's inside of me.
You stop every evil thought that dwells within me.
Such a good friend to me.
Just a friend to the end, *"and for that I'll always love you."*
O such a good friend, *"please be with me till the end."*
So just like that - just like this.
You're my friend forever, *"what is this I feel?"*
You're my friend, so can't it be.
That I no longer feel evil - "no more evil in me."
No more - no longer shall the devil rule me.

"Thank you my friend."

192

More

Stop pushing me away - stop pushing me away.
Don't push me away any more, any more.
Stop pushing me away - stop pushing me away.
"Don't push me again you fucking whore."
MORE!

Leave me be, set me free - all I want, all I need.
Is to see, why I care, God I wish it away - I wish away the pain.
BUT THE PAIN IS YOU!

So nice it could be - if it weren't so fucked!
So nice it would be - I am forever stuck.
Life is apart from me - seemingly I'm just dead.
I wish that were the truth - I wish it onto you.

Push me away, to this day - let me fall, so I call.
Call to hell, well "I'm not evil?" So who do you think you are?
Far in the depth of my soul - so cold it is in my heart.
Well, all is apart from me.
MORE!

Sane No More

Quit pushing me away, here I'll forever stay.
To make you mad, so damn mad.
So crazy it could be to see. "I need truth."
So walk as I do, to see a better you.
But you don't care, *Friend?* "I think not!"
Stop pushing me away. Don't push me away any more, any more.
Stop pushing me away. Don't push me again you fucking whore.
MORE!

More I wish, as I piss away my life. So here I seek to find your knife.
From my back I pull it out, I seek for you to shove it down your throat.
Cut your heart and watch you bleed. I hate you, because you used me.
Friends to the end, so the end is today... still I love this life of going insane.
MORE!

You Need To Kill Me

ALL I NEED! ALL I SEE! I WISH TO CRY! I WANT TO DIE!
See me alone with only hate.
KILL ME NOW! KILL ME GOOD!
DROP ME HARD! KILL ME FAST!
O dear God, don't let it last.
Dead bodies, dropped to the floor. Bloody fingers, *a knock at our door.*
Screaming crying, I hear children dying. To God I wish more.

Need I see, need I die? Would you care - would you cry?
"You need to kill me..."

Fuck the world, kill you all. Leave my body, kill your body.
Just to watch you cry, I need to die.
All is lost and can't be found. Bound to my only hell, "well?"

Need I see, need I die? Would you care - would you cry?
"You need to kill me..."

You See

Do you really want to see? What I have in store for you.
Do you really want to see? Open your eyes...
Do you really want to see? What I've held down for you.
Do you really want to be? Give me your mind...

Rip open your heart, sit back and fall apart.
I see that it's not over, give me your soul.
Fingertips on the lips of evil, would the light show a path?
Did my past pass? Why am I so alone?
You want to see? Open your body and set me free.

Do you really want to see? What I have in store for you.
Do you really want to see?
Give me your eyes...

Love?

You died for me. I cry in my dreams.
It seems I have only pain. Because of you I am insane.
I wish to die, set free my life. I wish to die, set free my mind.

You are the reason I bleed. Our reason to be was lost.
You must come back to me. But now I sleep - under six feet.
Your love has been untrue. I know you don't love me too.
Hold me true to the walls. Bleed me dead, crush my head.
I wish to die, set free my life. I wish to die, set free my mind.

God does forgive me. I do - not forgive me.
Sorry my love, I'd die for you. But it was you that has been untrue.
Sorry...

Set Me Free

Could you ever know my pain? Could you ever go insane?
Should I ever die? Should I set free my mind?
Life! Is gone! To me!?
Set me free, let me be. Please somebody, set me free.
Let me be, just set me free. Please somebody, let me die!

So here I am, stuck on the cross. I see what he saw and feel what he felt.
But I have hate and he had love.
Well here I'm stuck, I'm bleeding unjust.
Must I go to hell, because heaven doesn't care?
So here I cry and wish to die. Die out my soul and get rid of all the pain.
Was he insane, or is it just me?

Does God even care, or is this just his sick game?
To make me feel pain, "so unjust." So just let me die, let me cry.
I've tried to win, I feel only sin. Well, that's my life, "My life."
Tonight I die, with blood in the sky. I spit to the ground, it's only dust.
Must God forsake me? "Me!" So set me free, let me be.
Please somebody, set me free, let me be, set me free!
Please somebody, just let me go...

Life?

So I weep away these endless days. So I sleep inside, I am so crazed.
Well, it's only the truth, I've done my time.
I lose my mind day in and day out. I feel fear and I see doubt.
My life is but a loss and the price is me.
Death drops onto my neck; I feel the razor so cold.
Warmed by the blood running down my face.
I look at the world and see the disgrace. I touch my face, I feel so numb.
Am I dumb or is the world just slow? I am the God of pain, I so need to see.
Am I blind from pain, or are you just that insane?
My death I drop onto the world. I dig myself under the ground.
Moonlight twists in my soul; I feel pain burn my mouth.
Upside-down backwards-temptations; the hate is - insane then.
Well, the clouds don't lie, as I lie in this box.
My box is old and rotten but I'm still young.
I'll grow into the death, *"I'm done."*
Pull the blade from my eye and shove it into my heart.
Could the angel weep for me? Sleep as I die in my purgatory.
The growing pain is only the same, I am insane.
But that's only the truth, the truth is forever but *never will the tree grow.*
The water is running. The time is old and corrupt.
My path-past, forever fucked! Well, that's life - well, "mine."

Free Me

See - why can't you be? Why can't you just, "leave?"
Leave me be. Why can't you just let me go?
Free me, let me be. Why can't you just let me go?
I want to fall; I need it all, I wish to go.
Why can't you let me go?
Free me from the world. Free me from you.
See - you won't let me be.
I need to just go. Let me fall and die.
I wish to free, free my mind. I need some time God give me some mind.
I'm ready for forgiveness, I'm ready for rejoice.
I'm so alone inside, please set free my mind.
Why can't I move on? Why will I pass on?
Why won't you let me be? Why am I not free?
Please set me free. Free me please.

Smile

Smile sweet dove, falling through placid fire.
Call the hour; find the road has turned as the sands of time waste me away.
Questions bring me back to the knowledge of rebirth.
In my eyes I see the world turn, without me.
Endless days of suffering and regret, "yet I smile."
Turn the candle over and wax the eyes of mine.
Smile while I forsake the path I've hated.
You were the only reason I had to live.
Now I breathe only for revenge and sin. I am nothing just like you said.
I'm forever nothing, but an unfortunate sin.
Call the power, while gravity pulls me to fate.
Smile while the truth of all is forsaken.
You were my world, now I'm stuck in space.
Face the world, faceless on no taste of justice.
The most I had was you, and after all "I lose."
Laughter and tears of joy, I enjoy the life I hate.
So no more crying, only fighting, "I'll fight away the pain."
Wash my face, feel the world grow disgraced.
I taste the shadow, welcome to noon.
Soon I'll be at peace, when revenge sets me free.
So while I smile, you cry. "Forever I smile in life."

Pain Rush

I can never find a reason to breathe.
The world is beating me down, till I'm unseen.
The light is fading - reality is gone.
And truth drips off the edge of the knife.
Open one eye my love and let me out. I'm screaming forever to be free.
The ground is crumbling away at my feet.
The sky is red, I'm wishing to see. The dust covers my body.
I'm so warm, sleeping under six feet.
I'm falling deeper into myself. The world is gone or maybe it's me.
I know not whose face this is, even if it's mine.
I remember nothing of my past but pain and lies.
Hold my hand, put me to rest. I'm growing on no knowledge of this.
The water is rising, "God save me!"
Rush me faster away from the light. No!
I won't quit without a fight.

Tearless Cries

Love - will I ever feel love again or am I left with only sin?
Love - why can't I be happy in my life? From my back I pull your knife.
Love - will I never be known by the world? "I cry..."
I fall down to the gravestone and kiss my past goodbye.
I scream in a lost dark state of mind, behind the pain.
Bleeding tears inside, faceless inward cries, "I cry."
Blanket me - I'm so cold inside. Alone in mind, I wait.
I'm turning and seeking but I must be blind.
No more heart, only tearless cries. Inward *suffering*, "I cry."
Love - will I bloom the rose blue for only you?
Love - why do you push me down while I'm lost?
Laughter and crying, inside my soulless heart.
I might not be like everyone else in the world.
But I still feel all of what you do to me, "I can't see!"
Turn up the music, close the doors to the world.
I smile and cry inside, because I was right.
No matter how hard I try, no matter how much I cry.
Neither you, nor anyone could ever understand me, "*you never will.*"
You and you and everyone else are more heartless than me.
Well, Love - I will never be known again "*or maybe I will.*"
But still I know the truth. I sit here with tearless cries because of you.
Love?

Numb Tears

I shut my eyes, the pain rolls down my face, numb.
Turn me down then set me on the cross, "I'm done."
Push me two more times and I lose, "never will I be found?"
I the child cries because I will never know.
Why do you push me my love? "Turn over my gravestone."
Warm rain falls down onto my body, my spine twists, "I die."
Fall calling, I'm finding only your lies. Lay me to rest, I wish to wake up dead.
You give me air, only to watch me scream.
You give me life, only to see me bleed.
Said the white numb feeling that my heart is gone.
Push me down and I can only weep, "In my mind gone."
Push me to the north shadow, end me tonight!
She hates me so good, "*it's like a book.*"
Push me to the only truth, "never did I have a youth?"
I'm crying and frying, I'm wishing me gone.
Turn over the feeling, I'm oh so done;

Not one breath did set my heart free.
From my back I pull your knife and bleed.
Heart and hate, the world is no more. "I'm numb."
Done with fighting; only dying inside.
No body of my own, turn over my gravestone.
I'm not that bad, I'm just misunderstood.
Now with only hate I end this page!
"It's over for now..."

Dirt

Under the earth I crawl, fighting the ways of all.
Screaming low, the pain rushes through my skin.
Darkness grows, alone with hate and sin.
Clock tick me back to a child's mind.
Once in fire I lied, I die - never will you cry!?

Flow me reason, the light still gone.
My eyes are blank, so colorless within.
Shadows of a dream, seeing the failure of men.
Right between bone and flesh lies our truth.
Life so dirty, "you the world stole my youth."

Open the box, let me free to control my life.
Dripping down deep is my heart and your knife.
I lick the blade, you kill me indeed
So colorless dreams are me and the lie called life.

Under six stories is truth and pain.
Blood through the walls of what I call home.
Here I'm left, no home, no hope, only me.
You - you stare into my eyes as if I am faceless.
I need not to show you why.
Here I am with power, and the small angels cry.
Weep, I ask you to look within.
Dirt still covers and I'm left still with sin.

Crush Grind

Bring me the head of the man on top of the mountain.
Bring forth both arms of the man of the woods.
Bring me two hearts pure of lust and sin.
Bring me the soul of the child - dark... "Insane mind within."

Three left turns, candles black, fire rushes down dark and deep.
Flow the blood, feel the power grow "then burst!"
Said to the right and down twist of bone, "the owl calls for you."
Smile and laugh, twist the hatred back and back.
Two more grinds and the bones are dust.
Pull 4 children teeth and one child eye. "Crush and grind 2 more times."

Vibrations! The voices creep up my spine, cold in my mind - dark.
The smart demons enjoy fear and pain. "Flesh soon ripped away."
On large wings comes the cool death for you or I?
"Run my child and hide!" One north step and all will fall.
"Smile so sweet."
Rush the power throughout my body; it's so - so killing me.

I can't stop scratching... hold me down please! "Somebody save me!"
What evils have I turned loose upon the souls of mankind?
Hurry, we must stop the power! "The power must be mine!"
Fingernails crack and twist on the wooden door.
Regurgitation - I'm so seeing no escape, so soon I say!
No windows, the walls are crushing onto my brain.
Crush and grind down the bone, 3 left twists to home.
I call forth the power, to take me away!

"Good God..."

Paper

I love paper, it's my only friend. I love it when I can tell it my pain.
Paper doesn't ever question my ways. I sit here in my life of pain.
Paper love, the one done sung song of the only truth that I hate mankind.
Humans, so dirty and untruthful. I was and will always be evil, forever now a man.
I am now and will always be so, so alone.
Die - I wish to watch the world melt at my feet, I laugh while I burn.
Spiders run under my skin, I write my sin, on my only friend.
Paper - so the life I live so, so stuck!
Will I ever see a new reason to breathe? I hate the world, "people."
So - so I wish to watch them bleed.
Dark room spinning...
My paper love dances around me while I - while I cry!
So alone I die, die for the love of hate.
Nail me to the cross, on the cross I bleed.
So upside down, I dig so deep to never be found.
I love my friend, my paper love.
As I cry, she, it, we... all I have, is all I need.
I love my paper, the only truth. I sit in dark madness with only you.
My paper friend, you help me when I'm alone.
Hold me when I'm sick, I love my paper friend.
As the sin drops and blood rains.
Pains forever inside, left I am alone.
With an evil mind and my paper love.

Forehead To The Gravestone

Rushing in deep, "into the unknown."
With my forehead to the gravestone.
Spinning walls, the halls are deeper than they have ever been.
Seasons of the forever unjust; *the most I had was you.*
Draining time, the candle dims and the floor spins without me.
Forever unjust, ever I must, "deep in unknown."
With my forehead to the gravestone.
Forgotten times - forsaken minds - the only things I've seen are unseen.
Seep the hate from a world between, "life so, so unseen."
Crying and crying till only dust bleeds from your eyes.
With my forehead to the gravestone, "I wish I were known."
Bleed and watch the clouds fade and grow, "without me."
I wish to know, "forehead to the gravestone."
Never have I known;

So lay me on fine-comfort and sing my soul to sleep.
Blanket my pain; watch over me while I dream.
Deep down the dark halls I rush, a numb body is me.
Faded memories and the dream of life cannot be.
Drop to one knee, "oh lord please!" I wish to be known.
As I cry and bleed for you "for you." Never I'll be known.
Now a rush of pain... With my forehead to this gravestone.
Run away from the pain, hide inside till I die.
The ground spins and I'm left alone.
I wish I were with you, so my forehead to her gravestone.
Laughing at the pain, I feel so unsane, I can't see?!
Hold my hand Angel, let me sleep, "don't you weep."
We wished to be known, "so I sleep" and forever I will weep.
As I rush in deep, into the unknown, with my forehead to the gravestone.

Power

Power rises, the shadow seeps inside.
The truth cracks, so I'm burned alive.
The ghosts are calling me to shine, so through the Never I forever hide.
Down with sadness, crawling through madness.
The light dims, I so need to be alive.
Call my name and with the power I rise.
You are nothing, I am just nothing.
The faster I run, the more I wish to be alive.
The shadow grows; I'm growing with the knowledge of the naught.
When will you be done with me?!
I walk on water, was red blood. I rain the power, till my time has come.
You make me hurt, I search for reason.
The reason to be, the darkness is all I've seen.
Cut open my chest, rip out my heart.
The time has come, you tear me apart.
Power my hate, bring me to life. The reasons of me are hidden in life.
Shine me a path, give me the power.
Give me the reason, push me no more.
You must hate me, "was red on the floor."
Give me the tool; you're so full of hate.
Give me the power, it's now too late.
Shine me a reason, the power still grows.
Never doubt me again, forever you will lose.

Creep Behind Childhood

Drip the cloud down the back of my eyes.
Spin the candy-hate without a sense of time.
Fall to one knee and pray to the heaven's God.
Endless roads turn around; only on me "forever I creep."
Time clock ticking back and forth and back some more.
So many smiles turn upside down for me and me.
Into dark hallways, the singing takes me, "I wish to see."
The sound rocks the air, I feel the world move.
Which room, which door should open or close.
Should I leave my life to fate or make my own?
Knowing not where to go, swimming cold and alone.
Waist deep in sorrow and the only truth.
She and her and everyone else stole my youth.

Spin the knife on the back of my hand, "stop me!"
Let and enjoy the cloud drip down my spine.
I feel the twist of bones and heart within my soul.
Down the only truth bleeds the pain of the sane.
Weep the angels and watch me creep inside.
Sweet feeling the truth fold in my hand while closed?
Deep are the voices that find only the truth to behold.
Small little demons rip my flesh apart, one by one.
I spit blood into the sky and dream of happy times.
I nod back and forth in a painful mind state.
I grab the knife blade and shove it deep into my neck.
Wishing the path was still there, "it is."
But deep in darkness, I enjoy what I am.
Set aside from life and light I know only pain.
Spinning the blade on the back of my hand "under my skin."
I drop to both knees and speak to God.
"Are you listening?"

"This is who I am, this is what the world has made me."
"Thank you...."

Summit of Pain

At the summit of pain, no signs of release.
Place your hands on your temples and scream.
Flush the hatred outwards and laugh while we bleed.
No more delight in cutting myself. Taste the awesome gift called you.
So at the summit of pain, I choose my way.
I neglect the fire and enjoy the hour in between.

Tear off bleeding flesh; I rip out my own bones.
The sweat rolls down my face, I taste disgrace.
Hold my hand while I wonder away.
Deeper I dig, dig and dig to hide the pain.
My ways and reasons are now all forgot.
The time after time I fought just to lose.
So now at the summit of pain I choose.

I climb and crawl, I claw at my own grave.
I wonder what lies on the other side of the door.
The more I wait, the less I have to lose.
All I had was you, you and you and only you!
The truth is, there is no truth... only me.
I stand on the summit, smile and bleed.
Creep down dark hallways to find the world inside.
I climb, crawl, fall and fly only to die!
You nor you or even me will ever see past the summit.
I see now that I am on top. So I sleep. "Forever I will be."

Under Twisted Nerves

Let free my hands, sink deeper into the sand.
Sleek numb nerves go to war on me, the light is gone my love.
You are gone my love. Now I'm sitting on my gravestone alone.
I smile with regret. I enjoy the feeling I never had.
So living life on a lie, the lie called me.
Numb body falling to one knee, bleeding through my eyes.
One left turn away, pull the trigger to free yourself of pain.
Dance on stars and moons, Noon is so near.
Drop fear to the bottom of the lake, "take your time."
What a waste of mind you are, "far from ever being true."
So who could ever set free this numb feeling called me?
So I ball up in the corner of my past and truth;

You're gone now my love, you've now stolen my youth.
Left right twist of body, nerves are gone from me.
Deeper I sink into the sand, in a land called me.
Tear the light of life. I'm still here all alone.
Hold my heart in your hands while I wish for sanity.
The reasons of being me is forever so, so unseen.
The truth will be so, so forever in deep. Within a lie called me.
The sand covers me. I smile because I've known nothing else.
As twisting are the nerves of me. I wish I were seen.
I will never be, and you always will see.
Still alone on my gravestone, I smile nerveless.
So under twisted nerves I wait. Waiting for a new breath of life.

Friend or Foe?

Questions, why? Friend or foe, who's to know?
I am and will always be a twisting soul.
Knife point on my teeth; the bones hurt inside.
The light pours out of my grave, "rain the blood in the sky."
I see the end in a bloody kiss called you.
Shove me deeper down the hole of eternity.

The salt so sweet, the life is not complete.
The truth is gone; the far away is the pain.
Friend or foe, who's to know? "Not me."
So down the rabbit hole I run. Hiding from light, I avoid the sun.
I'm the son of a bitch you've made me out to be.
Down I dig, for my rest in purgatory.

Sweet tears roll down my face so warm like blood.
I cry in dreams and die in life.
I'm not to say who you are my "friend or foe?"
"Well" why do you love to watch me in pain?
Damn it, you drive me so insane, "away I creep."
Down dark halls of my mind and it cracks.
The knife called you is in my back.

You were my friend, now I only sin.
I loved you true, so who are you?
Friend or foe, well who's to know?
"Not me."

Hands On My Head Till Dusk

In grounded loss of our time spent on only your shit.
And I cannot move my eyes. I bleed nonstop in my soul.
Cold heart of nothing but my forever torn apart soul, dead.
Till dusk I scream, with pain and regret, yet you smile. "Smile!"
They laugh at me because I'm just a freak. They all clown on me - *"Freak!"*
Run more through my soul, run me cold on only lies.
Pain brought by my time. So no more time I waste with you.
If ever I had a way, I would have to say that this is it.
And nothing is left for me to do. Only lose and live in shit.
And I must be what you said. So until dusk I will stay on my grave alone.
Please someone help me die. Why do they laugh while I cry?
Hands on my head till dusk - the forever must be shown.
The knife must be yours because only you smile while I bleed.
And no one truly cares and no one ever will.
Place your hands on my head and rock me to sleep.
Put me to rest, and take away my breath.
"I'm just a freak - *and you laughed at me...*"

Dark Question

The darkness sets in. The hour of the mental twist is gone.
The questions are still lingering, the cloud is my only goal.
The cold body growing is mine. I'm forever alone within dark minds.
Warmth I wish, the deeper I still dig and dig to sleep.
Consciousness is melting, the chosen ones are here.
Fear and cold torment wrap around my warm icy body, *"I must be lost."*

Red flowing, warm sweet life with a heart of light.
The sands blow and rush down my throat, "open me."
Lightly cool metallic tools cut me down till I'm alive.
The wrong words spoken, and I'm cast away from the light.
Picky little angels sing your songs till you weep dust.
Laughter and cries, our mother earth dies, "you're all animals!"

We sleep, and fate creeps. Lambs to the slaughter we are.
Darkness growing, dimness be found to save my soul.
The reasons of the seasons of lust, hate and sin.
I welcome all into my heart, because I've known nothing else.
You - you push me away, I the dark child will soon rise.
The hour will pass and air will soon be gone;

Constriction of my neck, God please just set me free!
I'm so alone in this darkness called me. I need your guidance.
I'm not going to make it any further, am I?
Well, sorry to all but I am who I am because of you.
But neither you nor anyone will ever accept me, "I'm nothing."

Sorry My Only Child

Step by step, my feet are on the edge and I'm smiling, "all hates me."
The cool *fall wind* blowing across the land, through my hair.
Warm tears roll down my face, "please don't cry my child."
Years and years have passed and alone I waste away. "Don't save me."
I'm nothing by myself and alone I'll always be. "Forever just me."
My feet are moving, I wish to end all this pain now.
Now I'm falling and you my child scream so, so loud.
Time won't stop flowing, I'm burning out; I'll soon be gone.
Like a tree growing, soon I'll wither and die.
Run, play and step on stones that were once called me. "Be happy."
Open your heart to the truth. It's the path I made for you.
Sing sweet melodies. Smile while the wind kisses your face.
Upon the horrors of what I've done, "I'm sorry my only son."
Please just play and pray for the sun to shine one more day.
I'm dropping faster to the fate I've chosen. "Dry is the mind in me."
Grow strong and fight for what you believe in, "be a man."
Smile when the world wrongs you. Just know you're better than them.
Never stop living, always look passed the past, "live for me."
Sorry, I'm not there for you but know I'm with you always.
A grin on my face, I'm falling deep to fate, the light is gone to me.
Twist and bend the gravity, the sun dims - I'm fading, "sorry."
Red waters run throughout my mind. Deep hallways, "give me sight!"
Just one heartbeat away from grace, one piece of mind left.
Sorry if all I've done was leave you in the dark.
It's all my fault but this life has torn me apart.
I'm down to size, I know now all my mistakes, so sorry.
Live for me my only child, you the only thing I've had.
Smile my only child, even though I've fallen.
"You stand."

Under Gone Forgotten Life

At the bottom of wet dark crypts, creeps my mind.
Down lonely streets I walk, the trees blank and no longer alive.
No wind to run through my hair. You hurt me without a care.
No laughs as children play. Gone away I am from sane.
The same faces haunt my mind, memories of you stabbing me inside.
It's hopeless; I'm forever stuck in the dark dream called life.
It falls harder as I'm left here alone, lonely tears I cry.
So alone are the thoughts that brought me to life, "what a lie."
Fade me a new reason, or take away my air.
As angels rip away my heart, you don't care, you won't care.
Bring me a new dawn, the facts are forever gone.
Lord - lend me one hand of yours, "please somebody wake me!"
At the wake of the feeling so numb and forgotten.
The taste of sweet warm blood runs through my body.
This world around me melts; I'm nothing, "just a memory."
All was a lie, my life. I'm stuck outside looking within.
As this world crushes me, sin is once again taking control, "oh God!"
This is your fear, this is what you made. You shall never be saved.
Well now, I stand evil and without a care, leaving you without any air.
This is what you fear this is what you made for yourself.
Stillness falls over the land. No color or life, only pain.
The life - the light – they're all gone and faded away, "I am away."
Wake me at the beginning of the last sun rise.
Sorry if all you were, was a lie. Numb body and such a cold life, "why?!"
I walk over the bridge, the water smooth as glass. "Passing nothing."
The sky is gray, the light is dim, numb flowing and gone.
Six feet low, the glow of heaven is gone, but not lost.
In between I wait and try to right all my wrongs. "Am I wrong?"
Your memory lingers and haunts me till the end of my days.
I'm alone, the world is dead, or maybe it's me.
Deeper my mind creeps, to escape all the numb pains.
Life is forgotten, forsaken by all...
"Open your mind and breathe."

Never You

Torn away, left in dark shadows called life and you.
Deep away, red flowing hatred within your shameless neglect.
Love torn, you break me down till nothing's left.
Alone inside, all alone in dark sadness I weep and die.
Tears so cold, I walk through mindless winters called you.

Now at the top I scream. Nails through my flesh and bone.
Deep in fire, the hour is taking me back to the never.
Ever through the only madness, without human eyes.
Deeper in sadness, you break me down and eat me alive.

Small monsters crawling under my skin, "can you see!?"
I gave out my heart, like you gave to me.
Lift now my gravestone. Your heart so black and cold.
Now you match me, drain me like a burnt match please.
Nothing to see, no reason to breathe. "Let me free!"

Broken trust, I sit in dark torment and wait.
You broke the trust. You lied straight to my face.
So alone, no justice of what you have done to me.
Heartbroken, shove me into my hole and leave me be.
Here I soak, I bleed within dark memories.
You gave me all, then stole it away.
Now no sunshine. So I'm left in the gray.
Never more, you opened up and shut the door on me.
Never you, alone I am and forever will be.
"Can you see?!"

Chapter 9

Now Everything is Lost

Hammering Me Soulless

It begins hammering on my skull, what sins have I inflicted onto you?
Dark winged hatred flowing throughout all my being, I see no escape.
Through this gaping hole, shove your blade deep till I run cold.
I wish you to push me once more, till the light fades forever gone.
And my tongue breaks on forsaken words, *you torment my endless dream.*
It hammers on my skull, forever till my blood runs cold.

On no open truth I spin more and more. My eyes roll back till gone.
Sweet angels play their songs; they dance with laughter pointed at me.
Shame - my pride dies with a love for an angel, dark and gone.
Air - cool blowing through my head. Death is only an unseen dream.
Lay to rest the feelings you hide. Pride will consume and control again.
You hammer me soulless, with my cries so loud and numb.
Do all have deaf ears or am I just that far stuck under earth?
Birth of death brought with sweet taste; oh my sweet lust.
Must you leave me? Alone cold I cry. I see the world with a child's eyes.

Should the poison taste so sour and death feel so sweet? Numb is me. Oh more pain.
Time tick-tick and taking me away. Far - far from sane.
Why are the clouds red? This state of mind is all I've had.
I wish to rest, but hammering on my skull...
And this pain within my chest.
Give me reason but never doubt. "Do not doubt me!"

Small light fades and grows. Am I the only man who knows this truth?
It hammers on my skull, three small words stolen in youth.
It takes me time; it leaves me dark, cold and twisted within.
A love for an angel, taken away by her sin.
Now left in shadow, I sing with tears of pride.
In sorrow I weep and in happiness I die. Left only with pride.
It shoves deeper into my chest, from my back... I bleed in question.
You hammer me skull-less. I'm dark and left only to cry.
It hammers me soulless...
And my tongue breaks with forsaken cries.

Upon Your Soft Lips

I was there when you stopped and cried behind the tall oak tree.
I was there, and with you I will always be. "Set aside the differences."
On no more warmth dust bled from my eyes. "I tried to scream but cried!"
Your soft lips, sweet soft kiss. It brings me hope, you bring me to life.

"You cry," and with one hand I wipe away your tears.
With the other I hold you tight.
Never will I find someone so kind, "you love me" all differences aside.
We dance to our song, the moon so bright, it shines us hope.
I'll hold your kiss with me, forever in a *Knight's Dream*.
I love the way you hold me closer than close, "so warm."
Upon your soft lips, I feel love burn. "Always I will hold you."
What a twist of fate, you and me forever... "I hope."
I love you and you hold me, in your light, soft blue eyes.
It kills me to think I could lose you again, "not again!"
What could I say or do? "I love you," and always will...
Your tears fall and I have nothing to say, I love you; *"Forever this way."*
With you I see a future. Alone I see darkness and nothingness.

You stopped to cry, I was there, "why?!" That's all I ask.
I'm here with you, you have nothing to fear.
Upon your soft lips I left a kiss of life - light within.
You my love so close yet far away - in my arms yet gone.
To you I've sung this song, and we dance by the moonlight.
Soon you will be mine and I yours. I hope - I hope.
Never doubt your heart, never doubt me my love.
You stopped to cry, I was there to wipe away your tears.
With you I'm alive, and I have nothing to fear.
So warm in my arms I hold you, and you kiss me.
Upon your soft lips, I kiss an eternity.

Never Forgotten

It was on an old thought of her soft hand on my shoulder once more.
I took a walk to free the memory and try to find hope in a sunrise.
The smell of sweet morning; the dew still cool while the sun lies asleep.
I walked down a road I know so well. *"Would she be there waiting for me?"*
With no more drive, only thoughtless notions of her and I once more.
The sun not yet risen I move on to try. *Her house not yet lit, and still asleep.*

I came to a sudden halt one block away from her house.
And I couldn't understand; my feet wished to move no more.
And the cool-damp road of leaves pointed me away. *"Why" I asked myself."*
"Was I not good enough of a friend or that terrible of a lover?"
I could only think of the one simple truth of the matter.
"I took my only love and threw it away."
I wished to lay face first in the gutter.
And maybe there I could find a better fate of something...
So powerless I could do nothing!
Yet deep inside myself I found strength enough to move.
Not knowing where to. Still I could find no warmth and see no hope.
In the bright night, dark day.

Dark - damp - cold and drenched...
The questions lingered and I could find no tears to cry.
I need to free these cries. *So lost in-side I try to find hope of some better drive.*
Just a few houses away, would I see her face and hold her hand.
Will I ever kiss her soft lips again?
Her lightly golden blond hair, against her smooth - pale, *"flawless skin."*
I dream awake.

I've never forgotten the day I meet her in the park.
Her smile filled me with bliss.
I just sat there as she tried to ask me a question.
I was lost in her eyes, blue as the sky.
She smiled at me and I could say only one thing.
"Damn myself, if I never ask, your name."
I could only stare and I knew it was love at first sight.
But now I walk in question - "Dark day, Bright night."
I've never forgotten our first kiss.
We were friends and in a playful act our lips collided.
Soft - sweeter than any candy, warmer than any hug.
I felt true love for the first time that day.
On my lips she left a scar of what was and could never be;

"Well, at least for me."
I knew that I would love her always and forever.
"Little did I know," even if I was not there.
So there I walked, two houses away and the world still gray.
Day not yet awake, still dark-gone.
No hope I see, no warmth indeed.
Only cries of what I have inflicted upon myself.
Then in front of her house my knees grew weak.
And I wished to stop, but just couldn't.
The house still dark, the ground still damp.
With my pride broken I could only walk away.
I threw away my only love because of childish fights.
"We were both at fault." Now I walk with nothing...
And I could just die - for I was already dead inside.
And I just might have, if I didn't hear her soft voice behind me.

I turned - she was standing on her front porch.
She looked into my eyes in question - in question.
Yet she asked nothing. She only walked up to me.
And at the end of the street I saw the warm glow of the sun.
She put her hand on my shoulder and at that point...
The hope had risen - the sun alive - the day so bright.
I could say only one thing as she stared so deep into my eyes.
I felt so weak, "her soft blue eyes..."

"I've never forgotten you my love and never will I."
"I love you still and always will, you my life so bright."

She kissed me and smiled, I could only weep yet I held it in.
I hold it in - scared with love on my lips.
She took my hand - I held her hand and we walked into the sunrise.
"There I find hope."
And in the memory of her soft hand on my shoulder I can rest.
I no longer feel so empty in my chest.
We took a long walk down a short road.
And warm-damp from the morning dew.
I've never forgotten the feel of her and me.
And never will I - as we walk *Upon the Road of Leaves.*

216

With You My Angel

Can you hear the whisper of small angels upon the wind?
I hear their tale of a love so true.
Can you hear the voices of the forever in my soul?
Holding the forever in us.
Must we part our ways, must I live in shame?
Why won't you wake up my love?!
In the red pool of sorrow I weep. *The tears pulled down by shame and God.*
With you my angel, I feel so able.
But why won't you wake up from your dream?

Can you hear the whisper...
Of small demons on the last thought I held of a love so true?
Can you hear the voices of the Never in my soul?
Holding the nothing in me.
Must we part our ways, must I live in shame?
Why won't you awake from your dream?!
After the burnt were burned and after the dead found death.
In shame God took my breath.
With you my angel, I feel the abilities of so many things.
Please awake from your pain.

I remember the days I held you and you laughed in my arms.
Smiles sweet-forever. I remember the days we walked so long.
Down short roads and sang songs of our love.
I thought you were happy with me. *I thought you would never leave me.*
I thought you were happy with me. *I thought you would grow old with me.*
Why can't the Never set itself aside? Please my love, open your eyes!!

I can remember the days, with you my angel. We laughed and cried.
I can remember the days, with you my angel. We laughed and died.
Can you remember my angel, when you held me and I cried.
Can you remember my angel, when you told me we would never part?
Do you hear the whisper on the wind, of the truth you never said?

With you my angel, I just don't feel that dead.
With you my angel, I hold the thoughts of what we did.
With you my angel, please awake from your pain.
With you my angel, I feel not so insane - please wake.
Open your eyes and see the voices of the truth that I am dead.
And you just laughed.

This Knight's Dream

It was dark that day, in a mid-May haze.
Marching onward and hoping to see your face.
There was a love I left behind, now at war. In the flesh and in my mind.
I remember what I told you, and I hold myself true to the pledge I made.
"I'm coming home."
Hard roads and hot steel, I wear upon my shoulders every day.
Sweat pouring on my grave. As I have, and surely will once and again.
I fight to make things right, please my love...I hope you understand.
I am a man of my word and will see you once more.
Look for me by night or carried softly through the dawn.
"I'm coming home my love."
Sharp stabbing blades of friend or foe, I do not know but I feel weak and cold.
I see my brothers dying before my eyes. I hold myself dying and will not cry.
For I am a man and will keep my word.
Battle as I may, blood dripping from their blades.
I watched another man die by my sword just the other day.
This war is driving me insane, I cannot see. Sight taken and my body gives way.
My armor is too heavy...
My side stuck with enemy forces between my ribs and sheath.
For now this battle is over, but the next is but a breath away; "I bleed and fade."
Closing my eyes, I hear God speak to me.
I ask for forgiveness and he turned away.
He only smiled and left me there for dead.
I could only think of you, "I must stay awake."
I don't know where I found the strength but I stand and I know I've done my time.
Our lands are safe do to our fighting souls, and dead brothers keeping us aware.
For today we may be happy and dance till the sun shines alive.
I'm coming home my love, to hold you one last time; "I must stay awake."
Searching and calling, everyone is dead.
I am left alone on the battle field, alone and cold.
Somehow I arose and kept myself afoot.
I heard screaming in the distance but it faded.
I saw a man with his own heart in hand.
And a note telling of his journey to our land.
I know it's war but I found hell and wish to never look back, I'm leaving now.
My body broken, bones cracked, flesh rubbed away.
"Blood filled boots on a hot summer day."
And the thought of you is the only thing keeping me awake.
Someday I hope to find home.
Look for me by night or carried softly on my way home.
I will be with you again. Under a hill or in your arms;

I will not rest until you know I'm safe in your heart.
It's been years since I set way on this damn war.
Of damned souls and frail human pigs.
I'm on my way home, to hold you tight and never let go, my lovely drive.
Although I do not know if this is the right road, somehow I'll find you.
I ask you to forgive me, and understand that I'm doing this to keep you safe.
I can't wait, to hold you once more soft in my arms.
Smell of roses and morning dew.
I try to keep myself upright; I try to keep myself awake. "I'll see you soon."
This knight's dream is to once again kiss your lips.
And to never let you go. I'll never let go.
"I'm coming home."

<u>Given</u>

I hide form you the thing you seek.
And never will I let you receive more than what you've given.
Hold tighter than you ever have.
Open your eyes and see what you could have had, with me.
So many voices pointing me in every direction.
My destination I wait for, more I wait inside.
Alive I seek better reasons to give to all.
If all I had was you, then why now gone form me?
Ever through the madness I fall.
And wound after wound I learn something new; old is this feeling.
I've given you my heart, and you've torn me apart.
I'm now just a memory that could have been.
I have sinned as every man will.
I have given you all and now I'm left in hell - I'll never be free.
Sweet fire I taste, what a waste of heart you were.
Why has my life been such a blur? "Help me!"
Is all still inside? Am I even alive?
What road was the wrong one? So now my love is gone - done.
On your lips I see a kiss of death, why do you hurt me?
Please understand that I'm a twisted soul.
If ever I was happy, it was with you.
Now at the brink of lunacy I see no escape - it's almost over.
The sands of time run faster with every breath.
My chest cold - numb and heart broken, no more.
My mouth fills with blood, and I cannot swallow.
Never will I ever be forgiven - numb is me.
I scream and all flows out at once;

I need guidance or just put me to sleep, I wish not to weep.
More I see you happy with another love.
I die with my love for an angel that has never cared.
Years will pass and I'll still be the same.
Heart broken and in shame. I dig myself deeper away.
I've given you all, now I'm left with none.
I have sung this song before but forever no more.
You were my world; I'm now stuck in space.
I taste the sweet-death from a world between.
I hide all from you because you stole all from me.
I have given you everything - and nothing I've received.

<u>Shut Open My Soul</u>

It wasn't so hard when you turned - you watched me burn.
It wasn't so fun then, so why are you laughing, "at me?"
And it was hard, to forget your face.
The haunt stuck with my affection, "infection."
And it was you on open truth, you shove deeper your pain in my heart.

My mouth bleeds, my soul dies.
All that did shine, now dead faded and gone.
Shut open my soul, metallic love in my eye, did you or I fall to death?
Such a mind-loss of what I have given, I give now you my death.

Liberation within a nation of the dead, it grows so evil in my words.
It wasn't so hard to end what was over; *you drove me to the edge of reality.*
Silly little demon on my last breath, God will take away my home?
Homeless in the gutter, in the groove I move to your sick song of betrayal.

You hold the hand of a lie.
Smile while I beat my head till life is away from me.
Shut open my soul and I could and will always be cold.
What you did I will never forgive.
I drown in my own dedication to somebody that just doesn't matter.
I drew a picture on the wall, an angel holding my heart so high. "*I fall.*"
It was in the dark pit of my life, I found the light of exact evil-darkness.
I thank you, the pain deep.
The wax covers me until I forever slumber and smile.

I crack my tooth on the bone of a...
No matter what I say you push me away;

Feel the hell in my words.
Feel the depth in my burnt screams - then you laugh.
It wasn't so hard to watch me walk away, when you were already gone.
It wasn't so hard; you step on my heart and wipe it on the curb.

I was just a kid in the state of mind that I have always been.
I fought and died. I walk into the fires that you did make.
You now hold the hand of what stole you away from me.
I hear the voices grow and deception run rapidly...
Through my soul shut open.
I feel the dark pain in my only thought.
That you were mine and I was yours.
How did you become what you are?
How did I drive you to live a lie?

It wasn't so hard when your face was turned... *You laugh while I burn.*
It wasn't so hard.
To watch the one person who went to hell for you stay and die.
I ball-up in the corner of my room...
I would weep, "but I smile." I stand with my soul shut open.
"You betrayed me!" You stand with what I hate.
Now must I hate you too? Now will I always be confused?
Shut open my soul.
And I'm left cold in the nothing you and your new love made "*for me.*"
For me this pit is more than you ever were.

"*It will always be there for me.*"

On The Red Line

On the red line I breathe and see no further than the path before me.
Am I still alone? I exhale and watch the frost form on the window.
Is life a dream or just a recollection of my past?
Flowing and draining yet warm and growing cold.
Truth and pride are all that's left in my soul.
On the red line I walk, is light gone or just hiding from me?
What a sick game you play.
What am I to do? I'm just a man still lost and confused.
Consider one thing though - *I'm still me.*
On the red line I bleed, I ask you for warmth.
Yet angels stab me deep, so enjoying my pain.
Lust, deception and I'm still far from grace.
I still face the world faceless with a basis of truth.
It is true that no man can live under water.
Nor will any man ever know the simple truth of all.
On the red line I see, something of my past brought back.
Haunting my every thought and move.
Soon is noon and the dark end to such a short story.
Yet this is what I've selected and hold.
Pride on the tip of a knife, it cries my blood and bleeds only concert truth.
"Can't you see?"
Anymore moves and I'm bound to fall again.
And again I move to accept the outcome.
On the red line I move, it turns on me as it does for any man.
I'm just me, "can't you see!?"
Of all the dark thoughts and little white lies you've inflected onto me.
Still the angels stab me deep.
Dimming and fading on the back of my hand.
I spin the blade and so loud I scream.
Why do you still gaze up at the stars?
He's not coming back for you... You must find him.
And on the red line I search to find something of the war.
I need evidence to give forth.
I sleep awake and dream of only life and pride within my eyes.
Stone and dust are truth.
You can never imagine the images I've seen.
On the red line I lead - "I see."

This Hollow Void

Well, I'm still a man - I'm still alive.
Vacant holes of ambitions within my cranium.
The door ajar, as is the faces surrounding my every thought and dream.
Commence the countdown and swing me deep into tomorrow.
A whim of you - uncluttered, exposed and candid.
Are the roads leading further into the pit of yours.
Drip me deep into the hollow.
Drive me further from the hallow and sing me to sleep.
Dream the way to swallow; knives, blades and unfortunate things.
I break the trend and hope me above the sins of the damned.
Find me hollow at the bottom of this pit.
Fade me hallow, speak kind words into my brain.
And teach me nothing that I don't already know.
Damn my hands, ripping out my own eyes.
Cutting away my flesh and breaking the list.
Form me a tool more than just the nothing we have held.
"Take me deeper into hell."
A hollow man I may be but not far from the grace above and in the lime I see.
Bring forth the notion of forever the demon was.
Now I am just a breath that can never be.
Falling deep into this hollow.
Rushing deep within our hallow, will you follow?
Falling further into my fear, fading more into the clear.
Showing above all your fear and spoken like a true whore.
You took the words right out of my mouth.
And in this void I fade to the nameless section of my being.
Being told to stay away, in this hollow void.
Forming so deep in my chest, with a loss of breath.
In this hallow void, I remember the one thing I loved to die for.
But now you're dead.
In the hollow dead, I eat the remains of the angels and whatever is left.
In this hallow ground, I whisper words.
Remembering the days I smiled and cried.
This hollow void, a hole deep in my soul.
Breaking me down into a pool of tears.
This hallow void, a twist in my last dream of, "*hoping love.*"
In the nothing void, I fade to a nameless section of my being,
Being told I am away. This hollow void, a gray abyss... a home I call it.
"Here I would like to stay."

Wasted

Wasted - I feel so pasted to the walls of the tomorrow I thought I had.
Gray clouds of something hanging above the stairs swinging without a care.
Open mouth of wishing more than just your hate, spilt on the table.
Over the truth you hide a fable, of the nothing that anyone cared.
So wasted, I wait no more to see the bore and what a whore I must be.

12 hours of nothing we care for, murder dropped onto the floor.
Days of the haze we spoke of, and remember I'm still just a kid.
So wasted was the love I fueled, we stopped before it even began.
I take a look in the mirror and see what you want from me.
Purple days, of a haze, of a lie, of a life we once lived and now despise.

Grind me once more...
And bone-dust forever poured into the souls of the weak.
Drip me once more to the forever never bent and twisted.
Against the spine and over your lies, I feel so wasted, love taken.
My heart waiting, my skull bending.
And dripping with the sweet smell of new.
Pasted to the walls and halls of my mind.
I drip it back one more time.

"Must I hold it forever...?"
I hold it forever and dream of the days I lost and killed.
Memories of the nothing I never had but miss so dear.
I do fear the torment.
Of the small angels on my last one thing I never knew.
Wasted, I swim to the new.
The Never I knew. The forever I must.
I feel so wasted, and out of place I fell.
I feel so pasted to the walls of my eternal hell.

Open Heart Torn

Torn - born to destroy everything I touch, everything I love *"you and I."*
Torn - born to decay in a state of constant turmoil.
And no more will I breathe.
Broken over the edge of the pit, singing truth and forever that's it.
Days of words spoken over hot tea and warm milk. *I melt inside, "away."*

Open body and you are the disgrace.
Open my body and I find me out of place.
Of all the nothings you've once said...
Of all the times I beat my head.
Broken, I soak in my regret.
I know the outcome and nothing will be left.
Torn away from the place I would have loved to stay, *right at your side.*

My heart beating on my ribs and soon to give in...
I crumble at your feet.
I was born to be the one you would want to love.
But cast aside; I am the one in lost time.
Open body and nothing more.
Lay me upon the fine-comfort and shut the door.
Vulgar vices of the last night I will ever hold her.
What can I say to not fade away?

Torn - born to be the one who will hold all your lies.
And lay face first in hell.
Torn - born to be the one love you will never have again.
But you walked away.
Torn - born to live the life of the nothing I am.
In darkness waiting for a new light.
Torn - born to die a death that no man deserves.
Alone and old in a faded hole.

Open heart torn and nothing more from my mouth.
I cannot look you in the eyes. Open heart torn, and you smile.
While pissing away the days and years of love and pain.
Open heart torn, I was born to take this all to my grave.
With great knowing.
Open heart torn, I was born to love you for the rest of my life.
"But now I'm dead."

Was Your Loss

It was on a cool evening, as so many before it.
She came to me with only a tear in her eye.
I felt but confusion of so many things, "was I her reason?"
As the seasons of lust turn to dust, dead and gone.
I fade to a small nameless section of my conscious.
I feel a dark grimy, cold abyss grow inside.
It was on that thought when I asked the question.
The question that would damn me to an eternal loneliness.
On so untrue of a nature that you have inflected upon me.
Your dirty actions drove me away.
At the end of the corridor.
Above the stairs I swing in an eternal wondering "if anybody cares."
Care not you do about what you hate.
You hate me more than you breathe and you'll die on the thought.
Above bone yet under flesh.
What a harsh lesson you've learned over the time we've spent.
I feel spent, done with all that matters.
You no longer matter to me - so above the stairs I swing.
A happy thought of a smile on her face once more.
Yet she's dead now as is the one before.
More I need on the homely feeling her hand on my face...
Cold as ice - bloody nothing in my mind.
My hand on her shoulder and her fingernails under my skin.
You've clowned on me for the last time.
What a notion you hold of thinking it would be alright.
To do what you did to me.
In the purple mouth of a haze of a daze of the lie.
That you could love me true. *Never you...*
Madness forever deep in the pool that you soak in.
Sob as much as you can while you can.
Faceless I disgrace what you believe in.
I care not what you think. You were wrong, wrong indeed.
Mad I am indeed to think that you could understand.
"You won't understand." *You kill the notion.*
With emotion spelt in the ground, I feel bound to you.
The darkness under our sweet mother earth.
Ever more through the hole you've dug for yourself.
It was your loss, not mine, so deal with it.
I'm dead with the power of a mind of a lie I hold no more.
More I wish it away, away from grace.
Face no face and taste no taste on my tongue;

Your loss is my gain. Your lie is my pain, and you eat my brain.
Such a cynical thought of the tiny little demon under my skin.
Crawling and clawing at my only affection.
Infection within my soul, I'm dirty.
So unclean of a feeling your hand within my chest, you crush my heart.
Apart from the side to side twist of my teeth under soft skin.
You as dirty as sin, in locked with only me.
I hold you in such a pleasant place in my heart.
Cold dark and forever vice, under our earth I smile.
Was your loss, at the time you wished me away?
Was a cool evening as so many before it... so many.
It was your loss and my gain. You were my world and my pain.
It was your loss, not mine! Deal with it.

Death Flirt

Flowing red death through my heart cold-black.
Step by step, in front of my face and behind my back.
You push me further with your eyes, you lovely madness.
I wish I could just get over you, yet somehow you get under me.
I love the taste of your lips on mine. You drive me dead and over the edge.
All is now a waste of living. In the moonlight I feel the ending.
Please come back to me, I flirt with death, "it's only a dream."
You drive me so into love, and away from ever being with you.
I know you have comfort but remember, I love you.
All cannot end this way, it must be you and me but "that's only a dream."
I flirt with death because that's all I have. O I wish I were with you.
You lovely madness, you put me so deep in this sadness of nothing.
I have nothing but memories of you. So I watch the thought of our children die.
Oh God... I cannot do this on my own, "I need you."
I flirt with death, hoping it will bring me closer to you.
I wish there was more for me to say but I will love you always and a day.
Forever in this never ending dream I stay, it's the closest I am to you.
You're such a death flirt, and I hope to be with you but we know, "it'll never be."
I flirt with death, hoping to be with you someday.
Happy with me. But come on...
"I need to face the fact, that it's only a dream."

Through Sightless Seeing

Breathe, open wide my eyes and see through sights I've never seen.
I have control of my life from this point on, and on I move through this life.
Fate, control, destiny... Step after step I breathe and see the unseen.
I live to live; I open my eyes and see all of my life was a dream.
Awake I am, further down dark holes I dig to breathe.
This is it, all will fall into place and I face the world faceless.
Taste, test the taste of human flesh, blood of mine so thick.
Power rises up and down my icy warm body, numb I bleed.
Crawl, I crawl down my spine, I creep within my mind.
Lost, the drive was great, the price so, so much - myself.
I'll breathe, I'll move on and on till I'm the forever unseen.
And I can only think of the one thing stuck in my head.
I will never be good enough for the world.
I can only weep, yet I control my actions now.
And how would you like me to end this?
The forever I fall, so deep into the earth I wait.
Through sightless seeing I know... I know who you are now.

Fall More Through Darkness

Dark mother... Open your body and free the souls in bright night.
Small but still enjoying the slight burn in an eternal fright.
Constant filth - set aside the pride you believe in my children.
Steel warm metallic love, the blood grows colder with every breath.
It's hard to breathe, *it's hard to see further than this darkness called you.*
Constant crying to an angel, blank faceless with no warmth.
Fire dark, black burning evil of this soulless man, head first into pain.
Do I intimidate you? Do you fear me and my ways?
Far running deeper into the only prison you built with ever sin.
Brick after brick, you fall deeper in sound sorrow with darkness inside.
Haunt me no more with your light soft blue eyes.
Take my heart no more and leave me in this pit to cry.
You must enjoy, don't bother lending a hand, "I know you don't care."
You must enjoy watching me fall more through darkness.
Because you know you have the same fate as I.
Push me no more... Dark mother open your body and free the souls.
They deserve something more than this pain, and more they shall have.
And I know that I know that you know I will forever be stuck between.
This life and pain, hurt and sane. Must you haunt me with soft blue eyes?
Take me to the tip and I fall more through darkness, "that's all I have."

228

Soon Burnt Away

Small, faded light dimming. Soon burnt out and gone.
3 small cuts, soon my heart is gone, "I thank you."
Smile my love and look deeper within my eyes. Look within my mind.
Please open your soul and give me your hand, please trust me.
You stand in front of me, on my grave. Now I'm gone and faded.
The sky still blue, the world will move on and on. "Just breathe."
Step after step, life is still only to live and see - see?
This is the only way to get it out, even if it's already gone.
I wish you would go out with me and see, the stone is mine.
But the next door could be yours. If only you cared enough to see.
Soon the light will fade and all will turn to gray, once burnt away.
And no one will tell you how to get there. "But I will hold your hand."
If only you and the world could share the same thoughts of me.
But soon the end shall be and the world will move on - you need to see.
Life will always be the same. The wind will kiss your cheek.
Smile while you're young and try to remember all the fun thoughts.
The kisses and hugs of loved ones. The spread of joy around the world.
As I lay at the bottom of this hill, under a tall oak tree.
All soon burnt away and the gray it will always be.
3 small cuts, soon my heart is gone and "I thank you."
Please open your soul, just give me your hand, "trust me."
All can't be that bad; "remember the road of leaves."

Melt Me On The Cross

Sightless seeing, the rough torment that mankind has given to me.
Side mind lost beating... blood runs down my face numb.
Ice-body, finding me melt like human wax.
Rushing, flowing, never my mind will last, "it's past."
Dead grabbing your face, such a disgrace you were.
Throw your body on the fire pit, leave the feeling behind.
Fall forever into the abyss called my mind. "Finding light gone."

Round and around I go, finding no way to go... I'm stone.
Lay me on the knowledge of the Never I must, must I awake?
Lose your body and feel the disgrace grow... I'm unknown.
Singing and bleeding, I know not what I should do, "I'm so confused."
I put my feet on the edge and hold my heart while I scream.
I fall down the rabbit hole, just to see how deep it goes.
Hold me down and nail me tight, melt me on the cross;

I scream while I awake from the pain, life beating me down.
I nod back and back and back some more, till I'm asleep.
Need I go on to show you the reason of this pain?
I grab you by your face, I feel so disgraced and so "far from grace."

Under Stone

Watch me melt... Watch me drip deeper into hell.
The light is gone. I'm seeing no way out.
Push the knife deeper through my heart, "watch me snap!"
The forever is past me now. I'm just waiting to die.
I don't really care. I just wish to end my life.
Turn over the stone. Twist and let out the power.
The time to live is past. The feeling within did pass.
I'm smiling and laughing. The blood on the walls is mine.
The world is dying, I hear the angels crying; "I'm gone."
Hold me with two arms. I need the warmth from you.
Yet neglect me is all you do, "forever I lose."
I'm calling out to free this pain. All you do is drive me insane.
"Please let me out."
I'm so alone... Alone inside, alone in mind "because of you."
Darkness dripping down the back of my mind, "I'm lost."
The shadow grows. The walls fall, "it's growing faster."
Deeper I sink, I smile while I bleed.
The bones are broken, the flesh is torn.
The pain is grown. It's growing and holding me tighter till I'm gone.
I wish to sleep, this world is crushing me.
I need to put my feet on the edge and just fall.
All I've done, all I've said, it was wrong.

Past Rush Not Forgotten

Faster - dark corruption crushes down and falls deeper within me.
I'm running from pain and running from time. Harder you constrict my mind.
Little voices hold me true to the knowledge I've been seeking.
The sun blood-red, and all gravity pulls fate closer to my neck.
I ask you to let free this strain. The pain so close yet far within.
Nowhere to run, nowhere to hide. Within my mind cold-frozen.
Past brought back to my eyes. You stare deep into my face.
Pain, what a taste you own on the table in the back room.
On a shelf you hide the truth... Youth forever forgotten - "by you,"

Me, alone with dark memories. My enemy called me.
One step in front of another, I smile falling to fate and hate.
Rushing only within myself. Find me hell or heaven please!
Purgatory, I wait forever between reality and pain. "Unsane you."
Power flowing... Growing deeper in the back of my lonely mind.
Little dreams bring me only darkness and regret yet not forgotten.
Truth stolen by dark wings. Evil Angel so sweet and care free.
"Sorry..." I scream falling faster to fate and my sudden end.
Noon so soon rising above the cloud. Red faded and gone.

Abyss Called Me

Wide open, I see only darkness within myself.
Hatred growing, I fear I won't see the end.
Conscious dying, grab my throat and throw me in the abyss.
Voices screaming, seeping deeper into my brain.
Push me harder, I dig my own grave.
My destination I await... My future so unseen.
The questions are killing. Killing me indeed.
The monsters are creeping. Up my spine and in my mind.
The room is spinning. I'm living on lust and sin.
The fire is growing. Throw me into my abyss.
The time is coming. I'm now at the top of the list.
The light is dimming, "so this is it."
So unknowing of myself and all that's been.
Mother-Earth is dying, yet you still smile.
You will never understand until you look inside and feel.

With You Alive

So I'm dying, so I'm crying. Falling down, I am nothing.
Leave me to rot... I waste away and fade to gray.
Smile in shadow. Walking on glass and you follow.
Sleek falling madness. Down growing sadness, "with you."
Push my hatred up and outward and you laugh at me.
I'm so evil, I'm just a devil, "why!?" You hate me.
Down I slump and the ground is forming around me, "God."
You want me to stand and smile, "I love you." Then I smile.
With you awake, I am... Open eyes then so alive.
The sands are falling, time is running out. I wish I were with you now.
I'm so peaceful... You make me so alive when I'm with you,

So I'm dying, so I'm crying. Falling down, I am nothing.
Leave me to scream. I waste away and watch you fade.
Smile in shadow. Walking on glass - you whore.
Sleek falling madness. Down growing sadness, "with you."
Awake I fall, fading to the gray side of the nothing that I am.
But what am I to say? Everyway and day I fade.
The blood I drank, "with you alive...." I open my eyes.
To see who we truly are. Dead and not remembered.
Now the pain washes away.

Human Too

Drop me crying, only your hatred.
Free me screaming, untrue cries.
Open body... Bleed and creep till death - Apart!
You've heard so many things.
The thoughts ringing into your brain.
Of whom I am and what to say.
You broke the trust, the ever it must.
So many things ringing in your brain.
I'm human too, why are you confused?
So many things I would love to do.
I die to set free the truth... I loved you true.
Just remember. "I'm human too."

Alone

Sleep... Lay my head down to the endless gray.
All alone I've sat here with pain, I'm done with life.
Raindrops flow to me. Endless knives stuck under my flesh.
Here I am, where I've chosen to be. Left with only me.
Heart warmth, you with... I could just give you it all.
Sure, watch me fall to hell. I welcome the heat.
So many ways I've said the same old thing.
So many times I've tried to awake from the pain.
So alone I wait to dream but it's all unseen by even me.
I want to smile, I want to cry. I wish to live, yet I die.
I can hold only myself as I drift further into hell.
Rain flowing further into my soul, weeping whole.
Who am I? *Alone I weep...*

232

Nothing But Your Scream

Falling, growing, showing nothing but bone above flesh.
Knowing, flowing, I'm rising above the fog and lost in rest.
Brainstem torn on the razor's edge. I scream and see nothing left.
Nothing forming above our mindless feeling my chest caving in.
Sin for the love of an angle dark evil and forever mine.
Open your mouth and scream bloody cries, while I watch you die.
Four small cuts on your chest, "*my hand within* you," stealing your breath.
Your hair flowing, growing, not knowing an end, it will stop!
Bone above flesh, screaming until nothing's left. "I'm gone."
Gone away, I face my own grave, "smile and laugh."
Nothing but your scream rings through my head, gone-wasted.
It falls and the demon calls me to rise and scream.
Mirror black, no face to look at... Everything is gone from me.
Ever will I never set free the feeling so numb and dead?
Nerveless torment on my brain, eat my soul cold-wasted.
I hear the voices smash me, crush me, kill me "gone."
On the road to my dark, cold nothing yet home.
Mother of the ground, my fair wicked love holds me down.
In dark shadow I see I have no end to this day, gone and wasted.
Nothing but your scream rings in my head till nothing's left.
In my left hand I hold the blade, in the right, this pen.
Which do you choose to die by? Which way should you go? "Scream!"
Numb nothing, falling upon deaf ears. I fear nothing but your scream.

Razor Toy

Would you should you, drop me, kill me, hate me!
Small, tall, down I weep tears of dust, "must it be?"
The blade in hand, razor toy I love, "I love."
I feel the warmth run down my arm, "now I'm getting cold."
I wish I had a family. A love for me to hold.
I ask you to cover me with dirt and dust, "don't weep."
I love my razor toy; I play the game of rage.
I love my razor toy, I lay back - I tremble and weep.
I roll my eyes in the back of my head, "soon gone."
You laugh at my cries, you smile while I die.
All alone, six feet under earth and stone, "I weep."
Dripping the blood off my arm, from my heart, I look back.
Trying to see the nothing of me. I try to see a newer darkness of this life.
My arm open, bone and blood in clear sight.

To: You My Love

Dear sweet... My dear love, once again I wish to be at your side.
Time nonstop flowing, my heart still growing, "I need you."
What would I have to do, to hold you once more? "I love you."
You my love, who grows away from me, please don't hate me.
If I could, I would tear down the world for you.
I stand with pain crushing me down. All will fall, "for you."
If I could, I would go to hell for you, "deep into the pit."
I would smile, while snakes and spiders crawled under my skin.
I would lift my gravestone, crawl up and scream your name.
A million bricks falling down on my spine. *"Please my love, give us time."*
Bone above flesh, stone grinding on my teeth, I'd smile.
If I had one more kiss, if I had one more hug, I'd smile.
Dear sweet... My dear love, once again I wish to be at your side.
Nonstop, an ending... I scream in dark pain, your name.
Soft, lovely, warm and I would do anything for you.
Please just think about us, please try again.
I love you still, and always will, you my unnamed love...

PS: Times have changed, the time has come.
If you name it, it shall be done. "I love you."

Shock Me Cold

Shock my body and leave me on the notion of you and I once more.
Cut me bloody and the emotion is spilt onto the floor.
"We will never be again."
On the other spilt thought of you behind my back.
"Our love was torn away."
"Over the wrist we play with rage, under our skin we hide the pain, away-gone."
On I go waist deep in sorrow. I'm left alone, *cold-done, away from light.*
So I sway and say there is no future, only pain.
Twisted faded, gone and black.
Shock me cold and leave me on the tip of madness and regret.
"Open and shout." Shout out and cry to you I do, yet nothing I receive.
"I am nothing, just me." All alone in dark comfort I lean on no shoulder.
And I smile with tears set aside. Agony as my ally and I still wish to die.
And die I do, every day I'm without you.
Bone dust on the table and you're happy, smile with death beside you.
"Cut me and speculate. Shock me and desecrate. You're open and you disintegrate."
In awe I try to close my eyes;

Light so bright and taken away from me. So lonely I wait to awake.
Frail body and I hold only myself; no warmth, no heart.
Soon I'll be at home in the grave, eight heartless minds.
Yet mine is still most vulgar.
And all was in my hands at one time.
Now I'm alone with no tears to cry. Why so unknown?
You smile and laugh, you question my ways.
Soon I will be put to rest in my grave.
You shock me cold and I have no way to free this strain.
Only pain is true, so I'm alone and used.
When did all of this become your pain?
Why won't I stop running insane? "You eat my brain!"
And I try to stand, I try to run.
In my hand is numb regret and warm truth, "laugh at me!?"
In shadow I see, a new reason to bleed.
All is spinning and forever gone till death, "death is home."
Around me constricting...
In my eyes I feel the burn and the hurt in my spine,
End my time now! I gave you away!
This is the outcome to what I have chosen. I chose to stop, I'll never stop.
You say you love me, you said you loved me.
You wish to hold me. You will never hold me again.
Behind me then, but not behind me now?!
God my skull is crushing and my life is rushing away.
All was a lie? All in good time...
The blood is pumping and I see no sight, no light, no way out!
My mouth is dry and the sky is stagnant.
What a life, what a heart break, "and you're happy?"
You shock me cold and I can't believe that you told me you still love me.
You hold me dead, so all alone in my tomb I wait for noon to rise.
And the light to die, you kill my world with words.
On no sure path to truth and only questions upon questions.
You laugh behind my back.
It shocks me cold and I have no way out.
Enjoy my pain and lie in sorrow and my regret, "I hate it."
You shock me cold with your words.
Yet I question all your ways. Every day so unsane and, I GAVE YOU AWAY!
And I am stuck between worlds. Faceless and no future to wait on.
You smile and laugh. In front of my face and behind my back.
I'll never live again. "You shock me cold."

Un-love Me

Un-think the thoughts you have thought.
Un-know the things that you know.
Just remember the path and the leaves hold the truths.

Un-hold the things you have held.
Un-love the love you had for me.
Un-remember the thoughts you hold so close.
You must un-love me if you are ever to love me again.

Un-dream the dreams you have dreamt.
Un-desire the wants of a child heart in us.
Un-bear the thought that nailed me to the floor.
Wake me at the end of the end and squeeze my neck.

Un-kill the beasts you have slain.
Un-tend to the wounds you have nursed.
Un-heal the hole in my soul and laugh once more at my pain.
You must stop and see the truth in front of your face.

Un-love the child you once held while he cried.
Un-love the child you once held while he died.
Un-love this demon with angel wings.
You must un-love me if you ever wish to love me again.

Backwards Mind Fuck

I walked in not ready to see what I saw and you lie to me still.
I walked in not ready to except what I would see... You just stared right at me.
Smiles until you realized who I was, you just stared... You just never cared for me.

AND OVER THE NOTION OF YOU AND I.
ON I GO, TRY AND TRY, AS HANDS WERE HELD.
FURTHER I FEEL, DEEPER INTO HELL.
WHILE SMILES KISSED, HATE FORMED THE TOOL, "I WAS A FOOL."
AND IN THIS PIT I AM STUCK.
FOREVER IN A *BACKWARDS MIND FUCK*!

I walked in not ready to see what I saw, it was just too much for me.
I wondered if I'd ever awake from the darkness within me.
And I would like to say, "I fell insane." You - holding him so tight.
Blood and screams I wept while you kissed him nice and held him close,

236

SO OVER AND UNDER MY FLESH, YOU LIED AND I DIED.
I WOULD LOVE TO HAVE SHOVED MY PEN DEEP INTO HIS FACE.
I WALKED IN AND FELL OUT OF PLACE, FURTHER ASIDE.
BECAUSE IT IS MY PAST I HAUNT.
ON AND ON AND IN I WALKED.
YOU WERE SUCH A TRIP.
NOW AND FOREVER I HOLD MYSELF SO SICK.

In your eyes I watched the thought of our children die, they never knew life.
And I was pushed aside to the back of my head. Dirt and dust, death and snow.
Now I want everybody to know, the demon I...
Now stuck, "in memory of a backwards mind fuck."
What did I do to be pushed away? In my red tears I write today.
Of a love failed and a man stuck in hell. Well, that's what I did to myself.

I WISH IT TO LEAVE ME GONE, THE PAIN I HAVE CAUSED.
I WALKED IN NOT READY TO SEE WHAT I DID SEE.
YOU JUST STARED, YOU NEVER CARED - FOR ME.
"NOT FOR ME."
YOU'VE LIED TO ME ONCE AND AGAIN AND NOW I WEEP.
YOU HELD HIM TIGHT...
LIKE MY HANDS AROUND YOUR NECK.

Yet there is nothing more for me to do but step off the ledge and hold my breath.
Because I've had nothing more than you and this pain.
Now you're gone and I'm away.
I walked in not willing to except what I would see. You stared right at me.
And nothing but a smile while I screamed at night. Kissing while I bled in fright.
You loved him - I died. You kissed him, - I died. You held him - I tried.
You're dead now -"I cry."

It was on that thought that I knew I'd never love again.
In your memory I lay, in red-tears I write today, forever you unjust.
In deep I fell and now I am stuck, *forever...*
In this ***BACKWARDS MIND FUCK!***

<u>*And We Held It*</u>

Of the time I held close the feeling her lips, fire-red and hotter than hell.
I need something more. The war far from being over.
I need her warmth.
Young... We were young and had not a care in the world.
Young... I was young and held her close to me, in eternal devotion.
I could run forever into the sun and melt just like my heart.
I could hide, into the bottom of my grave.
And with her I feel at home.
Of the time I held her hand and would never let it go, "I feel her kiss still."
I need something more, of the war within me... Far from being over.

On that evening I walked to her house.
I knocked at the door, warm-red.
We took a walk to take in a sunset.
I set aside the time and the pain of an everyday life.
With her I took a walk, to feel the more of ever being just me.
I sway in my soul, the sky getting dark and the ground growing cold.
In the shadow of her I see a future.
I see a smile on her face. "Why?!" I do not ask.
In the hour of the day I felt her love, we were one.
I took a walk into a sunset with her.
To see if there was more in life than just my pain.
I took a walk with her, on the leaves we did lay.
I could no longer feel time, as if the sands just stopped.
The wind slow and gentle.
And with that I wish I could stay. In the sunset I stay...
Until the rise of our final day.

Chapter 10

Leap of Faith

Tweak

In the dark shadows as life beats us down.
All sound from our souls and our hearts lay on the table.
Us as one shall destroy the world, we tweak the future.
And the further we move through the good and the bad.
Us as family tweak together and move on without the bad.
I ask if you are ready but am I ready for you?
Not knowing where to go, or what to do.
The rush, we a family hold together. I'm dead without ya'll.
You my friends, my family, and us a band.
Together we tweak. "We tweak the future."

Once and Again

A short calling to the nothing between the worlds that I made.
Fall calling - was I nothing? What was it that you gave?
Deny me no more. I've been left behind, "once upon a time."
The ground shakes and I see my next end. "This is your sin."
Tripping over my own feet, I fall and the blade sinks in deep.
I trip over my own words. I caused all of this hurt.
The sun so warm in the night's cool breath.
Now and forever I will be in this nameless sin. "Once and again."
Knowing not what to say to you. I run so far inside to find only myself.
I return with nothing but loss and regret. "I see the ground move."
Soon I'll be at the end of such a short life.
"*Will anybody ever care about this*?" Why should I let you win?
The world is mine, death is mine, and life is gone.
I've looked within, once and again. Will I ever stand above myself?
Not over till it's done, not done till it's over. *When I let the demons weep.*
I watch the child cry. I push him down and look him in the eyes.
I tell him to stand, what a weak waste of flesh. "*I hate myself,* dumb kid!"
"Once and again."
I could not see, with my eyes buried under dust.
I could never move on, the world turns to dust.
It was all once inside, now it is just gone.
The forever was once and again.
I trip over my own tongue. I break my neck on the thought.
I hold this pen tight. I grip the edge and kiss my life goodbye.
I fall so deep into this abyss called myself.
"Once and again I roam in hell,"

I'm at home in the grave, soon to lay my body to rest.
I'll rest after I'm dead, once and again.
I have nothing but these words.
I trip over my own feet and fall in an endless night.
Shadows hold truth, you my only pain.
Under the sky of blood must I lie?
To an endless thought of the world I made, in purgatory I sway.
I've fought the devil and myself, you, the world and my hell.
I live in pain, you thought you'd win.
I control nothing... I hold the nothing within my sin.
"Once and again."

Spring

Over the years spent, smiles still counted sweetest.
I held the hour tight... Time slipping through my fingers.
I look now at my child, the one I hold dearest.
Deep in my heart I feel the devotion.
"Soft leaves against her warm cheek, cool day in the spring.
Light there - such a sweet beginning."

Such a green day with our blue sky.
I watch her smile, on this cool spring day.
And over the years spent, smiles still counted sweetest.
I held the hour tight, my youth now gone.
I hold my child tight, in the spring's cool gift.
I watch my child play... I smile still so sweet.
In the morning of her life I found affection.
In the spring of life I find it counted sweetest.

"Soft leaves against her warm cheek, cool day in the spring.
Light there - such a sweet beginning."

"I am so glad I got to be there."

242

Something Gone Forever

Tick the time through the clock.
Ticking taking me deeper into the shadow's memory.
Something gone?
How deep should we go to give the world what it owes us?
The *Ever* will grow within our souls till dusk.
Dust covers the hour that we wait for.
Time ticking and taking me home in madness.
My mouth dry - open and you clown on my feelings.
You hold my heart in your hands.
"You take me back." Ticking - taking nothing's left.
We have awaited this moment for the longest time.
Never will we stop fighting, we fight for what we deserve, "*something*!"
Why would you think you deserve more?
When I've given you too much already.
We stand on top, "are you ready!"
Fade the hour in the light of the time we found warmth in a sound of truth.
Truth is all we ever need. Need you see a better reason to go?
I show you the hour we have anticipated. The sand covers us day by day.
In the shadow's memory I try to stay awake. "You're just a freak."
You are only a freak of nothing we need.
Now we are on the road to something.
I know we need nothing but each other. The hour soon upon us.
Something gone forever and never will I feel a better reason to move?
We move on without doubt.
You doubt the fact that we are what we say.
You're just a clown, a fake with nothing more to say.
Say you're better than us. Must you push me to the hour you end?
In the end, nothing will be left. So tick the hour in my shadow's trip.
I twist and feel the nothing grow within my chest. "You best stay away."
Go! And no one could show us up...
They - the world could just shut the hell up and end the *tick-tick* lies.
Side-mind still gone in the swine-trip.
Left in the dark pit of nothing on my mind but your neglect.
What's left but only inquiry and dread?
I dread the day that haunts and hunts me down like an animal.
I am the creature forming above the notion of the forever just.
Just one more heartbeat away from the end.
Beginnings to ends, from dawn to dusk.
Must I show you, when it's already gone forever? Gone ticking away.
Grace, with her face so soft and unspoiled.
I wait for the answer and contemplate your forever suffering;

You must suffer the thought of why - why are the trees still dead?
Something gone forever and ever until the end.
We started with each other, and we'll never stop.
Tick the time through the clock, ticking and taking till gone.
Sanity you anticipate.
Just you wait for the hour when we grow above our dreams.
And that hour awaits us now.
You - the feeling so numb when I stand alone.
And alone I'll never be, "yet, still?" Something gone forever.
It is gone, the wait for so long.
Ever through the time tick-tick and taking till nothing's left.
Yet something gone forever...

Inward Growth

Sinister influence brought forth by violent regurgitations.
Your sight twists and lets you down.
The tool in hand, soon this machine will grow.
Till uncontrollable death fills the land.
I open my eyes to see the nothing of your world.
Will justice ever be brought with sweet warmth?
Alone I sit in my own box and reflect on the past I lived.
And the future in which I see only your end.

On end over end.
I dream of only the good wishes you've given to me.
Inside I smile and scream.
We cry dust and feel a sharp pain.
Deep in the back of our minds.
Will nobody help me?!

With truth in hand and the blade under my skin.
Look into my eyes and try to save me - just try!
The sky is still gray and I try to make it through another day.
Yet I stand motionless and weep.
Walking upon the road of leaves and into the cool breath of a fall wind.
Bringing only life and our true end.

Reason of Leaving

Was it such a loss of reason? I wonder if I felt it leaving.
Such a loss of feeling. Numb nerves gone and bleeding.
"And oh I tried, and I died. With a loss of reason."
"Did I feel it die? Under this forgiving sky. I need to seep away."
"Oh my God, did I feel the loss of reason? My soul is still bleeding."
I wonder if it will ever go away.

Was it you that left me? Was I the one who walked away?
Under such a reason. I run gone and I'm left with no reason.
"And oh I tried, and yes I died. With this loss of reason."
"Did I feel it die? Under this forgiving sky. I need to seep the pain."
"Oh my lord, did I feel the burn? My soul is still bleeding, *I'm leaving.*"
"I wonder if I'll ever go away?"

Was I such a demon? Was I the one with the reason? Somebody help me please!
Under this forgiving sky, still I wonder why. "I need to seep away."
And I feel the pain as you walked away.
Somebody in my soul gone and decayed.
"Did I feel it die?" Still I wonder why, "was it you who was leaving?"
Still bleeding..."Oh God why!"
Will I ever see a better lie? You my only reason, "I'm leaving."
It wasn't so fun with you; need I go on and move?
This is where it leaves you... I leave you.

Eulogy

He meant a lot to us all, and he meant just that much more to me.
He was a man of great words and good thoughts.
He was a great father to his daughter.
And he was a wonderful son to his dad.
He was a good friend to me, *his brother.* So forever in us he lives.
We have come far through the tears and smiles.
I ask you not to weep, but rather to remember his face, his laugh.
He was a great friend to us all, and we'll never forget his path.
He laid out for his children, for their children.
It's hard to hold in the tears. As I stand here in front of his family.
I ask you not to weep, I ask myself not to weep; *but rather to remember.*
Remember his words, remember his face.
My brother will live on in us all, so long as we remember.

Moon Trip

Side to side twist of mind, my soul cold and dark.
Dream and dream, open flesh and I'm torn apart.
I find no home, as under stone lies my body.
On my throne I find myself alone.

What a loss of time in my soul, what I need is nothing and you.
Gravity flowing within my soul.
What a shove down I feel.
I would never hurt you my love...
Yet it is you I kill.

Over the shadow I play with rage, under my skin I hide the pain.
Over and over and never again.
Taste the metallic warmth and feel the sin.

"On the moon I trip, now I feel so sick.
In the sky I die, on my mind is just I."

I hate the way I sung to you... I was nothing and I am me.
The moon in my mind, the pain on my tongue.
The shadow in my soul.
Never will I have a home...

"On the moon I trip, now I feel so sick.
In the sky I die, on my grave is just I."

Over the lie you told, in my body so cold.
Now I feel the end, on I feel my sin.
Fear not what you say but what you do.
Feel not my pain, my pain is you.

Over the moon I fall, deep in the minds of all.
Hollow is my heart, forever now torn apart.
What a loss of me, on I feel the need.
Still I wait, still I bleed...

On the moon's tip, in my tears I trip.
On I go, on the moon trip.
Now and forever I feel so sick.

Nothing I Can Change

Wait - where is it that the sky touches the ground?
"And where is it that the water runs cold down this stream."
I stood in front of you; I smiled, turned and walked.
I now am alone again, with sin and myself.
A long coat, a cold night, so once again I'm on the road.
And I seek only a better sense of drive. "*How is it that I stay awake?*"
"I don't know." The road is twisted and totality in a bind, like me.
I grabbed my meal for the day. I awoke in the morning's haze.
Cold in a summer's winter. This road is like the ones before it.
I walk to find what might lie at the end. "*I'm lying to myself.*"
My feet are tearing on the road, I need some hope.
I wish me not alone, yet I want nobody around.
I turn my eyes inward and try to find my home.
I seek a new hope on the tip of my madness.
I can only picture your face, you were my grace.
Now I'm out of place, as I seem to have been all along.
The cloud turns gray, the sky is black, the world is gone.
And I'm all that's left, "in my mind." Cold shakes on the roadside.
The time is running out, the sand pours from my mouth.
Who am I, I ask myself? *Where am I*, in purgatory or hell?
The road is turning and I'm still burning. Stroke the hour hand at three.
Set the stone on the ash and wait for the sky to touch the ground.
Pain - the lust I hold of truth and the roads I walk.
I walk and walk and see only my end.
Fight as I may, it's nothing I can change.
There was nothing I could do, I still lost you.
I looked into your eyes, smiled and turned.
You laugh at my pain. It's nothing I can change.
I walk now alone, I wish for company yet I drive all away.
In this gray abyss I stay.
Push me onto this once more then set the stone in place.
And drive the world into my head, now dead.
But what more is there to say; now my life is a haze.
Dark days are all that's ahead of me.
Where is it that the ground meets the sky?
The water is blood and I drown in night. all alone, *swimming in my own.*
The torment is just a part of my being. "As is your hate."
Your death drops and I walk away. I stay on this road I made.
I stay in gray, I stay awake, "how.?!"

Could Not Wait

Such a day of loss. I need to wipe away the frost.
And see something more than your world.
Now I push it behind me. I feel the cloud winding.
It falls acid and rains over me till I'm gone.
Was I so wrong to weep? I hear the voices so sweet.
It comforts me while I turn within.

All now gone - dead and covered. The trees are dark and gray.
I opened my eyes and this is what I see.
I could not wait for the world to change.
I could not wait for you to smile, "*just smile.*"
Far too much for me to hold.
I need nothing but a better truth in my hand.

I could not wait.
I will not wait, for all is gray.
Just dead faded and soon gone like me.
I could not wait to see - it is to be.
Must I hold you that close to my hell?
What a shove down in a spinal crush.
The bones are the only remains of what I did.
Could not wait for you to begin - so I end.

Back - back - back - back I need to move the feeling further.
The mother monster is coming, the demon just sits back.
He takes another drag and blows smoke in my face.
The dog just waits for its master to come home.
My life waits, "I'm no master."
I could not wait, so I took control.
The glass broke, now the wine is gone.

Hand to the-over... I need to see a better goal.
My mouth to a... I feel the nothing in my soul.
I could not wait any longer.
I need not wait - to control this monster.

To The Zenith

For someone who doesn't want to be left behind.
You do stare into the mirror and lie.
Thrust the casket into the earth, "death from birth."
Smile to frown - I creep into my hollow heart.
Rise to the apex, I feel there is nothing left.
Rhymes and riddles, knives and toys.
Line after line I've walked down these roads before; *you lie to me still.*
I seek a new reason, a better sense of drive.
I seek the zenith, to the top, above the sky.
In circles they play, while the heavens rain the blood of the damned.
I wash away the pain. I am at the peak if my being.
I am at the pinnacle of my self-destruction, divide and set aside.
To the zenith of my every whim.
I stand tall and watch over my children, "you are not forgotten."
Water in the reflection, the mirror cracked and the light faded dim.
Summit of hate I await. Death is just a dream; life - an eternal nightmare.
I wish to awake but you stand on my granite headstone.
Thrust the cloud over the limb; hang me with a rainbow noose. Colorless life, "hell."
Try after try, tear after tear; all crumbling within my broken soul-pit.
I sway in a lifeless being, stones being thrown.
They beat me down and down till I cannot stand; I'm broken.
Mouth torn on a razor's edge, twisted life-form...
Climb I will until my very end. *Lie to me no more*!
I seek what you hide. I live on pain and pride.
No man is as wicked as I, but you try, "you try."
The whore did sing me a song.
I wish to relax and pass away with no notions of you.
I seek my zenith, a truth of forever being a part of this sick twisted reality.
"Vanity is my soul." I wish to reach the tip of the top.
The top of the tip and see what I want to see.
Nothing could ever change my mind.
Forever I will be turned backwards and inside.
I asked you once to tell me the truth.
I asked you twice to run and hide, "hide - hide!"
In a way I am what you seek and dream.
In a lost turn of events I destroy what you seek.
I am the one you love - I am the one you kill.
I feel these wounds will never heal.
You've grown without me being able to stop it.
You've grown and I age with no profit,

I see in age that I've never changed. I will stay the same, *I seek my zenith.*
To the top, to the north, to the zenith with my every whim, I fall now so-so far.
I've had to suffer. I've had to break the door.
Now I am what I've grown to be.
Weak you little demons on my tongue.
Wink at the end to our world, whisper in my ear.
Tell me that I can awake from this hell someday.
Hold me and say it will be okay. To find the truth, to reach the end.
To find the top, to prevail with sin, "life - hell."
I will die before I lose my pride.
I seek a new reason of drive, on I leave the light.
To the zenith of my every dream.
Of being a true spirit of hallow truth and growing strong.
For someone who does not want to be left behind.
You stare at the mirror and lie. So seek the zenith and end my time.
Seek the zenith and end the lie. Seek the zenith and it's me you'll find.

Open Mind But Nothing More

Leave - leave me to grow alone. Set in place my gravestone.
Drop only for the love of God. "Lord take me home."
Running through the tall blades of grass.
Running from the pain, running from my past.
Rush me deep into madness, forgive my sadness.
"The soul of me?" I the child is twisting out of place.
In clear mirror, I seem faceless.
I turned and the world was gray. I stood and just fell.
Nowhere to run, I find the moment aside.
Shove the hate done and I smile inside.
With the thoughts wrong. I smile still set aside.
Within this old broken hole called home.
Brown-red, dark and damp. What could I ever do without you?
Upon the thought of broken truth, I head first into lost madness.
We are broken, gone forever because of me.
Look into my eyes and tell me something I don't know.
Laugh while I weep, betray while I sleep.
Could you ever be more? I wonder what could become of me.
Could I ever be more to you, why do you hate me so?
Could I ever be more to you? Please just never let me go.

When I Needed You

You walked away when I needed you most.
You left me standing... Heartless, no hope.
I hope you are happy with how you left me.
I - the monster now unbound and ready.
"I can't believe you're gone."

One Step Away

Why is it so hard to understand me? *Why does the world crush me deep*?
Faceless I scream to a love that does not care.
Crawling only into madness, "the shadow grows."
Find me on the dark wings of evil. The taste of lust must be set aside.
Aside I am from the world, "the world between."

Little demons crawl in-side. Mindless I sit in my dark room.
I rock the world of mine, "set aside?"
I wash myself in the blood of the Just.
Face torn on the pencil tip, "this is it."

Around me spinning, faces of the damned.
The low dark voice whispers to me.
The face of my love haunts me so clearly.
Clearly I'm mad, mad at the one above.
Mad I am at my one true love.
Broke - I soak in tears of sadness.
Forsaking the truth, only in youth did I love?

Fingertip broken on the paper.
Watch me drift away, face gone in my song of me.
Only I can cry to myself, because the world cannot hear.
Here I wait for my time, singing myself to sleep.
Weep the sorrow, with only my hollow-self.
Deeper I dig me to hell, one step away from grace.
The mirror cracks and faceless I wait.
One step away...

Rains While We Weep

Standing above you, it rains while I weep.
I clinch my fist - it rains while you weep; never will you be forgotten.
Please forgive me for not getting to say goodbye.
Sky dim, would you like me to smile?
It rains while I weep - cold dark; much like me.
Would you like us to smile?
It rains while we weep.

"Good-Bye"

I would like to say goodbye but you're already gone.
Just until we meet again, it won't be long.
Life - a stream; time a ripple in all.
I wish to say goodbye, to us you were "everything" and forever will be.
I wipe the tears from my eyes, I say goodbye.
Just until we meet again. Not too far, not so long.
I'll never give up, "like you I'll be strong."
Until we meet again, "I say goodbye."
Until we meet again, in heaven's light.

Scream

Was to kill - the demon I am; "I smile."
Was a pill - now I feel the monster I am.
Run to the north, crumble my soul.
Was to the... I crush the... scream - scream - scream!
Now bleeding, I seep evil truth. Scream bleeding, I am a demon-man.
Shut open the thought of the ever I can.
We were once a life of truth, now justice raped before our eyes.
Was to kill - the demon I am; "I smile."
Was a pill - now I see what kind of monster I am.
Run to the north - rip away my soul.
Was to the... I crush my soul and scream - scream - scream!
Just waiting to be free, just watching you hang my dreams.
Just wishing for a better end, it was a sin.
Now I scream and watch it end.
I scream - I bleed, I scream - I cry, I screamed - *you died...*

Faith Test

It's a test is what it is, to see how much pressure and strain I can bear.
To watch my head cave-in and see me crumble away into nothing like he is to me.
What a sick game you play with my head.
To you I've given the name of faith.
Struck down in the prime of life.
Stuck in between wishes and lies, "I question you."
Push me over the edge!
This cliff is high enough; you take away everything but me.
You watch me weep in the corner of my room.
Beating and bleeding; the wall creaked red.
You test me to see if I care, you bleed me, hurt me.
Stabbing me with needles and I rip out my own hair.
I await my fate; I sit here with no home, no heart, no hope and no faith.
"Face me you freak!"
It's just throwing rocks. You push and shove, pull and break.
Now the hourglass is slipping.
You test my faith, I taste the blade - I test my fate.
The slate is broken "I'm broken." I am what you would call an evil man.
I am what you would call a heartless child.
Neglect and regret are all I've known.
It's just throwing stones, "but why at me?"
It's a test is what it is.
A game you play with my head, driving me to death.
Suicide of life, hate or suffering.
I ask you to leave me to my own tools, "you fool."
Breaking down in the middle of a lord trust.
I breakdown in tomorrow's hate lust. Faith test, wasting my last breath.
I have no more heart to give; you've taken it all.
Now my world is gray, forever I am stuck in this haze.
Dark days are my fate. I the monster now grown...
I've shown you the path to forgiveness, "just leave me alone."
I am alone; I am a cold waste of flesh. I wish to breathe no more.
I want to fade away, I stay in these dark days; no color, no life, no love.
For me I have felt only hate. What a fate, what a thing I hate.
You my lord with no face, no words spoken for me to hear.
You leave me alone, dark with only fear. You test me, hurt me, kill me!
You have taken away everything that mattered to me!
I'm alone with a hate-lust for you, what am I to do?
I guess I just need faith...

Picture On The Wall

My eyes burn, my stomach hurts, the room is spinning.
"I need some sort of grip."
Ice on the floor, the paint dark and chipping away.
In the mirror I see no face. So why are all the voices here?
What did I do to deserve this and why won't the pain stop?
Cold and damp, the room broken and soon to crumble away just like me.
I weep - the tears roll down my face.
At first warm but at the end so cold, "alone like me."
Nothing in this purgatory but me.
I'm all alone in the thought of what was and could never be.
The wall's dark-red tint, the floor a slightly faded blue.
The room so motionless, "I still weep."
In the corner I ball-up and cry myself to sleep.
Why won't the world just leave me be? Cold and damp - ice and hell.
I walk in place; the wall spills the feel of only hidden truth.
Behind open doors and beneath a frozen lake.
Might you find what it is you are looking for?
In this room I sway and in this mind state I stay and sway.
"Nothing to comfort me but hate." My mind crumbles away day by day.
The life of what you've given is all I despise.
Why so alone am I? Why won't anybody hold my hand?
So alone in this room, so cold is I.
Weep as I may but you laugh at my pain.
Somebody please hold my hand! Never did I have an arm around me.
Never did I have warmth surround me, I need more than this.
The room's color dark, and the air so dirty.
I have nothing, am nothing; will always be away.
Tears flowing nonstop, my body trembles.
I feel that only dust could bleed from my eyes, with such an abrupt halt.
I see something behind the red and in front of my eyes.
A shade of light yellow and bright green. *So quick I am to get to my feet.*
I try to run to the wall, I try to reach out and touch.
My body gives and I fall in bloody cries.
Struggle as I may, I get nowhere fast.
I reach and further I fall back. "I need strength."
Deep in the pit of my soul I found the power to stand.
I focus and stay in place. In the mirror I see an outline but still no face.
I move step by step and seem to never reach.
In the time's horrid hand laid the tool. I spoke to the voice in my head and it said.
"Leave to be only me and my fate...
Behind open doors and beneath a frozen lake."
Such a hard hit;

My fingernails scratched at the wall so fast, three broke off.
Crawl and claw I did, to reach what it is I seek.
The colors growing, the wall showing something new.
More shades of green and a light, so bright blue.
White and yellow, orange and pink.
The dark paint chipped away until only this, what I found would show.
A picture of a warm lake with so much life. Doors open with no secrets to hide.
I saw a sky with not one rain drop in sight.
Life in the sense of truth. Life in which I lived my youth.
I held it so close to my heart, the picture on the wall, was it my dream.
Did my mind grab that brush and paint that hidden picture?
I feel tears form under my eyes, yet all of them now run warm.
I have a lot to do before the world is to share my thoughts and sights.
All not yet gone, the room half dark like me, still something's a miss.
I need a hand to hold while I weep, I need an arm around me.
Much like the picture on the wall.

Time Taken

Red - it was the last though I held.
Life was the only memory in which I'd dwell.
Looking through this hourglass.
Watching my time crumble and pass, "I have nothing."
In my hallow mind, in my broken heart.
I gaze at the actions that form before me.
You think so little of me; all my dreams are torn into nothing by you.
You were the one for me, now on my grave I lay. *Done with all your hate.*
You push me and I fall down. You cut me and in my blood I drown.
My face broken on the edge of reality. My body faded and it flows down the drain.
You laugh at me! You smile while you betray.
You stole my heart and tore it apart.
Life taken, time waiting for me to die, you hate me. "All alone I waste away."
Round in the pool of what you see. I walk in the memory.
You think so little of me, you think I'm nothing.
You stand above my grave and smile.
I am nothing to you; I was not the person you loved.
I am just nothing but done. Time taken, life wasting away.
The sand flowing, never knowing an end.
Deadication to you I had, now I wonder alone in the time sand.
I am nothing, you stole away my dream. You walk with the others.
In my soul growing weak, the beast forming inside.
Time is all I had and nothing I need.

In The Absence

I could drop it onto the ground that you stand.
I could stop it on the thought that you'd win.
I could run until the sun grows cold.
I could fight until it is your heart that I hold.
I could sleep until I can never awake.
I would weep, but it is you that is late.
In the absence of reality, I hold your breath in my hand.
In the memory of your absence, I ball-up in the back of my mind.
In your last wish, you asked who I truly am. *"Forever I'm away."*

I could drop it onto the ground where you lay.
I could drop it, in the world's dark haze.
I could love it but you push me away.
I could love it, until the end of gray.
I could sleep until I never awake. I could weep but it is you I seek.
Should I have told you the truth? Should I have held you that close?
Should I need a new drive to my end?
In the absence of reality I find no sanity...

Nursery Rhyme Me Truth

Cry - the hurt has developed since the last time I was inside myself.
Over the bridge I walk. In my heart I feel the pain stalk my soul.
Nursery rhymes are forming truth, the head twist I held in my youth.
Why has nobody told me the truth? The hurt was the only thing I knew.
Abandoned by the world, my only way to get away from the gray is gone.
I wash away the roses and memories of the thing you gave.
The ways we sang and played.
I love the lie - why can't the dream be my forever?
I want to breathe under water. I want to live after death.
Nursery rhyme me truth, take me away.
Give me a better youth; give me a better way to stay.
Take me away, take me away.
Give me a better taste, give me a better light.
Stop the voices, the scream in my childhood memories.
Take me away from the cradle and place me in the grave.
In the mud where I lay.
In the depth where I want to stay...

This Reminder

It was on that thought that you reminded me.
Of what I was and could never be.
In my hand I held it, warm with awareness and grief.
"Why won't you leave me?" It was over before it began.
Deeper I dig myself into the sand, in gone awareness.

Sleek something, over the ground it pours.
In the mouth of madness I find the bore.
Never on the tip of what you gave to me.
You have given only hurt and damage.
Would it control you before it controls me?
Would I break as I fall to my knees over your shame?
Pain - such a taste in the back of my mouth.
I swallow the razor that gleams in my eyes.
It was on that thought that you reminded me.
That I am nothing but flesh and frail bones.

Under my tongue I taste the gift.
Memories of pain that was shoved beneath my skin.
Sin is the name I call, so deep under the earth I crawl.
And in the hour between I scream!
Of the time you held truth, never shattered in youth.
You spoke true pain, you lovely pain.
God I need, to guide me through the never pit of sorrow.
"Damn, this reminds me of you."

I would and could but never will free the strain.
Pain in the deep hollow called me.
Me on the tip of madness, shadow me with sadness and regret.
Yet I bleed still.
Steel through my hands, I'm nailed to the wall.
This reminder of you drives me to hell.
Hell I wish, it's better than where I stand now...

Given Down To My Last Tear

What am I to say? And if I were, would you even care?
Long flowing hair, you the one I hold closest to my heart.
You my love that has torn me apart.
I have spent many of hours, on this feeling so numb and dead inside.
I will not give into this feeling. You will haunt me no more.

Love you as I may...
But I will not watch you crumble into nothing before my eyes.
I will never give you a second to think, I will not let you breathe.
No one will understand but you.
I hold you in my arms forever in a *night-spell.*

Into heaven or hell, I ask you what outcome you wish.
If yet ever I would know. No, not ever shall I fall again for you.
Your knife I hold deep in my heart, you tear me down and away.
You the love I have killed, now in regret I stay.

Hoping that someday I may awake from this lie called life.
Dreaming of the day I kissed your lips and held you tight.
Nights in which we were one, our bodies together.
And never will I let you go; never will you see me go.
I hold you - I need you - I love you; my dead bride in my arms.

In my soul, the dark crypt... In my head, the wish.
I wish I were with you, my pain I threw away.
I wish I were with you, "please somebody let me die."
I wish I were with you, "please someone take away my life."
I love you, I need you, I breathe you.
Forever in my tears rolling down my face; I hold you, I miss you.
I remember the days we thought of only each other.

Now because of what I've done.
I sit here and cry, given down to my last tear.

The Last One Given

Mouth open, leaves flowing.
The dim side to the story given to little angels.
Smiles broken, dust flowing. The wind is the life that's left *and always gone.*
Years taken and the bones twist-bind... Head over *the open door to the pit.*
And if blood dripped down the fang of the angel's evil smile.
Who would care? And in the eyes of the damned I drift and flow.
Into the hell fire and cool spring air. The pull to the last breath taken.
The hour, in which I held her hand, I hold only hate.
I was the last one given, "fearing the mother of monsters."
"And down the throat of the snake."
Red moons in the back of light, down in the side-set.
And you laugh, "Not taken." Now I take the blade.
In the reflection I hold the past; the pass of emotion.
And the little angel's arms torn off from her body.
Legs eaten while she was still alive.
No one around to hear her scream, no one would even care.
Her wings *red* - now gone. I the monster created by the world.
I hold her soft face in my hands, she weeps.
I eat at her remains, "God weeps."
I tear at your pain and I lick away the blood.
Call me evil if you will yet you are what made the leaves form the path.
I was the last one given and you all laughed.
Without a breath in your smile and you drown in your denial.
The rough jagged tongue across my neck.
You lick my life away; you haunt me even in death.
"I - the last one given." And giving me something to hold.
Other than the knife in your spine, not mine.
And lying in a pool of tears.
The angel ripped and raped in her darkest fears.
But you were the first one taken.
You are the only one that knows true light.
In my back I found your knife.
And in spite the demon smokes the river down to his soul; *he waits for me.*
Little angle torn down and held while she screamed, it seems I laughed.
You the angel, you the world.
All my pain is here and I throw it in my grave.
And you would like me to die.
You would enjoy seeing the murderer be put to justice.
It's only a joke, "life and death."
There is nothing more than the pain that binds us.
Leaves point me to the north side of hell;

And there is where I'd find your cries.
In the *Forbidden Lost*, is the true stream to the *Always & Forever*.
And never will you hold another hand.
Yours in my mouth, "screams and I smile."
You will never get that far, you will never know the end.
Only the... what you want to see.
Because I was the last one give, you will be the first one taken.
I held the angel; wings gone, blood mine.
Life is the ever and never is it given?

On The Brighter Side

On the brighter side, there must be a sun to shine and a heart to beat.
On the brighter side, there must be a son to cry and the end of the day.
And on the brighter side, there must be someone out there to hold me.
Has it been years since the ever twist of sweet sorrow and *madness-joy*.
Has it been an eternity? Will it be infinity until I once again give out my heart?
If memories are all I have, and they are... Then what is there for me to live for?
The butterfly on the tip of my tongue.
I see the wings spread; I see the skull of the Ever Dead.
And on the brighter side to this morning,
I am mourning the death of my child, me. So in the fog I reach my hand.
I try to hold something more than this monster named me.
I wish I could kill this zombie.
As I walk dead and decayed. I pull off my face but on the brighter side.
There must be a meaning for all of this; it can't just be my fate.
It is my fate to lose everyone who is close to me; I free this soul of nothing.
God save my soul, give me a new hole to crawl into.
As mud is man I waste away. On the brighter side, it's not your fate.
As faith fades away, I would live anyway.
And no one's here to give me a better truth.
And I drink away my youth, in smoke it fades.
And the green to gray, from me to this. On the brighter side it's not you.
And on the brighter side, you were not used.
My head is twisting and you just pissed me away.
I have no one to hold me. In the slump to the life that no one cares.
I tear out my hair and I weep, I weep.
So many tears running down my face. So many times I fell out of place, no face.
So on the brighter side, you did love.
You loved hating me; yes I see, the pain indeed.
And as it rushes, the monster blushes.
I feel the alien pit in the stomach of my fear;

And my fears fell on the table.
You told me the fable and our notion just fades away.
In my jaws I taste the pleasure.
And the acid pressure comes home for me.
I let it roll down my throat, will I choke?
On the brighter side, you won't care.
On the brighter side, I won't live with it forever.
Just the rest of eternity.

There Is Nothing To Say

I stand on the edge of everything I once thought; crying dust.
I hold it on the tip of my affection, dripping deep in mind.
And she walks away with another hand to hold, I weep dust.
Walking as far as the eye can see. Holding nothing close but me, on I weep.
If light were an object, it would be the one thing I never held.
I will always be in hell. Never held, never taught the truth, only lies.
Only your cries and my blood pours.
Pouring into the mouth of what I want and need.
It is what I hold close to me, me, me, me!
And she is a mind tease; she was a love to me.
I am a demon still and always will be because all that mattered to me.
All that had meaning is now gone and buried deep.
And here I stand on the edge of my every whim; weeping deep within sin and me.
From start to end, I feel the overload and the undertow; far away I drift and stay.
Heading deeper into hell and further away from grace.
"Me" I have no face. I look at you and expect something more.
I cut myself and bleed on the floor. If yet ever more the darkness was.
If yet ever more the hatred is inside of me.
And she walked away with another hand to hold.
I pushed her away, I lost my faith.
Now fate lay on the face of a coin, a toss to see; there is nothing to say.
I kiss her and lay my hand on her face. I wish I could wash the pain away.
And I do, by walking away. She I loved, she tore me insane.
And you could say there is nothing to say yet so much to think on.
I walked away, her face stuck in mind. Time after time I lost her and will lose you.
Because I'm just that evil, I'm just a stupid kid; lost so deep in sin.
Nothing to guide my way, nothing to cover my pain, "I have only pain."
I would love to hold your hand and kiss your lips, *"hold you close to me."*
I would've told you how I felt but again I would have only opened hell.
And you do not need to be brought to my world.
I look you in the "Eyes." And there is nothing to say...

Home Is Just A Breath Away

Most honestly I say, that you are the one who is crazed.
"You lying waste of flesh."
Play your games; waste your head on thoughts of false truths.
"Waste yourself with someone else."
Grip the tip of madness and fall into the hell pit like me.
"Scream while the world laughs."
Do nothing to pass the time. I've wasted my time with you.
I should weep... "But I'd rather smile."
So I grip my teeth on the bone.
I rip and tear the flesh and lie on the stone, "welcome home."
I push my fingernails harder and deeper into your skin.
I watch you bleed and bleed and bleed.
Such torment these little monsters on my skull give.
I take it all, scream and laugh.
I rip off your flesh and watch you scream your last breath.
You're almost home now. Wow, what a skull twist.
What a side-breath of fate. I have waited far too long for this.
Home is just a breath away and you say that I never cared.
You say that I never tried.
I grip my teeth on your neck. I tear out and sallow your flesh.
Then smile while you bleed and bleed.
Ah, to see the look of fear on your face.
Just before life is completely gone, we're almost home.
Most honestly I say, that you are the one who is crazed.
"Such a waste of human emotion."
Play your games; beat your head on the thought that I could have cared, "I did care."
Grip the tip of sadness.
And fall just that much deeper into hell like me. "I laugh and scream."
You do nothing to pass your time.
I'm done wasting time with you! "I should weep, yet I smile."
I pity you not. I will never give you what you want.
And you smile while I turn inward and scream.
I waste no more time with un-sane you...
Has God forgiven me and my emotions? My devotion is dead.
This is what you get for pushing me that far.
My past has come back to haunt me for the last time.
Damn the devil inside me, the angels grip their blades and stab me deep.
Would I smile or weep? I light the fire and watch you burn.
"I told you to watch what you say and do." Now you lose.
With you and "your loves" in the dirt I can rest.
I will - I will and you're almost away;

The ashes I swallow and take to my grave.
You're a waste of human emotion, burnt and your loves decay.
Home is just a breath away and you said that I didn't care.
You said I didn't try! "Smile and die."
Most honestly I say, that you are the one who is crazed.
"You are blind and will never see again."
You played your games but I won in the end.
You think you're strong; "you weak waste of flesh."
I grip the tip of sorrow and wait for tomorrow to come.
"Soon I'll be at home in my grave." Through all of the insanity and pain.
Through your blind actions and childish games you should remember.
"Home is just a breath away."

Ever Child

And all was not forgiven; the trees now dead as I walk across this pier.
I tremble on the thought of what you have done to me.
On the summer leaves dead in the fall.
I place my hand on your heart. Angel's sweet cool breath.
The emotion brought forth on outrageous rants.
I hold my child in my arms.
A ripple in her eyes and I break down; a teardrop in her mind.
I flow over the water in a way that shows me only doubt.

I would be your father, I would watch you grow.
I would clean your wounds. Forever I would hold you while you cry.
I would wipe away the tears.
If you feared then all monsters would come to know my wrath.
Alone I walk on this pier and peer into my future.
I gaze deep into the water, would I drift above it?
Or would I sink and swallow?
You my ever child I hold. You, the ever should I go...
You the thought that keeps me alive. You, the light in dark night.

I would be your father but will you ever be my child?

"Within" You Now 2

Dark times, dead minds, my soul torn away.
Broken fingers, my soul lingers, 2 heartbeats away.
Lies told, I've lost my soul, it chips away.
Lies told, I've lost my soul, it chips me away.

Tell me you love me, spread wide open your legs.
Remove your clothes, wet opening; let me in, let me in.
Friction smooth, warm sweet oozing, heart beating.
Fingernails under my skin.
Scream louder, harder I hit and hit, *faster-slower.*
You hold me tighter. I am within, I am within.

Now when one becomes two and two become three.
And I await a sign of compassion; within, within.
Dark times, dead minds, my soul torn away.
Broken fingers, my soul lingers, one heartbeat away.
Lies told, to hide the truth, lost and chipping away.

You on top... You and I connected, so deep within I stay.
Is there no end to this dark day, mad time - you mine?
You so wild biting my neck, kiss my mouth, suck my tongue.
Fingers in your hair, you consume me with no care.
One now two and three from us, one is me and two as you.
You held on for far too long; let me up, let me up!

Now when one becomes two and two becomes three *"Family."*
But I'm not ready for these dark times, dead minds.
Within, you now 2... Away, gone and confused.
Heart beating, sweat bleeding, warm love, sweet taste.
Open yourself for me; let me in, let me in.

Chapter 11

As She Drove Away

I Did - I Did

I would start it, I would end it, I did, I did.
You smile so sweet, I crumble - I tumble, I reach within my deceit.
I call out the monster. I've formed the evil beast.
I would let it free, I did, I did.
What a deception, you lie and do not blink.
So I turn my head, blow a kiss and wink.
I would crumble, scream and tumble, I did, I did.
Biting my own tongue, watching it bleed.
Fire on my gravestone, smoke under my eyelids.
You walk - one foot in front of the other; two feet gone, I fall.
Lying on the concrete in a school yard; mean faces above me.
You were against me, I would end it all, I did, I did.
Shooting at angels, watching your dreams fade weak.
Now it crumbles my world dark and beating on me.
I would start it and I will end it, I did, I did.
You - just another face in the crowd; you spit on my wounds.
In the Salt-Graveyard, the tall trees crumble and tumble...
I am a demon, wings of untruth and lust, greed and pain.
I open my eyes and wipe my tears from my face.
I consume the world and watch it end... I did, I did.

Shoot In Sin

Must you hate me? Must you break me?
Smooth eyes covered with wax; consume my breath.
I lay back further, "hold me father, stop weeping mother."
I shoot in sin and watch the world dim; consuming my sin.
I shoot it in and watch reality break and tumble.
My flesh flakes off my body. I'm exposed to your disease.
Blood forever flowing, shoot the sin within me.
I am melting, "human wax." I am burnt, dead and gone.
It's nothing, my teeth fall onto the dirt, "my home."
Grave - it's alone with me; tears I hold and seep.
I shoot in sin, the world slips further into my brain.
My body is just a lie. My mind was such a waste.
It was fun, "I sat in front of the mirror and tore off my own face."
Now I'm alone, I am home in my grave; cold so cold. *"Feel the hurt."*
Endless shakes "I shoot in sin" and watch all end.
I the child now gone, under blood and washed within.
Your words mean nothing to me "I speak evil - do I,"

Numb screams, only to me the sun dies; "it weeps."
Demon mother, Angel - my lover, I hold your death.
Razor, needles, pills and smoke, I smile on the cloud.
"You wish to change me. I hope you die just like me."
Unspoken, untaken, never far from grace; I waste.
I shoot in sin and laugh at yours "and or death of mine."

Soft Blue Eyes

Soft blue eyes haunt my dreams, I scream and scream!
I lay back, my hands on my face, on my last breath.
I seem so alone "I am" I scream at night, blue eyes...
Hold my chest, soon I'll be in my grave, I lay in my grave.
Home is a breath away; I hope not to let it pass me.
Soft blue eyes, sweet warm smile, I cannot sleep.
Hair flowing, never knowing an end to my pain.
I lay back, hands on my face, "I feel so disgraced."
Every time my eyes close, I see her face.
Now I fell out of place, I need faith.
Please God, let go of my neck, "let me live!"
Soft blue eyes, I would hold her until the end of light.
Now at the end of noon, dawn is here.
I lay back in my grave, end my pain, "please!"
"Somehow I will find a way out of this world."
"And into her arms."

Me On The Mic.

I feel so out of place, I feel the dirt on my face.
I need the warmth to hold me, "please somebody hold me."
Now on the stage I ball-up with rage; "it's given."
I take in the sights of the back of my mind.
Back my eyes roll, "I scream!" Blood dripping off the mic.
You in the sea of faces, "standing out" so cold...
You my love stand out, with another kiss on your mouth.
Fingernails deep in my skin, my face now torn open.
I shake, I tremble, I crumble, pulled down by hell.
Down deep in the pit; sorrow dripping off my face.
On the mic I scream, on the mic I bleed, "new hope." Hope?
What a funny notion, as you hold somebody else and laugh.
Upward spiting, dust and mud, downward falling;

"Me on the ground."
Lights dim, the sea of faces flows back and forward.
Colors red and black, the music rages in my soul.
My hair flowing, head banging! "I feel so alone."
With my lover, with my brothers, song and band.
My soul in the gutter, me without a lover.
She stood there with someone else and "I wish hell."
Me on the mic, I tell you a story; "truth and pain."
Time soon over and we live on without a thought.
Me on the mic, feeling out of place, numb-forgot.

The Person Next To Me

Deep down, sorrow pains and I find the light dimmed and me alone.
Sound, loud - my hurt and pain.
Blood pouring out of my mouth and into my grave.
I look to the right; my brother, my left hand.
I look to the left; my brother, my right hand.
I turn my head back; my spine, my soul, my brother, my band.
I stand in the front, as sound crushes my skull.
Demon-angel, my lover, my pain, my soul; it's dimming.
The person next to me; my brother, my band "all I have."
If I could paint it on a wall; green, black and red with blood.
My eyes roll into the back of my head, "now ours to take."
Soul up for grabs; cut my heart, cut my neck.
Down in the deep pit of my thoughts - I think only truth.

The Girl I Want

The girl I want, I cannot have. The girl I have, I do not want.
This lie I live... I want to sleep. This life I live... I wish to not weep.
The girl I want, I cannot have. The girl I have, I do not want.
This life I live... you cut me deep. This world I hold... pain I seep.
I sit back in a cold room, dark and dim. I wish it to end, I wish it to end.
I run from the world, my pain is me. I run from the world, my loss is me.
Could I ever awake from this dream? Could I never find a grip to keep?
Would you ever open your eyes and free your mind?
The girl I want, I will never have. She does not know I even exist.
The girl I have, I'll never lose. She wishes I did not exist.
Hold me somebody, let me see the light.
Cut me somebody, please let me die.

Dead Skin

Show out - slow down - shoot in - dead skin.
Scream low - end flow - down blow - dead skin.
Broken heart - crumble apart - welcome sin - shoot within.
Mangled flesh - hole in breath - I try to die... break the sky.

I watch the world pass me by. I watch the light dim and die.
I scream and see the flesh torn from my body.
I laugh un-feeling the torment you inflict.
I go on no more of the madness inside.
I try, I die... you smile.

"Earthworm Love"

It was on her last day of holding my hand...
It was the last way, of showing her a better end.
Sweet shadow given in the back of my throat
Sour dripping, the hour dipping deep to dawn, I'm down.
In soft blue eyes I drown and smile with death.
If I would have kissed her lips, would they crumble to dust?
In this world of slime; the filth of man breaks the trust.
But she is gone now from my side. She is gone now and I bleed.

She was my love; now the mirror monster.
The water red in the freezing dream.
I was the last one who could have changed.
Now in the dark and gray I lie, kissing the earthworm sand.
Yes it was my love, now decay her smile.
The slow-while I lay on her bed.
The leaves form a blanket and covers from foot to head.
Sour dripping... deep down dipping further in me.
If I would hug her, would God forgive me?
It was on her last day of holding my hand.
That I learned I loved her, "I'm such a monster."
I kiss the earthworm sand "once my love."
I lay on her bed, blanketed in the fall.

Jesus

As many miles were walked, feet bleeding on fiery - gray stone.
He smiled, holding the weight on his back.
Living life to be murdered, for his brothers and sisters.
Setting aside a place for you and I.
A smile while nailed, metal against bone.
He knew what had to be done. Now we have a path given.
"Will you follow?"

Heads Will Roll

In my world everything would be exactly what it isn't.
Heads will roll! Am I late? Am I late?
Heads will roll! Am I late? Am I late?
For what path to take, how should I know?
Should I drink from the hourglass?
Or should I just lie down and eat away the back of my eyes?

The world in my dreams seems a lighter gray,
The world in my dreams seems to have a darker scream!
What do you want from me!? What do you want from me!?
Am I late? Am I late? Is it fate?! Is it fate?!
You're too late! You're too late!
Heads will roll! Heads will roll!

Remember to chew your water and wash the dirt before you eat.
Remember to play with your food and watch it scream!
In my world everyone is dead, in my life I'll lose my head.
And everything was a blur seen through the looking glass and I feel the burn.
Remember me, am I late? Remember me, am I late?
Remember me, you're too late...

As She Drove Away

And as she drove away I could only smile.
Because I knew my life was over and a new one would begin.
I'm still myself; I am just a demon in hell "*Sorry...*"
As she drove away, I could only remember her face.
Because I knew I would never see it again.
And I know I will always be by myself.
I know I will never love again or maybe I will just feel like shit.
Until the day that I get over it.
But unknown to the things to be.
As she drove away, I set my soul free.
To the knowing that I was once happy.
Once... *Sorry.*

How Much More?

How much more shit can I take?
The walls are falling.
The world is calling me to rise.

How much pain can one man take?
How much further can I fall before I hit?
How much more... in this life of shit!

Will there never be an end?
Will there ever be an end?
Will I ever be known?
Will I always be un-shown?

Please take me away from this fate.
Please take me away from this face.
I know that it's mine; I know that it's here.

I rip off lumps of flesh and wash your body with the blood.
I rip away my face, hoping for a better fate.
I know that you're fake; I know that it's fate, I know I have no faith.
"God!"
How much more of this shit can I take?

Bleed Me More

It wasn't long ago, when life flowed through my body and soul.
But now left with only hatred and the lies you so believed in.
I believe there is something you forgot to say.
Something you forgot to do, "yes there is..."
Cold-blue yet still flowing within my dark crowded mind.
Still the question lingers.
The truth pulled down through my eyes, "I bleed."
There was something more for you to do, "I do believe."
There was something more for me to say "but it's clear."
The nothing I hold in my arms tonight.
The something I wish for, deep in my fright.
These ways were once a man, wishing for a love true and pure.
Now I bleed just a little more.
Bleed me just to see the end of my fate. Bleed me just to see me hate.
Bleed me just to watch me die. Bleed me, just watch me cry.
A little more I wish to fall. Just a little more in this summer fog.
Just a little blood to end the truth. Bleed me more and drain my youth.

Tongue Stuck To The Wall

Time after time - soul wasted, heart taken; you laugh at me still.
Road after road I walk and see my soul slip; I fall deep within.
Crumble and break down until I'm dust and rotten flesh; hollow chest.
With a nail I grow from hell; tongue stuck to the wall, I scream!
I hammer my body to the cross, I lose and toss.
Grip the eyes of the moon and I drift from home.
Time after time soul wasted, heart taken; you watch me scream - bleed.
Mile after mile I walk and see no further than what's in front of me.
I fall down and break away into ash and dust decay.
With no more hope, I nail my tongue to the wall.
With no more drive, I see the blood in the frost.
I watch the world fade and myself crumble into tears.
Tongue stuck to the wall, my life and fears.
Tongue stuck to the wall, I find it forever in my arms.
Nowhere to hide, I scream numb and forgot.
No one on my side, I nail myself down and watch it subside.
No one on my side, I weep and watch myself die.
No one on my side, tongue stuck to the wall, *forever I'm aside.*

No Where To Go

What to say, what to do. I lost my eyes and lost you.
Broke my heart, you tore me down, now sound sorrow.
No sun to shine, no wind to blow, no life to live... Grass to grow.
No words to speak, no life to taste; no love to hold, so on I wait.
No sights to see, no food to eat, no thoughts to know; I don't know.
No soul to keep, no body of my own, "I'm all alone."
I run away, I try to fight, I run away, "out of sight."
No kiss to remember, no child to cherish, "I'm away."
It was the darkness; I was a lover, now I'm dead.
It was the monster; I am another, now I am dead.
No sound to hear, no voice I scream; on I bleed.
No bed to sleep in, no mind to dream in... only sin, only sin.
No life to live yet still I die. No tears to weep, still I cry.
Nowhere to go, no heart to hold; only an empty chest.
Nowhere to go, no heart nor soul; no tears to hide, still I cry.

Boxed Numb

Rage and I beat... I live within hell's heat.
I rip and I tear... your flesh, blood and hair.
Crumble as I fall... deep in the minds of all.
Down and I tear... crushing without a care.
Soul let down, lift and we'll drown.
"I wonder, in thunder; lighting and insane."
I love her, with another; she lies in her own grave.
Scream now, scream loud; die numb, scream numb.
Little child, my only son; now I die, done.
Scream little voices, boxed inside my head.
Now I look to the shadow in my room, "soon I will eat my own brain!"
And the world will fall, the world will laugh.
Did I do the wrong thing, what should I have said?
I feel my love dying, I hear my love crying.
But I'm not sorry, I'm not asking for forgiveness.
Now I'm sweet chosen, boxed numb in my skull.
The room has no light, the walls feel cold.
I'm bound to this fate I seek. "Dead and alone."
I'm now at the end of my sanity, "I smile."
Now I shove this pen into my eye, boxed numb in my mind.
I'm boxed numb, now just throw dirt on me.
Throw dirt on me, throw dirt on me, on me, on me, on me...

Face Me

Faces, faces - numb face sound.
Places, places - call my number and I'm out.
Racing, racing - I try to go and rush my life out.
Faces, faces - numb face sound.
Place me, place me - you just throw me down.
Hate me, hate me and then shove me out.
Under the wing of my demon lover I speak justice and truth.
Lift me with one hand and tear my flesh off with the other.
Eat my body, bloody death and I smile. Eyes shut open and drip.
Faces, faces - numb face sound. Tasting, tasting - the blood from my mouth.
Kill me, kill me - crush me please. Drop me, drop me - under the sea.
Faceless, faithless - time running out. Faithless, faceless - *without a sound.*
Crush me, kill me; "face me please!"
Under all - was I a lover? I await the next.
Over none, have I said the wrong thing?
Face me - taste me - rush me - crush me, please!
Like clay, like my faith; *God understands.*
Even though I'm dead, I have not forsaken you.

I Bleed A Little

To watch the truth flow out of her eyes.
Time stops for nobody but I, "I bleed a little."
Roads turn inward and I wish to leave.
To watch the life pour out of my eyes.
Time wasting, my world pasted to the floor.
Blood dripping off my teeth, "I bleed a little."
Leaves blowing in the wind, on the whisper of an angel.
Demons calling within "hold me *Angel.*"
Fingernail broken on my love; paper / pen.
Brain-cell stolen; I bleed a little again.
I wish to run, I wish to hide. I dream to live, I want to die.
I scream numb sound. I lay back and drown.
We stand tall, till we're broken on the cross.
Faith and fate, love and hate; death and me.
There was nothing we could do.
Torn apart, you stole my heart, leave me be.
I bleed a little of the truth out from my soul.
I weep a little and still I feel cold. I bleed a little and wait for dawn.
I bleed a little and find myself gone...

Cut Me And Gone

What am I going to do? Where am I going to go?
The devil may be evil.
But I am the one who rules hell.
Or is it the pit between sanity and you?

Push and shove me once more.
Hit me harder, 3 more.
Cut me deeper, throw me to the ground.
I need a hand to hold.
I need a sweet voice to tell me everything is okay.
I need a hammer, to end my pain.

Nail me to a cross, I die with these words.
Cut me and gone, now I burn.
Scream while I cry, laugh while you die.
Love behind my back.
Leave me nothing left.

My soul melts like wax and I wander.
I wonder what is next in line.
Am I next to live, or next to die?

I run from your words and "you laugh at me."
I run and I burn, "you laugh at me."
Cut me and I'm done; cut me and gone.
Please somebody hold my hand, "please love me!"
Don't leave me, don't hurt me; don't leave me, don't hurt me.
"Please."

Sick Sight

I sit here watching these people.
They indulge their gluttony on a day to day basis.
Stuffing their pockets and faces... repetitively they masticate.
They'd rather stay in their own little world un-open to all.
They disgust me; I'd turn my head away.
I'd regurgitate on their sight.
Their gluttony is such a waste.
Their greed is such a disgrace.
I sit here watching them waste away.
Soon they won't even be able to walk.
These pieces of shit control the world; un-open to all.
I'd rather turn my head, I wish there wasted lives dead.
They'd rather just put me away. I spit on their disgrace.
Their greed and gluttony is so sick; their sight is so disturbing.
I'd walk away but here I stay - I point and laugh.

Know Wrong

As I know, the worst is now.
I feel the hurt and I...
Scream bleeding, God! *I loved her.*
She used me, abused me.
I bleed from my mouth, "I..."
Die-cry in the torment!
It has bent me wrong.
So sorry, I loved you.
So kill me, "God kill me!"

The worst has come and I am dumb.
The dead child... in a while.
So forsaken and waiting.
To bleed and forget the...
God torment, I am bent.
So save me; give a shoulder to cry on.
I'm sorry.
I am gone.

Spinning The Bottle

With this bottle, spinning my life into misery.
Now I'm hollow, drinking the fears you gave to me.
"You could have been my queen." Now all is unseen.

I know what I should have done. I know what I should have said.
I know I should have walked away but my love for you.
It drove me to this fate. *"Now I rip off my own face."*

Rub your fingers on my eyes, to know what I think and hold.
It is you I despise; all the lies you have told.
To give me nothing, eating my heart and brain.
To say the nothing; "you should have stood there by me!"

Picture

Picture, picture; soft is the sound I feel in my soul.
Why can't I feel your hands on mine?
Time is running out and the sun burns on and on.

Picture, picture; the wind tells a tale of compassion.
Why must it linger... the only thought of my past?
Childhood was - life was and will always be, so tells the wind.

Twist, twist; I will hold it on the tip of my soul.
Open the shutter and see the truth.
I walk more and more and my feet want to give in.

Twist, twist; I picture a soft face I held.
Why do you walk away, *was I that bad of a lover*?
I'm full of what was, I'm empty and always will be.

Scream, scream; I hold it in my hand and head.
I hold the picture, a memory of what was.
I picture a smile on her face and wish it so much.
Picture, picture; soft is the sound I hold in my soul.
Why can't I feel your lips on mine?
Time is running out and the sun burns on and on.
Tick - tick and away.

Monster You Found

Heading further into what you are. Running deeper, inside so far.
I am the power that you do seek. I am the demon, inside growing unseen.
I am the shadow that hides your sin. I am the monster you found within.
MOTHER!
Power growing, never knowing. No! No!
Power showing, ever moving? No! No!
We... forever your drive! We... are the ones who decide!
Deeper running into the stars. Forever showing who you are.
And I am the feeling when you're too numb.
And I am the logic when you are skull-gone.
I am the water to wash your skin. I am the monster you found within.
FATHER!
"And the tiny blade was in her hand."
"And the death was sweet of our forever sins."
Shadow trip! This is it! Calling the time! Rushing your mind!
Running in far! The power you seek! I hide under your skin!
I am the monster you found within...

On This White Line "Gone"

I've been down, this lonely road "with you."
And I've seen how, you treat me, I feel so used.
And I don't need this "shit" and I won't live with it.
I just want you to go away; I just want to end this pain.

I've been down. this lonely road with you "show me."
And I've been there, suffering only you "you're wrong."
Moving on, to give the world a better view.
"Welcome to a better view," *without you.*
On this white line gone, I move on and on.
On this short life gone, you push me gone and gone.
And I've seen how - you fuck me "I feel so used."
On the down-twist of my soul, "cold dark never."
Suffering the truth, suffering my youth. *GIVE IT BACK!*
"Never..."
On the white line gone, time passing "away."
On this white line gone, you push me away.
Time past! Past! Time past! Past! On this white line.

Sway - And Say No More To Me

Now what could I say? What could I do? "Somebody hold me."
Was it your right hand I held; *why do I even care anymore?*
I walk on the roads you made, I kiss the air and die.
One hand on my heart, one thought on my mind. "*Please hold me.*"
Alone as I have ever been; colder I feel now with every sin.

Touch my face, run your fingers through my hair, "*make me feel that you're here.*"
Please don't let the evil control my actions, don't walk away anymore.
You hurt me so easily; you cut out my heart, you tear me apart.
I fold my arms in - my legs crossed; I stay here alone forever.
You could hold me but you'd rather just let me cry.

Sway and say no more to me, all alone my tears run warm, red blood.
Now what could I say? What could I ever do to get you to hold me?
Somebody put out a hand, help me rise; in death-drops I die.
Watch the power leave, watch the air bleed through my body, "help."

Blade, blade - I twist and scream; you laugh and smile at my pain.
Hurt, hurt; I throw-up and it is only blood I see.
On the wall, you smile inside while I fall "damn you."

Could you ever know anything more than what you tell yourself?
I scream as loud as I can, three inches from your face.
You blow me a kiss and still you turn away, "away."

I stand under the sea, I stare up and weep; "God let me sleep."
All alone, I have nothing; the world has walked away from me.
I now know the truth; I know it's real "still alone."

I've lost everything, all to me is gone; "you laugh."
I sway and you say nothing more to me, "nothing."
I could just die "and I have." With nothing but me.

Never Ending Search

In the purple mouth of reality and your dreams I seem to know no end.
I felt the blade on me; in my heart I know no end.
Such a downward push of my affections, such a slap in my face you gave.
What a taste you left in my mouth.
Never will the search for compassion end.
Over and under my tongue goes the emotion.
I feel the emotion, I sway and sway; I feel so sick.
The world is so untrue, the world is so sick.
Never did I know where to go, now and forever I am lost.
Such a downward shove of my affections. Such a slap in my face you gave.
What a taste you left in my mouth and never will the search for truth end.
With dying compassion I wish an end. With a never ending search I fail.
I'll never give in but I will never find what I seek.
I seek only truth, I need only truth.

Story of You

Through the door, screams bleeding down the sound.
Left with nothing; bound to all your lies.
Over the table, you told me the fable.
You were just my world, now I stand alone because of me.
I would say sorry but I know what I did.
I know what I said, you were my life but now I'm dead.
Light was all, now in fog... I scream numb sound and you don't care.
Nobody cares and I'm all alone. You left me with only my thoughts.
Demons crawling and clawing me, just like your wrist.
I was sent to hell, I am left in hell, I have only myself.
Only my dreams to comfort me; I have only me.
You drove way and I would live any way.
I still bleed on and on and on and on and under my grave.
Screaming and dreaming of times past.
Dreaming of wishes and they pass me, you just pass me.
Gravity on the tip of the blade, have I any reasons to live anymore?
Have I any reasons to care for myself?
The world is a gray abyss much like the pit in my mind.
I have driven you away; I said what I had to say.
I did what I had to do, I know what you think and I love you too.
But go away, go away, leave me insane.
I would grab the blade and shove it deeper into my eye.
I love the pain; it's all I have at this time.

Just Go Away

Why won't it all just go away? Why must I cry and rip away my face?
Why did I throw away my love?
Why is my heart now gone, why won't it all just go away?
Please someone give me a better way, show me a better fate.
I need to see further than the fires of hell.
Why is it that no matter what I say or do...
None of these feelings will just go away, please just kill my heart and pain.
I want to be a normal human, no longer a demon.
I just want to be a normal man, without this gaping hole in my chest.
Why is it that no matter how hard I try.
No one is there to help me up when I die.
Please just go away, leave me to rot and fade.
Please just go away, leave me to my fate.
Just go away, I sit here and rip off my own face.
I drift away from grace, I lost my face.
Why won't it just go away?

Only So Far

I hope you know I can only be pushed so far.
Your words dripping deep into my ear.
Running wind with the dogs down the street.
They seek the better taste of the world; life running from my body.
What did I do to drive away the light?
Water creeping on the road, the loss of grip and sand forms stone.
Because we are dust and nothing more.
Ashes from our mothers and fathers.
"Keep on speaking," I can be pushed only so far.
And just as the fish scurry when they are disturbed.
You like the wind in a hurry; you flop on the ground just like a fish.
And what a hurry, in the ground I am buried.
And the dogs howl at the moon's gravity kiss.
The taste of meat, salt when ripped from bone.
You keep on speaking; I hope you know I can be pushed only so far.
And this is why I'm locked away.
In the ground where you'd like me to stay.
The world must have a better taste yet God forbid if I ever run my tongue across it.
So here I lay, as I hear you play. You the world with such a sick game.
Keep on pushing me with your words... They will get you only so far.

Chapter 12

Forever Wasn't so Long

Mistakes

The given, the broken, the living, I'm leaving!
The heart-take, this mistake, my own way, you're away!
As open envelop is your skin, it's given!
And on any open thought, we're away!
I- say, I- stay, away, mistake, heart-take, I-break, hope-wait, away.
And I am given nothing more. I am crying forever more.
Hope my love, hope my death, help me stop this hopeless-ness!

God given the lust of the damned.
And the left hand to the north side of heart.
I fall down and head-loss; I'm lost, don't leave me!
You were the light, now I fall, now I fight the...
Loss and I will grow the... No! Here the world was and now the demon is.
As she held him, the... I-will-just die.
And as she loved him, on and on I cry, given the inner knife.

I'm in the inner twirl, a twist of fate and the only pull to the right.
I lost everything and more, you treat me like a whore.
Throw me down, in my-lost-thought; my last-hope.
And numb I crumble into a fire and find in the last hour; it - away.
I-say, I-stay, in-pain, this-time, this-mine and you're just in the dust.
And no one cares to find me. No one cares to help me, "God save me."
Is there a reason to all of this? Is there a better lie to shift my wrist?
Nothing more I wish, just hope and an end to this helpless-ness.

I would drift away but am I already too far gone?
Oh this mistake, my-own way, you're away, I'm-in pain.
And no one cares to see any further than this monster in front of their eyes.
I am a demon with angel cries, I wish a better lie and I need a new light.
And down the rabbit hole I fall, into the lemon-drop of nothing else.
This mistake, I hope a new end; my mistake, dear God save my soul.
Will I ever get out of this hole? Should I continue or is this all?
I-say, I-sway, in-take, hope-wait. I-am, away and in my grave.
And I rest my head upon the moon; my true love I do not regret.
The moon and this side-said, "was it to the north - and bone take?"

No One

No one to hold me, no one to show me.
No one to guide me, no one to hide me.
No one to love me, no one to need me.
No one to feed me, no one to embrace.

Nowhere to go, nowhere to hide.
No one to show, no one in mind.
No love I hold, no heart I behold.
Only tears I cry, only tears I hide.

I hide myself behind the mirror.
I hold the mask in front of my face.
No one to guide me, it is me they hate.

No knife to grab, no heart to stab.
No blood to bleed, no one holds me.
No soul I'd contain, if ever I stopped the pain.

I blanket the hurt, cover my wounds.
I blanket the burn, cover me soon.
I blanket my life, uncover the truth.
I blanket the knife, in my chest I consume.

No one to hold me, no one to love me
No one to need me, no one feed me.
No one to kiss me, no one to miss me.
No one to guide me, someone just hide me.

Put me on the back burner and leave me be.
Put me in the last thought you held of me.
Leave me to the torment I deserve.
Blanket this child and watch him burn.

She Untrue: "Still I'm Used"

I take my time, the ever will I - and the notion of us.
Nothing but a slap in my face.
She laughed while I cried, she cried while I laughed.
This feeling will never pass, and I only hope it to die.
I wish to lay face first into the flames of hell; this fate is mine.
I pushed her away, to another hand to hold.
In coal-black dust called my heart, I weep.
Still I'm used and she untrue to me...
"Make that an error," a mistake I made.
How could I call it untrue, when I threw her away?
It takes time I say; now I fall so far from grace.
This face you slap, in a taste I despise, what a surprise.
Now I beat my head once again.
Another reason, a new season of the lust of you.
You held him tight, you kissed him nice.
"YOU FUCKED HIM RIGHT?!"
But the worst part was you lied to me. "My love - with my enemies."
So now in this open sea, the seed of forgiveness was pissed away.
Further I drift from you, I weep so hard in me.
You loved him, you killed me.
You feel nothing, so I run to the room in which I hide.
I turn my head from you and love, my heart is dust.
Can you turn it to stone? You laughed at me, she untrue, "*still I'm used.*"
Somebody help me, "let me go!" But you lied to me.
You get pissed when I sing, you held him nice while I screamed so sound.
You threw me away, just as I have done to you.
You drove me insane, "I feel so used." Can you see the light dimming?
The world wasting away, crumbling into me.
Everyone around me has a love to hold, a heart to beat.
I beat my head till I'm dead, and I've tried so hard...
To show you some better way but you just shoved me aside.
I tried to show you another face but I fell deep into disgrace.
Away from affection. I screamed at night, you loved him good.
I bleed at night, you fucked him good!
You were not with me at the time yet you lied.
You lied, I cried. You lied, I died. She untrue and still I feel used.
The only way of not my suicide, not my time.
I could end it now but I only weep, I feel so used. "She untrue to me."
How many more times will I venture through hell?
Will it ever stop? "I think not."
I did this to me, all my pain rests on my shoulders;

I want to just roll over and die.
I was held down and my emotions raped while you laughed:
I screamed and you laughed. You were supposed to be on my side.
But you as they; so Goddamn two faced. "Me, I have no face."
As I walk away from grace, I hear a voice in me, "I am used."
And the end to me shall always be.
I know I will never be loved again; never a love pure-true.
You untrue, still I'm used.
And the world turns on and on without me.
"God save me." I have put my head into the inferno.
And I've seen that I am not loved; even if I still love her.
She was not with me at the time but she lied, but I died.
God she lied to me and laughed! You and the world laugh at me.
"I lay naked and raped on the floor, and you used me."

The Only Way

The only way, now I have nothing else.
I hold only me, dear God save my soul.
I hold nothing inside, indeed I see only the fire and on I go away.
And I am nothing; I see the only truth of the matter.
All is gone but me, all is dead; all is free. Even the twist of my mind.
Only the truth of the times.
Alone I wait to die, in the dark I wait and cry.
All alone I beat my head. In the dark I wish for death.
Death to me and I have no one to hold.
I lost all and you and you and you!
I have only truth, I lost my youth and no one holds me.
I have no one on my side. In the blood of this demon I lie, the boil of hate.
The steam I contain, in the last word.
In the only word spoken, I will never walk away.
I will never leave and die. "I'm already dead..."
Now I hold only the truth, you left me and burned my youth.
As you hold them, skin against skin; warm and hot, smooth and fine.
You fucked me real good, you fuck them and I want to die!
You loved me and I wish to die. I must die, please God save my soul.
I cut open the roof of my mouth, just so I can think of something else.
I break off the limbs of little lambs and feast upon the murder.
I lust upon the dead... I shoot the shit with Beelzebub.
I hold the phone and question God; "*have I done wrong?*"
All of that and dozens of more lies.
So I love the truth of the forever and I lost my life,

I hold nothing else; I wait to die, I wait to cry, "I wish to live."
Yet you get under my skin.
The only way to say it all, all I had was my life.
And now it has been taken away, so is there any other way?
You stole my sanity and broke my heart. You hold them, you loved me.
You fuck them and killed me. It kills me, "I kill me!"
Because I am just a shell of a man, I wish to tear off my skin, I weep.
I wish there was another way, this is the only way!
I have nothing else, so I wish hell.
I rip out my own eyes, to make the pain go away.
I can only think and remember the pain.
I pull out my own teeth, I feel my soul bleed.
I have only the right, to leave your world.
I have no other way to stop this.
I wish death... I hold this knife in my chest.
I break off the blade under my skin and I find this to be the only way.
"Dear God stop the pain and show me some hope."

To Take Away The Air

To take away the air, you took away my care.
To take away the light, you took away my life.
To take away the moon, you brought upon our doom.
To take away my soul, now in ice red-cold.
Of rushing and crushing the bone between teeth.
The life of the never, and never will it leave.
Just the nine in the-mine; and the eight that I ate.
Being held down to the wall, knives thrown at my skull.

No one wants to hold me. I have no shoulder to cry on.
Ever in the morning; the sorrow of her need, and I fall.
In a purple left twist of something left in the back of my ear.
In the ever let out, I drown in the depth of all my fears.

To take away the air, you left me without a care.
To take away the light, you left me bloody in fright.
To take away the moon, then laugh upon our doom.
To take away my soul, I have no desire for you to hold.
You took away my air; you hate me without a care.
You took away the light; you left me with no path to find.
You took away my love, my heart ripped and raped in youth.
You took away my soul, now in ice red-cold.

Lonely Dreams

Small lips, a warm kiss, shattered dreams, lonely screams; I did this to me.
I run my fingers through your hair; I twist the love around our fingers.
I kiss your lips, I taste the fire; I see the hour and I know it's because of me.
I drift above the stream of sadness; I flow in the tears I cry, in a child's eyes.
We were one but forever I've done the deed.
I killed you because you killed me.
I kiss the stone, I lay on my grave; I eat the dirt, my soul now stand.
I kiss the earth; I feel the flow of gravity running across my body.
I look into your mind; I rip out my own eyes because I did this to me.
Small lips, a warm kiss, someone true for me to hold and lonely dreams...
I see only in this child's mind. I weep because I found your lies.
I see my torment around your neck. I sit alone and wait for death.
And it rips out my spine, you raped my mind and now I can only scream.
You tore out my tears; I drown in the realization of my fears, alone.
You in bed, you in love, you at home, as for me; "it's done."
I can and have walked away. I have and shall burn for my sins.
Lord Jesus, save my soul. Wash away the pain and the shame of my life.
Lord Jesus, I dig this hole. I bury my face to hide this disgrace, "save me."
Can I never know a better life, soon dead?
Will any of this even matter? All alone I seem to cry.
Can anyone even care to see a better lie? I plummet profoundly...
Into the dreams of a demon's wing lifting me to hell.
In the dirt I lay, in the gray and consuming haze I sway, "God save me."
I am alone, I did this to me.
Someone, take me home; in the dark I weep.
I need someone to hold and guide me to the bottom of this hole.
Fill the abyss, the heartless soul I am, hate me you do; "I did love you."
Now I lost and now I'm lost, the devil I may be; you still haunt me.
And I have no one to hold me. I have no shoulder to cry on.
"I weep alone."
Small lips, a warm kiss, shattered dreams, all alone I scream.
No one hears me; no one cares to know what I feel.
I have everything but you; now alone, I am dead.
I need to go further than what you gave to me.
I must go, I need a new hope.
I must leave; I will and have set it free.
God I must die and leave this pain behind.
Lord shall I ever know one true?
Alone I weep, in this hole I made for me.
You with happiness, me with death.
I'm so alone, dreaming of our first kiss.
"And you laugh."

Violent Vibrations

Violent vibrations, in soul secreting.
The years in yearning, a lecture to learn.
As hands held the hammer?
The plummet and pull to our mother earth.
Steel and stone, heart and bone.
The sole proprietor of the notion.
In nauseous notions of the grave.

Then in spite of sprits and child charms.
In the love and loneliness, in salt and soot.
He gave to you and I, a choice to scream or cry.
In steaming seeming swallowing sorrow; violent vibrations.
On death and dedication, to a life of pain and grief.

Though he wondered in with pain.
More and more.
To live and love.
Speak and seek the notion in child charms.
Pushed and punished for being a being.
Of not their pretty picture.

Just a *"Just"* life.
Must is must.
And never die.
He opened the option to both you and I.
Through the violent vibrations.
Singing the songs.
Leaving this world...

So far behind.

Always & Forever

So sorry, I tried to make you happy.
I'm sorry, that I was never what you needed.
I am nothing, a puddle of spit and tears.
I'm just a child, realizing my biggest fears.

As I stand here crying in front of all these people.
You hold the hand of all but me, laughing while I weep.
And I wish to die, I wish to try; I want to die.
I have no one, I have nothing and you just turn your head.
I see you kiss him and no one will miss this demon called me.

Always and forever, you said you would love me.
Does he know, I held you so close to my heart?
Do you feel as safe when in his arms?
Now I weep; realizing what I did!

So sorry, I didn't mean to hurt you.
I love you still and always will, "so sorry."
I am the one you wish to kill.
I am the one you buried on top the hill.
I am the asshole that you say I am.
I am nothing but dying within.

As I stand here crying in front of all these people.
You hold his hand and I crumble away, melting my faith.
And I wish to die, I want to cry, I want to die!
Because I have no one, I have nothing.
"Dear God save my soul."
You just turned your head; I die inside because of what I did.

So sorry, I loved you but now I'm going to die.
I did not mean to - to hurt you but I guess I did.
I loved you, my only - so lonely I weep.
I wish I had a shoulder to cry on but you laugh.
Always and forever, I wish to hold you my angel.
Always & forever I wish to die.
And you just turn away...

Dead & Faded

The life of the never is gone and forever.
I wish it would all just fade dead-gone.
The soul of the monster, the dream of this child.
I need it gone, dead and faded.
Malevolent words spoken with benevolent truth.
Those words embrace me in my youth.
The stream of forgiveness.
I drown in the blood of her youth, now dead and faded.
Locks of her ever - devoted to the wicked and the forever.
I just washed it all away.
Miles I walked, with bloody sores on my feet.
My mouth cracks open and bleeds; now through the looking glass...
I spit in the air and forget the light, now dead and faded.
I scream in the moment past, looking through the hourglass.
Kissing goodbye my life.
Now the torment, the suicide in the eyes of my love.
Cutting myself and wishing hell.
Better than you in front of my eyes, staring deep into my soul.
Now dead and faded; the lock of my jaw and the break of my tongue.
Now it arrives and forever it's done.
I always just spoke the wrong words.
Always I sit here and watch my flesh burn; so you are my human clay.
Now I mold my faith and see the other side of the moon.
I weep as the angel walks away.
She used me and stole my face, now faithless.
No hope I hold in between my teeth.
No hope I hold because no one helps me.
Dead and faded, away to the back of the smoke.
I say no one cares but I - true I die on grizzly minds of the fact.
The always and never I will consume your youth.
I'm left now in the dark.
Crying and wishing an end to this torment I made for myself.
I the monster with no heart in my chest.
I have no soul and wish I had a home; so drip the candy-hate.
Melt this metal heart because I have no other alternative.
Please somebody save my soul, I need to see a new light.
Dead and gone - so faded away...

In The Back of My Mouth

Unknown to even myself, what the outcome will be.
The world and the numb feeling in the back of my mouth.
The ever twirling, I'm forever burning; you just threw me out.
I have nothing to live for, no one to hold my hand through the dark.
I have only these words and this numb feeling in the back of my mouth.
I know you just used me, I know you don't need me.
I know you just used me, you never loved me.
You know you just fucked me, you never loved me.
I know you lied, so now I free my life, on open pain of the forever is now here.
It was the ever, nobody cares to hear.
And I cut open my heart, I gave it to you.
I opened my body, now I feel so used.
Abused and I ball up in the corner of my room.
I cry and I cry, never getting where I need to be.
I cut myself, I wish for hell; "you just fucked me!"
The numb and the unforgiving. I will always be here to give *EuQiNu*.
I will tear off my face. I am so out of place. I am just so not in place.
So just throw me away, just throw me away.
So just throw me away, just throw me away.
Throw me away, leave me in pain!
And I'm away and I'm insane. I'll go away, I'll leave this face.
I'm away, I'm in pain. I fell inside and I died.
And razor toys in love with dust. In the memory will I find a truth?
In the past where I left my youth, I hope to find one true.
Maybe you and maybe I will die.
God give me a better lie; give me a new reason to stay.
All I have is... This numb feeling in the back of my mouth.
And forever I wish to stay insane.

Now Everything Is Broken

Now everything is broken, just like our love.
Smile sweet and sound, take the time and let it out.
Leave it out, leave your mind.
Your body dead - leave my heart, burnt and dead.
I'm screaming all day; "no one hears my pain."
Time is wasting; here I'm hating your ways.
Someone just take me! Please take me - *Away*!
Nail my hands to the ground...

294

Must Be My Fault

Find me on the truth of what I need.
See no more of the darkness and weep me, weep me.
I see my brother with, my wife, my love, her knife, in my back.
"What a lack of reach." Now I bleed, in the eyes of my family.
They hold the knife deeper in me. I tear-roll and tear the flesh from bone.
Would it make God happy as a pig in shit to see me die?
Would it make you happy to watch me shove in deeper your knife? "Would it be nice?"
And I could take the time to find a better reason.
Yet you give me only a season of lust and death.
I have no heart in my chest; dust pours out from my spine.
It's time to set the records straight!
The truth is - I had a world of what I needed.
Friends of brothers and a family I could trust.
A life, a wife, a love, a mother, a brother, a lover, another.
I lost her, the monster; help me!
Cut me, suck me; shut me out in the dark.
Kill me, heal me; throw me back into the water.
I sink and in the eyes of my family I drift away.
Further and further away from grace. *Disgrace* must be my name.
Blood must be this taste in my mouth. "*What a tang so sweet.*"
Sour faces hold over my bed - *Grave*, call it what you will.
Under the hill and tree; I have nothing in my life but me.
You push me, you shove me; you don't love me.
The demon could come and I would be left behind.
You stand above me; I cry, I cry.
It must be my fault that all in my life that is good was given to me.
All of everything was given to me.
I didn't ask for this life. I wish darkness, not light.
I didn't ask for this pain, leave me insane.
My lover with my brother; her sin, his mouth, my death.
"I won't leave a damn thing out!"
Her wish, his late night. Their come together and my break away.
I ask for night, rest I need, razor I seep into my wrist, we become one.
Your knife must just not be enough for me.
It's my fault all these things happen to me.
It's my destiny of what I could never be. I'm stuck behind a glass wall.
Watching everyone grow and fall; watching my life fade dim.
I see the paint on the wall, red with my blood.
Lost with my love, it must be my fault.
I'm a dumb kid, I'm a sideshow freak.
Watching people press their faces against the glass;

I feel naked and I hear them all laugh.
Pointing their fingers, I hold my breath and wish for death.
I ask for more drive, I ask for more life.
Please put away your lies; put away your knife.
Why must you kill what is already dead?
Why must you watch as I hold my breath? I turn blue, my life fleeting.
My body crushing under the water; the eyes of you kill me.
I drift away, in the eyes of my family.
They are not my blood, they are not my love. I loved her; I need you brother!
Yet you shove your knife deep into my spine. *"I tear-roll."*
And my tears roll down my face day by day.
It must be my fault you went away, "Angel."
You my love, you my dove. You my lover with my brother.
You push me to the back, away.
Find me on the truth of something I don't need.
Feeling drunk, drowning in my heart-of-weed; finding that the water was LSD.
Finding that the mushrooms were not enough to kill the pain.
The pain of it all is just me.
In the must be, in the kill me, in the death-roll, under the stone.
My grave, my ways, my life, my wife, my light.
Dimmed and doomed at the start; no stars.
Find me on the truth of what I need.
See no more of the darkness and weep me, weep me.
I see my lover with my brother.
She wants him, he has no one at the time and I end up alone.
It doesn't matter, it never mattered yet I still beat my head.
I don't matter, you'd rather kill me.
You tore my heart from my chest, my last breath called out to Angel.
She never called back; my time-sand is heavy.
My time-loss is ready to just take me away, just take me away.
Far into the darkness of what you have made for me.
You gave to me, you do hate me.
Now in the last point to make, I push you to your mistake.
You stabbed me deep, through my spine and heart.
You stabbed me deep and you tore me apart; I remind you though.
You may have cut me, you may have fucked me.
You even let me drown. "You smile now."
Yet you forget - you let me live on in this pain.
I live on insane, in pain; I bleed on in rain.
It must be my fault that I didn't die.
It must be my fault that I watched you die!
Must be my fault that all this happened.
It's my destiny to lose all but knowledge.
"Weep me..."

I've Got the Life

Back and forth I sway...
Rolling my eyes into the back of my head, forever white-gone.
The words of brothers ring deep into my brain.
But I am nothing, just thrown away. Call me trash and cast me aside.
Call me last and I wait in the abyss called my mind.
So brothers I ask; what did I do to drive you away?
Brothers please don't leave me this way, *I am nothing*...
As I sit in my room cold in a September mourning, why am I alone?
As I push away my lover, now I lost my brother.
My demon-inner called the way.
Please no further and evermore will the Gods of sound beat me down.
Until I'm on top? So far away I ask you to return.
I bite my cheek and watch it bleed; so, so far away.
I will never know a home other than what I have.
"I've got the life but now I'm dead." "Forever got the life and I stand."
Because you walked, I will stay forever in this haze.
Hair beating on my face; hot sweat pouring down my face.
So now in grace I turn away. As I crush and grind my teeth to dust.
The fire calls and I must, I must! "I'll never quit."
You walked away, I fell insane. I ask my brother, will you return?
Don't leave me brother, I have a plan; all will fall.
"And we rise again." Forever us. I have come too far to give up now.
And never will I walk away, never will I change; I have only you few.
One, two, three, four and nothing more to hold me down.
I've got the life, and what more would you want me to say?
Deeper into my faith I sway. "It was on a September morning,"
That I awoke ready for the day; "no more pain, no pain."
The side of me I should give; for now, one leaves.
But will he return, please return.
So now I scream and burn, in a desert fire.
I ask the other to keep your head, stay awake.
I ask another, my oldest brother; now I need your help.
Now I ask you to stand, once again.
Life has just begun and now you feel it's done.
Never walk away from yourself.
I sat up and grabbed the tool; and forget the fools who walked away!
We are not them. What more could we do but stand.
And show the world what it did, we must stand.
Please, I need you. There can never be an end to what we have started.
My heart and mind. You are the all and I am nothing without you.
I now more need you at my side, with my mind as broken as it has been;

My life taken and I will not live in vain.
Keep your body strong and your mind clear.
We must make what needs to happen, happen; we must stay together.
We must show the world what it did, we must stand.
We've already got the life, and I say.
Forget the fools who walked away; they were not true.
They were nothing but fools; the world is just a reach away.
But in an abyss called shit! Tell me brother, one who is true.
Will you forever leave or return to beat the world.
We will have our revenge and it shall be sweet.
We will have our revenge forever sweet.
So stay here, fight forever loco.
And the sound Gods shall have no choice but to bow.
"We must fight back."

Manufactured Tolerance

I threw it down, I shoved it out; I gave it all away.
I pushed it down, I stamped it out; I gave it all away.
How much longer can I hold this in!? The pressure is crushing me deep.
The life of what I've seen and over again I play with my brain.
I spin it on the back of my hand, I keep it deep within.
The anger is building and I feel it filling my body.
I feel it growing, still I'm holding; I will not let it out!
Should I let it out? Would you even care? Does anybody want to hear?
No one is there for me. No one would stay to help me.
I need some kind of hope, a light to guide my way.
The hate and anger, it's growing and deeper in me it stays.
The heat of hell and the fire does glow. I know only this...
Have I a love, have I a home or is this shit all I hold?
Would you step aside to see something more?
Would you set aside your feelings to see, or am I just a bore?
Treat me as a whore; I do not have anything more.
And the anger builds up in me, I hold it in and you care not to see.
The ways I know will never change, the ways I know will always be.
I want to leave this place. I want to leave this face, I would rip it off!
I should walk away, you ask me to count to ten.
That's just ten more ways to kill you.
So I think I will just lie here and waste away.
What would you like me to say?
I have put up with this for far too long, much too long.
I feel a monster stirring in me, a demon I would like to be;

What, are you mad at me? Am I mad, crazy to think that you cared!
I rip your body down consume your flesh and watch you weep far down.
I have your body; it's all over now, the anger buildup!
I wish you would shut up!
Please just let me walk away. Let me forever be this crazed.
I hold the anger inside; I never let it out.
I feel the burn and God get it out.
I wish I knew a better you but I cannot change the world.
I wish I could free the strain, the pain I hold so far in me.
I have given you a sight on the truth; I wish you would even care.
Now on the torment I cry, I wish to die, I'm dead inside "I cannot love you."
I do not love me! Why can't you see! You did this to me.

Inner Worm Torment

Dark to the truth.
The worm in my brain, twisting and consuming my world.
Reality is but a bastard's wish.
If God ever gave to man the choice; I choose to decay.
The world so green with greed.
The truth so deep in the pit I call my soul; in this hole.
The one I held took me to hell, as is every man's end.
To be destroyed by a woman. I was falling deep into the life I created.
Her voice was the only thing I could hear.
Now the worm in my soul, this parasite I will never be rid of.
Until I die, I weep. Wax over my eyes, dust covers my body.
Skin falling off of my bones, this is my fate and funny to think I had faith.
Now so faceless I wait to die or be free from all.
Torment - and I descend to hell.
Will you like to see me cry; me in the corner of my mind.
I am just a child wishing to die.
The worm crawling through the caverns of my soul.
I have been told a story of an angel that once had a life.
An evil angel sent to destroy.
I find this to be a fact yet I see now that this is that.
I am the angel, evil in this light.
I am a devil you just wish to push me out of your life.
Smiling with your love and I wish to decay, rip off my face.
This parasite I can never stop, I cursed myself.
This is the truth, I did love you.
But the outcome has come to be, I have now only me.
God give to me a blade of fire;

Show to me the hour in which the pain will subside.
The inner worm has been giving me only nights of fear and regret.
I threw her away but she wanted to leave.
Who would truly wish to be with me? Who would care?
God take away my air and stop the endless torment of my skull.
God take me home.
I sit here now in front of an old love now gone from my grasp.
Wishing for death. Lord take the given and show me the way.
Please lay me to rest and maybe just maybe.
Someday I can awake with no recollection of this, God save me.
Please, I ask you; the one in front of me.
Save my soul and heart, please help me.
I do now fall apart. I do now have no other way to go.
Please don't go away. This worm has been eating at my life.
My body now falling deeper into the abyss.
The fall has been true, it is all true.
I am nothing but used, I am no one be me, Dead.
The inner worm controls my every thought and move.
Please, you in front of me. Grab the blade, please kill me.
Please kill me my love, "kill me..."

Near Nothing

Near nothing, I look and see an angel in front of my eyes.
"So what else is new?"
Near nothing, I feel the room spinning; what else is there for me to do?
Fear nothing, well I had all once but now I can only dwell in the memories.
I remember when I was just a child; I felt my first kiss, warm and tender.
When I was just a child, I felt my first loss.
When I was pushed down and spit on.
I've been kicked, and I've felt the truth from a very young age.
I've felt only pain; but I always dreamed of being the bigger person.
And standing up for those who are weak like me.
I have always dreamed of someday having a real family.
A mother and a father...
I dreamed of having all these things under one roof.
But I know now, a dream it will stay.
Near nothing, I wish there was something more for me to say.
Other than my pains, but all is not as dim as I make it out to be.
I still have all of my memories.
Of loss and regret, pain and death, the hurt and the cold; numb and forever just alone.
I break everything I touch, my heart and yours;

Near nothing I throw me away.
I wish I had something more to say and a better lie to live.
"Give me something!" Or just let me end.
I see so many faces around me.
But none of them seem to care; they all just pass me by.
I wish I had a better way to get out of this life.
I need to make some new memories.
Good God give me an end to this world.
And stop the torment of these new faces.
New lips to kiss, new fights to lose.
New pain I contain, well; now I'm confused.
Near no one, I dream of having someone to hold but I find only tears.
Near nothing I see a hand I want to hold, a shoulder I wish to cry on.
So on I cry with nothing more than me, I see smiles; it all eats at me.
Near no one I weep and she laughs at my pain; I cry and you push me.
I wish I had a hand to hold, I wish I were a better person that you might like.
I wish I was alive, dead I am inside; dead I am in my mind but no one cares.
Near nothing I stare into eyes I adore but nothing more, nothing more.
"Not for me." So what else is new?
I am still and always will be left with only memories.
I wish it could be, but so near to nothing I am.
And with this knife I set it free. The strain I can no longer bear.
I dream of the days I held someone I loved; "I'm now alone."
Near to nothing but the blade in my hand.
I look into the eyes I adore but nothing more.
I sit here and weep the tears of memories.
And find that I will always be alone.
Near to no one I hold the truth up with pride.
I kill myself and wish you would cry.
But only a dream is it all, and I fall and I fall.
With no hand to hold or a shoulder to cry on.
Near nothing I weep, and no one cares.
No one helps me, "help me."

My Love Is Dead

More of a loss, more of a frost on my grave.
More of a fight, more of a night in which I fall to my grave.
More a death, less of a breath for me to intake.
More of a whore and she will never be the same.
My love is dead.

What a hopeless act, in my back you placed your blade of hate.
What a hopeless thought, that someday I could be happy.
You with a happy face, you have grown disgraced.
My love is dead.

Help me mom, I need to hold someone before I die.
Help me mom, I need a shoulder on which to cry.
Help me love; the smoke and music raging on forever.
Help me love, but now she's dead; dead forever.

Give it back, the life I gave to you and them.
Give it back, my childhood and thoughts within.
Give it back! My heart from my chest and you watch it bleed.
Give it back! All of my lost breaths and it was you I need.
"I loved you." But now she's dead.

Save me God! What must I do to stop all of this pain?
Save me God! Why am I in hell, screaming for the past to reply?
Kill me God, I wish not to exist any longer.
Kill me God; in hell I feel the lust and the must.
"Just stop this!" My love is dead.

Most I had was you but now I see the truth.
Most I had was you but now I have only what lies in my hands.
Must I die so confused? What did I do, besides love you?
Must I die so confused? What did I do, to lose you?
My love is dead.

I see the forever and the gravity pulls the fate I await into my hands.
I see the forever, a tunnel of lights and I feel numb within.
Because I cannot take you with me, I wish you were here.
I loved you; I must - need - see the sea of the damned and me.
My love, "*I'm dead...*"

Another Page

This is just another story of what I have lost and gained.
This is just another story of how I have died and cried within.
So down the halls I walk, holding the tears within, trying not to be seen.
The only thoughts I hold are of you, I cannot sleep so forever I'm confused.
You wound-up on my front door step, smiling and I die inside.
I see and hear you're not alone at night while I die inside; and you try to lie.

Why lie? I threw you away, the only love for me.
But you're now out of reach. Please I ask, come back and hold my hand.
Hug me tight, kiss me nice but all that is - is a dream.
Because we could never be again, not anymore.
You say you want to be my friend, "don't lie to me you fucking whore!"
So sorry for what I said but what would you expect, I'm just an asshole.

So this is a story of what was and can never be again.
This is a story of how I loved and died within.
You were my friend; you were my every reason for living.
You were my everything.
I gave you the world and my heart, "was that not enough?"
But what does any of this matter; I will be alone, "always & forever."
I have just the rest of my life to waste in the dark corner of my head weeping.

Why do you act like you care? You won't be there, why would you care?
You don't love me, you never loved me the way I loved you.
You don't love me, now and forever I lay awake and confused.
I am dead now to the world, all of what I had has pushed me away.
I wish to leave and start a new day but that's only a dream.
This is just another page, in the long story of my loss and fears.
This is just another page, in the book in which I hold so dear.

All I had was you my love but now you walk with another hand to hold.
I scream so loud yet I hold it in, because I know what I did.
Just a test, yet you failed; you were supposed to have loved me.
But now what can I say; this is just another page.
In the story of how I found the most beautiful angel.
That angel that loved me so true.
And I just threw it away; I sincerely hope you will be happy.
"I'm so sorry." But for me - this is just another page.

Benevolent Betrayal

So far, so good... And the light still shines on the edge of the mantel.
As the sorrow sweeps, sound and slowly to the south side of my sanity.
The west way was once forgotten and forbidden by the voice above.
Devine torment reaches deep and pulls on my small intestine, "I scream!"
So benevolent is the word spoken with no one around to hear, no ear to lie in.
And dark was the last sight I saw.
Swinging above the stairway, in the haze I smile.
I would have held her, but another hand she found.
I would love her, yet to hell I am bound and no one seems to care.
Ignorant to the notions I once spewed from my head.
I scream now to the reflection in the lake, I am what I truly hate.
To the north way, and watching the water wash the blood down the drain.
I would hold her hand and be there till the day comes, in which I fall.
I say nothing and hold it in the deep ditch, watching the shit flow by.
Was I once and again the one you just drove by? Caring not if I live or die.
I tried to tell you how I felt but the words just never seemed to surface.
God I hope I can just awake from this pain and someday find some truth.
So said some that say I saw the end swimming past.
And I piss away the life you gave. I sway back and forth.
So sick I am, dreaming of holding your hand, you're not here.
Here I fear the forever falling further into this un-forgiven.
"And my eyes melt away."
My skull broken with benevolent betrayal, I loved the...
And what more have I now?
Only this scar on my heart and the pain in my soul.
Always and forever I am alone. *So far so good....*
And still no one knows who I am, the child you pushed down.
I tried, lied, died, cried and buried myself in the sand box.
My soul now locked. Away I stay and embrace the past.
Because that's all I have left to do, in my wounds.
The brainstem simmers.
Smiling so sound in sweetness with stationary sanity.
My mother I wish, my life of the never-forgive.
I shall punish them all, my loves.
My heart stolen with benevolent betrayal.
My skull broken on your words.
You, the young beauty standing in front of me.
I ask you now; could you ever love me, but what does it matter?
You and I can never be, because you have a hand to hold.
And I dwell forever in my integrity.
It is the unstoppable truth of my always and forever;

The answer waits on the back burner and there I might find some hope.
I must and shall take control of my life, because you will just push me down.
With benevolent betrayal I stand.
So this hand I hold does not exist, because of what I did.
I love you little girl, the one standing in front of me, my dear sweet.
I love the way they say sorry that they stole my life.
They stole my heart and soul but I will be a man, and I will stand.
With benevolent betrayal I see the Zenith; "*and Hope I await.*"

My Placid Heart

Do you like the grin on my face? The smile when I'm around you.
Is it comforting for you to know that you will never be alone?
I will always be there for you, ready to wipe away your tears.
I'll always be ready to fight your fights.
Why act so concerned when I come home late? *"The traffic was heavy."*
You stare so lovely into my eyes, my soul melts and I for once feel warm.
You are the glue that keeps me together, the paint on my canvas of life.
Does it feel nice, to know that I love you now and always will.
Smile my love and your wounds I will heal.
As you lay to sleep, I hold your hand and feel your heart beat.
I would not trade it for the world.
If it were possible, I would give you the world.
But for now I give you myself, my every thought I wish to share.
Our every kiss I wear on my soul while I rest awake.
So, do you like the grin on my face? The smile when I'm around you.
My placid heart when you run your fingers through my hair.
The peaceful thoughts, when you kiss me and wash away my fears.
For you, any task is just a reach away. I love you, forever and a day.
Till the end of time, our love shall wind down my spine and make me alive.
Because I love you now and always will.
Still you kiss me and I melt away. My eyes are blinded by your splendor.
Such loveliness I hold in my arms.
I wish us to be never apart, and our child shall know the same.
As I hold and kiss you, so warm in the rain, then you look at me and smile.
While our seed grows, I would like you to know. "I love you."
I wish there were more to say, I may be a poet.
But I just can't seem to find the words.
To describe just how much I love you.
So I will take the rest of our lives to show you.
I wish to grow old with you and fight over all the little things.
Like who loves who more;

I just want you to know, I may not always be there at your side.
But I am always in your heart.
I just want you to know. Only death could keep me from you.
In dreams I lay peaceful when I hold you.
I need you my addiction, my love. You are my every reason for living.
Please wipe the tears of joy from your eyes.
And know I will be with you always, in heaven's light.

SomedaY

If I hold you, will you ever look at me the same?
If I told you, will you ever speak to me again?
I think the years have turned, and this heart has burned.
I think the world has turned, I think I want to burn.
And I hope someday you can see what I see.
Feel for me the way I feel for you, someday.
I hope to maybe hold your hand, to kiss your lips.
I dream of maybe being at you side and you at mine.
Maybe if I held you, you would see a different light.
But if I told you; you might never speak to me again.
I fear this, and I said never again, and without you.
Well, I think these feelings can be cast aside, maybe you and me.
I speak to an angel, a pure and simple goddess of the earth.
Fire and hail, dust and mold; all the elements blanket me.
And I see only death in me; I feel the hate in me. Please make it go away.
Help me return to faith and give me a face and eyes to see.
Give me love, and help set me free, free me from the strain.
Free me from this pain. I hope to God you see someday.
I pray to God you see someday.
And I toss faith in the air, my coin, my life, this heart, this knife.
And heads or tails, call it in the air,
Pull me down, and run your fingers through my hair.
Please someday see the truth that I had a chance with you and I pissed it away.
You hold another; I just fall away from grace, my faith pissed away.
And fate is brought to me on the wings of dark, and I fall apart.
Hope, I feel so hopeless, and see no outcome.
Alone I shall always be, please someday I hope you see.
But if I told you, would you look at me the same?
If I held you, would you ever speak to me again?
Please someday I hope you see.
And feel the feelings within-side me... Someday.

Just A Life of Screaming

Just a life of screaming, and I wish I could hold her.
My eyes revolving, the hate is evolving into a new tyrant.
I will cut off my eyelids... God, please wash away the wounds.
If I had the chance to take it all back, I would; because it's mine.
I guess I was not good enough of a lover for you, "I tried to be there."
I did it all for you, but you just never cared; you doubt me still.

Just a life of screaming, and I feel my soul fleeting, my body and grace.
You tore away my face, and left me with no faith.
I wish I were with you now.
You were my life, but now I scream alone in this room.
Can you see justice; was it *Just,* the hell they put me through?
I can never stop thinking about you, you haunt my every thought.

I wish I were with you, but now and forever I am lost.
This life of screaming, seeming to never end.
"Please God, make it go away!"
I did love her but now I am away. My soul I wish you had saved.
I ask you to have a heart; "*hold me,*" I'm crying, I'm dying - inside.
Dust and the sands of time pull a blanket over my head.
"I hold my breath."
Just a life of screaming, and seemingly I will just break off the edge.
Because I know the end, and I will always love you but just know.
"I hate you."

Heavy like a thousand bricks, I try to hold in these tears.
Day by day, it breaks me.
As you beat me down, into the earth. I feel the burn - and I know it.
But won't it just go away; won't it just fade to gray? *"I LOVED HER!"*
Stuck behind this glass, naked and the whole world laughs.
I watch you steal my heart, I watch you tear me apart.
Please stay out of my life.
I wish I had a life, I wish I had a knife, but it is all just a dream.

To see, to bleed, to love, to die. I tried, I've cried; please God save me.
I watched her walk away, and I knew my life is over, "yet I smile."
I watched her drive away, and I knew my life is over, "I smile."
I smile while the blood drips onto my lips, this taste I adore.
Please - somebody; take me home in my grave and let me rest.
Just a life of screaming, as I feel my heart being raped in my chest.

Torn And Raped

A demon you hold, in the eyes of a child's love.
Torn down in his youth and spread over the land.
Raped in his mind and beaten while he cried.
You smile, you laugh... I am the child, spread across the lands.

I hold the blade in my chest and wish to never breathe again.
I inhale while in hell and deep as a well I fall through you.
I held the nail, to cover me in noon, blanket my root.
You can never hide who I am; you may try but never win.
You can never hide who I am; you raped my mind.
Now I'm dead within.

Till the word is spoken and the tears are wiped away.
The voices will control and my soul has been raped.
God you wish me to hell, torn in my youth.
Break me and I scream, but you laugh while I bleed.

A demon you hold, and no more can I rest.
You fucked me real good, with your knife in my chest.
I am the freak - as I tear off the meat; salt and bone, heart and stone.
You can never cover my roots. You will never hide who I am.
Why are you so mad, "you all made me this?"
A worm in my brain, a girl in my pain; I will never live.
I can never know what it will be like to have a family.
I can never know what it would be like, to have a friend.

Torn down, on the edge of nothing. Held down by you and the world.
In the presence of demons, the blood of mine; I tremble and weep.
You never loved me, you only fucked me; "and now I bleed."
With only a tear in my eyes.
Only the pain in my mind and no heart to hold.

Torn and raped - held down by the girl I loved; kicked and scraped.
Now I live with only hate, forever I wait.
But you can never hide my roots. You fucked me out of a youth!
You created this monster; now spread over the land.
Raped in his mind, buried deep within...

Toxic Ways

The ways I know are, troubled and faded.
The monster is now, here and I'm waiting.
The death of my soul, the hour you hold a brick.
Throwing my skull, into a death of love and shit.
Nowhere to hide my face and last wishes.
Nowhere to go and cover me with poison kisses.
Toxic heart spewing out the last memory you hold of me.
Undying ways of breaking down in tears of the unsane.
You want a better toss of faith, on the fate of my justice.
I'm hoping for justice and the most I had was you.
A demon I hold in every brain cell, clawing at my tomb.
Bringing me torment, I know it was heart-sent.
I have no other alternative than to rip out my own spine.
I scream day by day but I shall only give it time.
In half the worry and half the shut up, "I'm such a fuck up."
What did you think was going to happen? What was on the edge of the blade?
Where are you going? Please place me back in my grave.
A world of nothing, a face in the teeth of a dead dog's howl.
The moon is fading and I have no way out.
God I need some better way; the hour I tried to save.
"Place me on toxic torment and shove me down - down - down."
I had a love, I lived above but now it's done and I am away.
Covered in tears of blood, dripping from my eyes, why am I so away?
I scream on the tip of a monster, I love you but now it fades.
I scream on a trip of nothing else, only in my hell I stay.
God given and no one takes the time to care.
All is going, and no one is knowing; God save my soul.
I hold the hour, I punish the one I held in my arms.
I wish I were a better person that you would have cared for.
But I am nothing, just a dumb reject of a forever bore.
Please show me no more toxic ways. "*Never shall I ever be saved?*"
I am no one - I wish you would love me but now I am away.

Dope Me

Drop me, dope me, love me.
See me in the back room, with only hate.
Soon gone and wasted.
Love with every breath.
So forever wasted.

Hold Me So Far

I can't find the right keys, I cannot even see.
I feel so sick, I need some air but you don't care.
Will talking of this ever get old?

Give me a better view, show me a better you.
Take me to a nowhere land of dreaming sweet.
Taking the awesome gift I gave to you, "I want to die!"
I just need to take a walk and free some strain from my mind.

Why do I write this? Does anybody even care?
No one helps me, so easy it must be to say everything will be alright.
All I hear you say is, "move on and free the strain."
All I ever hear you say is, "there is always another day."
All I need is for you to just go away.
All I want, is another day.

Shove me, break me, hate me, leave me on no more truth.
Hate me, kill me, fuck me, leave me with no more truth.
Leave me, beat me, let me show you another youth.
In backwards death of living and leaving the loss lost.

I hope the outcome will be better.
Better than what I hold in my arms now.
I need to be free and pull these thorns from my mouth.
I would show you but you think you already know.
I would have told you but I'll never find a way out.

I hold the light, I need a light. I need a life, so give me yours.
I hold the knife; I need a light, to shine me a better tomorrow.
I will never know what it is like to have a family.
So I will just make my own.

Grab me with one hand and hold me over the edge.
My life is in your hands, and you wish me to never breathe again.
Grip the blade in the other hand, and smile so sweet.
I fall tumbling through so many memories of you.
Hold me so far and does any of this even matter?

<u>*All Against Me*</u>

There is nothing new for me to say so I think I'll just repeat myself.
There is nothing new, I still hurt you and I will forever live in this pain.
With this lack of sleep, I stayed up trying not to lose you but I think I did.
I know I fucked up but you will never forgive my sin.
"I'm so sorry my love." I never meant to hurt you but I did.
Now I have my one and only love against me.
I was just that pissed off with Me!
I did something so stupid, "please forgive me."
I'm so sorry but now all is against me.

I find that I was probably right, I will die alone.
I will lose you, all because of me.
I never meant to hurt you. I will forever love you but I fear you hate me.
I love you still and always will; forever in this knight's dream.
With all against me, I can now only sit back...
And take in the torment of pens and needles shoved in deep.
God please don't hate me, I only love you.
I need only you because you are my everything.
I'm such a fuck up and I wish I could forever just shut up and drift away.

In the last thing I said.
It is the only thing I hold close to me, "I need to sleep."
I feel my eyelids falling. I feel the power calling, "I want to kill myself."
I only need to awake from this hell and wash all this pain away.
Because nothing really matters.
Just the fact that I love you and you love me.
Is there anything that really matters? I wish you could understand.

I can only say one thing through all of this... I love you and that's it.
I can only picture your face every time I close my eyes.
I can only think of you and goodnight - goodbye.
"Please put me to rest." Please place my heart back in my chest.
I'm such a hollow person.
Tell me, will he love you as much as I do and if so, "lucky you."
I hope to see you happy. I know I can be the one to make it so.
If only you would just give me the time, I will spend the rest of my life.
Just so you can see, I love you. I will do anything just so you can smile.

I need to just take another walk and see a hope in a sunrise.
And there I might find a hope of some better drive - there I'll find light.
But all is against me and nobody truly cares;

I can only love you and wish that you would care.
But all is against me and no one wants to help a dead soul like me.
I loved you then and always will but still you throw me down.
This is my fate...
I lay here with a new faith and I know I can fix it all now.
But all is against me, all and you - no one cares, not even you.
You were right, "I will die alone."
All because of me, all against me; all and me.
Please somebody kill me, I just so need to sleep...

Could You Ever Be With Me Again?

Could you ever be with me again?
And spend the rest of your days knowing I love you.
I wonder if you could ever know how truly devoted I am to you?
Days to weeks, weeks to months and months to years.
The years I've spent loving you.
I wish to spend the remainder of our lives showing you I care.
I just cannot bear knowing that you might not return my love.
I wish you to spend the rest of your life, treated like the angel you are.

Far from ever stopping, I can never stop loving you.
"No matter what you say." I see you holding the hand of another man.
He could never love you as I do. I know all the secrets you hide.
And I share the passions you hold in your heart.
I've deadicated all my work and being to you.
And I would eat dirt to prove myself.
So tell me, should I kill myself to confirm my love?

Could you ever be with me again?
And spend the rest of your life knowing I love you.
Could you ever move on knowing that I'm dead without you?
"You my forever love." Could you ever be with me again?
Watching our children grow and play.
I would so enjoy growing old with you, fighting over the little things.
I know we are meant to be but I fear that it is too late for me.
You are the only girl I love, such a beautiful woman.
I will always be with you, even if I'm not there.
Could you ever be with me again?
I will always love you forever and again...

312

Poetic Nonsense

So many ways to lose all that matters in life yet I care only for her.
I've strived to make a path for us to follow.
As I sit here and dream so hollow, I crumble at her feet.
I lay on the broken glass; I look up at her and weep.
There just isn't anything more for me to do but move on and lose.
"I've lost it all." Is there anything more for me to say?
I already lost her, "please take my last breath away," as I hold the cloud...
I feel it dripping sweet mushroom smells of candy hatred in me.
Held to my human nature, I despise this rotting body of *feeble & frail* loves.

I hold the hour in the time sands now forming stone.
"I'm just *Bones against you...*"
I have fallen and there just wasn't anyone there to catch me.
I just fall in discreet and no one is there to help pick up the pieces.
The world laughs at me. I'm pushed aside because I'm just a freak.
I'm just dead meat so throw me away. I could stay here and speak of this all day.
But there's no ear to care of my pains. I know I pushed her away.
But I'm too late to fix the wounds I've made, now in hell I must stay.
I know what I did and forever in this hell I shall sit and pray.

I hope that someday she could be happy and I see that it happened yesterday.
The truth is she's comfortable and I'll never again see another smile on her face.
I so wish her to be happy. As my tears hit this paper my heart breaks in two.
I wish I could have been there.
Holding you close and forever true, "I love you."
Though I speak of it, I fear that she will never hear me.
I'm just crying to air, I know that nobody cares.
And never will I know true love again, "I'm just a sin."
So please somebody throw me away, please somebody leave me in my grave.

I hold the nothing deep in my soul.
I know that there is nothing left for me to hold.
Please somebody give me grace.
Please somebody give me a face and hold me true.
Deep under the hatred and in the acid I consume...
The reason for living is leaving; the knowledge is nothing.
I am forever just a nothing pit of despair but you don't care.
No one will ever take the time to help this weak child in loss.
I'm just a loss of reason, I need a better season.
To guide me further than this poetic nonsense - I'm nothing.
Just lift your head, take away my breath and throw me back into the hell pit;

Fire and the nothing I will forever be.
The torment is all that I made for me. Because I took the only one I loved.
I pushed her away and now I'm too late, she moved on.
There is only death I hold in my chest.
And I wish I were dead because I don't have you.
Call me stupid and cast me away.
I fear the forever loneliness in which I must stay and I wish I had a face.
I wish I knew grace and could lay with her forever in us.
But all of what this is, is just poetic nonsense.
Because I know I will never know true love again.
Such an unfortunate sin I live.
I will forever die in this story of truth and shit.
It's just poetic nonsense that I live and dedicate to you.
"The love I lost."

Walk Through A Midnight-Sun

She fell away from the grip of angels.
She fell deep into my heart where she should stay.
Devotion was the only object, the one thing I held true for her and now I lose.
I lost the affection... the deep in my soul...
The gaping hole where my heart should be. I tried to show her a better life.
I tried to kill the sickness yet it spread; now she's dead.
She fell away from me, I could only hold on for so long.
Now in the gray I lay and weep, as she fell away...
The ring I now hold in my hand and the memory of a slap in my face.
I walk through a midnight sun. It shines a shine that only the damned can see.
I take a walk through a midnight sun.
I spread my arms - I look inside and see, "I love her no more."

Years spent on the only wish I shall never realize.
You must realize that I mean more.
Nor you or the winged hate that consumes my soul...
The decay of the dead child. Never more I hold that whore.
What a bore I keep as my life, in my back I find the knife.
It is where she left it, I held her and she killed my...
So tear out my eyes and realize I'm me. I hate these words from my mouth.
I hate the lie you told and was then found out; I know now.
As she fell away from the angel's grip.
In the blood of man I am dipped, "this is it;"

And the nonsense was and will always be. She will never be herself again.
Again I'm lost, not ever will I find an outcome better than this quest.
I must find the light of darkness and on I walk through a midnight sun.
It was for her I lived but now it's done, it won - I'm dead - away.

Through the moon's gravity kiss... The death of my soul is my only love.
The decay of my heart is once again done; I lost - it won.
As she fell away, I knew only this... I took a walk through a midnight sun.
Maybe it could guide me over the edge. Maybe I could sleep until the end.
Please, someone fill the hole in my chest. I have no heart, God save me!

"I love her no more."

Chapter 13

Upon the Road of Leaves

I Need To Relax

Maybe I should just take my time, wait it out; open my mind and relax.
Maybe I should just wakeup now.
And stop beating my head on the concrete.
Someone could be out there waiting on me.
But I just sit here drowning in shit.
Someday I'll find someone to fill this gaping hole in my heart and soul.
But for now I just need to take a breath, one, two, three; I need to see.
There must be more in life than just my demented self and these pains and sorrows.

The truth is I wish to stay in this utter loneliness; it's all I've ever known.
What would you expect from me?
Did you think I would just smile and be happy?
Maybe you don't know me that well.
Or maybe you just truly don't care; it could be so many things.
But I know now I need to stop killing myself over her.
And release the pain I have for all the people I once cared for.
I know that they were not my true friends.
But on the brighter side to it all, "I got the last laugh in the end."

I did push her away, and this zombie is all that's left of me.
But there is nothing more for me to do.
But just sit back and free my mind.
Death and pain are not all there is in life.
I just need to relax and free my mind.
I feel so bottled up and the pressure is constant building.
"I need the filling of my heart."
The truth is I just need to relax and leave all that was in the past - past.
Maybe I should just go and maybe I could let it all be, to set myself free.

I am my worst enemy and there is nothing for me to say or do.
Because I just don't want things to change.
But I know I need to move on; it's so hard to get over the girl I love.
But she moved on and so should I.
There is no meaning to all this nonsense, but I live it day after day.
I know I need to get over it but it's just so hard to shut up my heart.
These pages sometimes just don't seem to be long enough.
I still have more to say, with all these faces around me.
Yet I seem to push them all away, I am a disgrace.
And maybe I will find a face to cover this shell of a man, I do need hope.
And maybe I could find someone to fill this gaping hole.
This hole in my heart and soul;

Just maybe I could find someone, who could deal with all my shit.
It's a pretty picture I paint in my head, of someday being happy again.
I hope, some girl could find it in herself.
To be loved every day by this reject from hell.

There is nothing left for me to do.
But relax and get over the fact that I am alone.
I know that I pushed away the girl I love. She moves on and I go insane...
I know that she wants me to be happy.
Yet I only want her, but that's just a dream and my life was as a blur.
I know I need to move on but I just want to stay.
Maybe I should just relax but I'll never forget the past.
Because that's all I have. I may move on and find a new love.
Twice as great and to her I would dedicate myself.
But for now I just need to get through the day, without breaking into tears.
I now live my biggest fears but I'm not dead.
I just need to relax.

The Dream

Damn - I seem to have nothing more to say.
I've lost her forever and I just want to get away.
There is no reason for driving myself over the edge.
I've lost all and her but now I have everything but you.
Damn - what am I to say, I moving on in this haze?
These dark days that lay ahead of me... it's okay.
What more would you want me to say?
I've pushed her away and now alone I will forever be.
Okay - but the words will always linger in my brain.
The memories are far from ever being gone.
I can only live in sorrow for now but it's all just for now...
I just want to move on and free this pain.
I know I'm just a sad little child inside, but hiding in deep the pain.
The blade was yours but now I've grown, and flesh covers your lies.
I'm lips are scared with love and my mind scared with the thought of you and me.
I know I am who I am and being happy was the dream.
Damn - would you like it if I just stopped writing these things?
I would like it if I woke up to that dream, but it's over.
I know I will and mostly have moved on.
There truly is nothing more for me to do.
I pushed her away and now in this haze I stay, in dark days.
I know I had all at once and then watched it fall through my fingers;

I slowly realized that I still have a family, a friend and a love.
The love I live, is the songs I sing of the memories of her and me?
So for now, in the depths of the dream I wish to stay; I must get over it.
That's all that is left for me to do; to be the one to rise.
And live life on the road, "See the sights and know."
That is the tomorrow and the life I wish is the dream.
To be happy with the girl I love and smile without a care.
It could have been the best in the world. I did love her with all my heart.
But now as it lies bleeding on the floor I can only step away.
There's nothing more for me to do, these dark days are my home.
The only thing I need I have but will forever wish more.
I just need to move on and awake in the dream, I know it to be.
I just need to move on.
Before I lose the next one that's standing right in front of me.

Cut Open Eye

Finding new reasons to stay.
The mounds of the tomorrow are dripping in me hollow.
And I fade to the hallow, the hour in the abyss called me.
Finding that yesterday was a dream.
In this void I find me numb and lost. I only wished to smile.
"Now all is lost and forever gone." So I took the pain.
My feet bloody as I dragged them across the road and leaves.
That's all I've seen, stones and bones. The ashes I taste in my mouth.
Your body is in my mind and it won't get out.
As it begins so splendor, I feel it splinter in my brain.
Spinning the torment in a joyful mind state.
Shower the thought behind the dream.
I feel the hurt bringing the steam.
With troubles I stay, just another day. I feel so hopeless now.
On open truth, in the buried behind our youth.
I scream the pain, I love the hate!
We are and always shall be in the bottom of my every wish.
Take me to the last way.
Please take away the pains and drive me to a new view.
My world now gone but new reasons I seek.
To stay in state of a hopeless dream.
Lost numb dying fears; blood, sludge, hate and death.
And my fears are taking me away.
Take me so far away to that tall oak tree on top of a hill.
Where I sleep, where I weep;

Somebody find the hope, there deep in the sand.
You've beaten this man and I'm done.
Cut open my eye.
Leave me to the last thought and bring me a new light.
I fade to the hollow.
I fall from your hallow and drip deep into your hell.
The void will never be filled.
I've lost the drive, the one that kept me alive.
Now I just need to awake yet you cut open my eye, so in blindness I wait.
You who I wished to keep, now you're away and I can only weep.
I knew what I did, so now I hate myself.
I cut open my eye to see a better light.
Somebody take me away!
Please somebody show me a face, find me new faith.
So I await fate, loving the hating of you.
Now I scream! I want a hand to hold but I must wait.
So into myself and you; just take me deep and I lose.
I'm only doing this for me, because my mind loves the pain.
I cut open my eye, to see a better way.
Please give me faith and take my fate.
Will anyone ever love this demon?
I think I am just a dead man on the edge.
I'm wishing for light, I'm hoping for sight but I've cut open my eye.
So far out I've been all my life.
Looking for a new way to die and a better death.
But all I have is life; all I need is light but you've cut open my eyes.
You've walked away when I needed you most, so now I'm just a ghost.
So I just fade to the hollow, dripping deep into this hallow.
"Someone take me away!"
I need a kiss on my lips, a hand on my chest, a thought on my breath.
A new reason to move, a new and better view.
But I fear that it's only a dream.
Until I have that heart again, in this hollow I shall wait; weeping deep in hate.
I've cut open my eyes, to see a better tomorrow.
But all I see now is this hollow void...

I'm Such a Bore

So you came to my door.
I felt the scream, "I'm such a bore!"
So you came to my room.
The red numb walls, the blood filled moon.

So she came up to me, smiles of pain unseen in me.
I felt the twist of my spine, as I weep and I die.
She only wanted what she came for.
So I'm alone, "I'm such a bore."
Just throw me down, "I'm such a whore."
So she came to my door, "I'm such a bore."

LEAVE ME TO DIE ALONE!
WATCH ME SMASH MY FOREHEAD ON THIS GRAVESTONE!
I KNOW THE TRUTH IS HERE!
IT'S TIME TO FREE MY FEARS!
I'M NOT HERE! I'M NOT HERE!
I'M NOT HERE! I'M NOT HERE!

Is it too late to tell you how I feel? "Yes."
Am I too late to walk away from this hell? "Yes."
Are you so happy without me? "Yes."
If I'm that evil, then God set me free! "Please!"

So she came up to my door.
And I broke back into myself.
I know there's more out there than this hell.
Why won't she just leave me be?!
Why in God's name does she still haunt me?

I'm not a faded lump of flesh.
I'm still that hollow in my chest.
Time has passed and I've grown to know.
As I spit blood - on my gravestone!

I need to break me over the stone, I'm not home.
I just need a little more, "I'm such a bore."
You fucking whore! Fucking whore! Never more!
"Someone set me free!"

Behind Me

So many words spoken yet so little said.
I just wanted to say goodbye but you turned your head.
So much I would have loved to tell you.
But now you're gone and in this sadness I stay confused.
You hold another so happy, I die inside every day.
You loved me. I love you. You hate me. I love you.
You kill me. I bleed inside. I killed you, "God let me die!"

I fall back into my pit of despair.
I fade back, into the smoke and purple tears.
I drip the awesome on my tongue.
The power rising, with pointless hiding.
"Open the door, *I ask you - please.*"

Behind the torment, I find the reasons.
Behind so *whore-bent,* I find the reasons.
In the rose bloomed blue, as I gave to you.
Behind the scars on my lips, that you gave to me.
Behind the disgrace, you'll find me.

I wait no more; I want no more, no more!
As I dream of that day when I was wrong and you walked away.
You should have been mine - *It* should have been mine.
You should have been mine - *It* should have been mine, God please!
Someone just take me away, throw me disgraced and let me burn.

I stand here in this cold, I weep here in this snow.
Building a snowman and watching him melt away like me.
Breaking down into a puddle of blood and tears.
Now today I live my fears, so alone I wish to die.
Nowhere to go, nowhere to hide, "God let me die!"
I just wanted to say goodbye, I just wanted to live - not die.
I just wanted to hold you one last time. I want to live, "I die!"

I fall back into my pit of despair.
I fade back into the smoke and purple tears.
I drip the awesome on my tongue.
The power rising, with pointless hiding.
"Open the door, *I ask you - please...*"

Never Too Far

Never too far, to give into the one in my way, I take in all the pain.
Never too far, to know that I am only me, in the depths of your mistakes.
Never too much, pain of the three cuts on my chest, to rip out my heart.
Never too much, to tell you how I feel. I'm just a broken man on the edge.
Just one last thought in my head. I know I would love to hold you once again.
Just one last thought in my head. Now I am just that much more dead.
So throw me under dirt and take me to my place of birth, "*Home.*"
The never too far to drive me under earth into the dirt, I hope to find you.
It hits - colliding across my skull, faster and faster!
Thoughts and voices ringing in my brain.
My eyes turning black as my heart; forever I am broke like that.
"Why won't the voices just, PLEASE GO AWAY?!!"

Water - water flowing, burning fields of mushroom loves dying.
Pain - pain flowing under my tongue.
Melting away my spine, winding me down.
Home - home is where the heart is, so I guess I will never know.
I have no heart, I have no way.
I know I'll never go too far, because no one listens to me.
Only child cries, only I die and no one will be there to hear my last words.
I took the hourglass and smashed it against my head.
To give myself some life. You could say that I've wished to die.
I know I've flirted with suicide. What more would you want me to say?
I think I've already said enough.

Never too far, never will I ever find a better reason to breathe.
I live to die and die to live. I love her now but never again.
I seep the pills, in mushroom loves dripping under my flesh.
Worms eating at my brain, these hogs digging at the roots of my pain.
I tried to remember what you said, but the smoke is all that's left.
I took the cigarette and put it out on my eyelids, to see what's new.
I keep myself open, my chest bleeding, my soul dying, "God crying!"
And someone rocks me to sleep, someone sings me to sleep.
So far - far away I seep, the dream of kissing the girl next to me.
The hope of loving the next one to be, "someone save me."
"*PLEASE*!!"

Hope

I hope you're happy with how you left me.
Standing in the rain; no heart - know pain.
I hope you're happy with how you *fucked* me.
Standing there in the rain, walking in my endless pain.
The finding her standing on my grave, smiles while I rot insane.
Take me more into the haze, the bitter taste of my sorrow.
As I swallow down my hates, drinking away all my pains.
What a tomorrow and I find it today, drowning in this haze.
All has been dark days ever since our nightmare before Christmas.
I feel hate winding, I see time winding, I know hope is dying.
Find me deep in my grave; take me so far - far away from grace.
Someone took away my face, thrown me out of place.
Hope I await but now the leaves are turning black. "I'll never forget."
I hope you're happy with what you did to me, left me standing alone.
I hope you're happy; you with your new family. "Someone take me home."

I see so deep in the eyes of the abyss, the hour in reflections of you.
In the pain I twist, breaking my wrist and knowing that, that was it.
So it's over now, and you have what I hope you were looking for.
I know you'll never be alone, as for me; I live under this stone.
Drowning in the realizations of my fears. So I drink all these tears.
Look into my eyes and see the pain of how you left me.
How you were, how you've been. I miss the girl who stole my heart.
But give it back, I'm broke and at a lack of reach with the world.
You haunt my every dream. I hope you know how I feel.
You with your new family; me with my life of pain and hurt.
But the truth is, I have everything I want in life.
But now I can never have you because I threw you away.
And now I have only these days of hard drink and soft death.
I miss the dream I had of being the one who gave you it all.
But now I'm awake and knowing the hate. The truth you left for me.
Please get off my grave, step away and.
"GET THE FUCK OUT OF MY HEAD!!"
I just hope you will be happy, as I stand on your gravestone.
Flesh below bone and blood above everything.
I swim in the knowing of this.
I wish I could have been the one to give you everything.
But I hope... I hope you know that I loved you once but now I step aside.
Because you were my everything. But now you're nothing in life.

326

Crimson Wrist

Wow! What a taste I awake with in the back of my mouth.
Old smoke and a peppermint spice.
I awake trying to swallow back the past.
Lifting the amber glass; no rocks, hard shot.
As I lay in bed, staring at the back of my eyelids.
Dripping back to twisted high-ness.
My body shakes and bones begin to ache.
What a taste I have in my mouth, of memories gone.
What was I supposed to say?
Ringing echoes of the morning birds in my brain; I cannot wait.
I drag my body out of bed, I moan low.
Beating my head, remembering what you said.
Looking down as my tears and blood hit the floor.
Drinking the smoke of the never more. I found it on the last sheet.
The words she spoke and hung up the phone, she was right.
Was I right to walk away from all of it?
Now weeping and seeping with crimson wrist.
My neck hurts, and what a burst of sadness.
Sadness that falls upon me in the early morning; as if the night could.
I stay standing on the edge of my sanity hoping I'll find hope.
I wash my face and nothing can replace this taste I have in my mouth.
"She laughed." I awoke with the same feeling.
A feeling I've always seemed to have. Weeping with crimson wrist.
I shower... Hot beating on my flesh, burning my body numb.
Hoping for a new sun to rise.
I awake in the early day to try and wash away the dreams.
Nothing seems to help me. Could I ever wake up just one day?
And not feel this endless pain in my head forever now?
I just wish it could all stop ringing in my ears.
My head won't stop flushing down; my hope was and never can be again.
This world is now gray and forever this is it.
I put my shoes on the wrong feet.
To make me just that much later to where I need to be.
I smoke another clove, I drink another drink.
I sink into this reality I made for myself.
To try and push back the knowing that I no longer have a life; yet I live.
"For only now." I've come so far but all it was - was shit.
This pain I live with such a burn in my mouth.
I place my hands on their face.
And know that I am forever and will always be this way.
I run my tongue on the ground;

Feeling the glass bringing me down, down, down.
I'm stuck grabbing my face.
Rubbing my eyes and remembering that day - that day.
Drowning in the bottles I shoot.
The shots I take rushing through my blood and feeling my lungs caving in.
Weeping over these crimson wrists, until I drift away again.
I live with this burn in my chest and this taste in my mouth.
The knowing that I will never get better on my own.
It just kills my heart and soul; running day after day in my own brain.
Wishing for a better tomorrow, "that's only a dream."
In the mirror I stare at crimson wrists.
Wishing that I could awake; drowning in the moon's gravity love.
The haze I push my way through every day.
In night I live and in life I die. In love I wish she were alive, "sorry."
Knowing that all is dead and so am I.
Knowing that I pushed her away - away I cry.
Feeling the forever has past and the never is now.
I go to bed every night with the same thoughts.
If I wasn't myself, would all still be this way?
Was it my fault or is it fate? I go to bed now...
With this blood on my wrist and a peppermint spice in the back of my mouth.
With crimson wrist I live and in life I die.

The Day She Died

I remember the day she died.
I felt like someone ripped out my heart.
I remember the feel of her warmth; she kept me so down to earth.
"I miss her." I loved her with all my heart.
And nothing will ever fill this hole in my soul.
Nothing could replace the girl I loved, as she lies above in heaven's light.
I remember the day she died, my heart was crushed and forever it shall be.
I know that we'll be together, forever in a knight's dream.

Balling up in the corner of my room.
Weeping these days away, I hope so hope it away yet no one is there.
I hear a knocking at the door, no one was there; "no one cares."
The day she died, was the day I knew the answer to all my questions.
The day she died, it was the day I took the last step over the edge and fell.
And you don't feel the feel of feeling the numb torment inside.

So hopeless I wait, I know that she will be missed, *my love forever gone.*
She was there for me when I needed someone to hold;

She was there for me when I was alone.
She was there, she did care and I see how hopeless I am.
It's pointless for you to think otherwise.
I remember the day she died. It hit me like a ton of bricks.
"Every day it hits."

Do you remember the day she died?
I could only walk endlessly in myself.
Knowing that she was taken away from us, "forever she will be missed."
She was the one who lent an ear when I needed to talk, she who I loved.
Forever on a walk of smiles and orange leaves in the fall.
She I love, forever love.

God I ask, why was she taken away from us?
Why didn't I get to say goodbye?
Hopeless I am, just a broken man.
Remembering the days and years I loved her.
She who was always there, she who always cared.
She who I hold in my heart true.
She was the most caring person I ever knew.
The girl I once loved, the girl who everyone knew, "I miss her."
Why can't these thoughts of pain just fade away?
The memories comfort me.
I remember the day she died but "you" were not there for me.

She was born when heaven shined and died in early August.
She was the closest one to me, "I didn't even get to say goodbye."
I remember the day she died, and where were you?
I've struggled from that day forth to live, because inside I die.
I know that she would want me to be happy but it's just so hard.
The day she died was the day I died.
And the time I realized who, "*you*" truly are.
This world will never be the same without her.
I am not the same without her, but I try my hardest to move on.
On her grave I lay, remembering that day. I miss her so, so much.
But I remember the day she died and the life she lived.
Forever she will be missed, by everyone and me.

I Want To Stay

Day pumping the life back into my body. Night fueling my every thought and move.
With torment waiting, would you like to smell the fresh human death and sweet truth?
Rusted walls of chain linked fences.
Blood spilt on the floor, screams in the distance.
What more, what more could I do?
She asked me to tell her, what could I do?
The bricks fall on my thoughts every day.
She whispered to me, "I want to stay."
Should I have told the truth? Why am I so young yet at a loss of youth?
And I lie here on a velvet bed, silky sleek sheets with roses laid on the covers.
Soft comfort on her lips, the taste of sweet innocence on her body.
She whispered and wishes of love and the never end of us.
The rub of numb nerves that tweak. The change of one angel to another.
Her body once mine, she loved the awesome; "a gift I gave her."
A thought I once lived but now I burn, so she whispered in my ear...

Day pumping the life back into my body.
Night fueling my every thought and move and the rocking horse dances.
The hourglass speaks small rhymes and poems.
And rushes the nonsense back into me day after day.
She once told me, "I want to stay."
Halls deep in the asylum called my brain. Demons weeping at my feet today.
Should I have told her, what should I say?
She came to me and whispered, "I want to stay." *Here I would like to play...*
The body of a child called me, dead and nothing else.
The child was once called me.
But youth now stolen and my memories are all that's left.
Would you like to play? Swinging above the staircase.
The body stiff and cold; here screaming at the end of my madness.
Cries at the end of the hall, should I have told you?

I would like for you to know, soft was her body and pail sweet flesh.
Blue eyes so deep, I swam in the oceans called her mind, my only vice.
It would have been nice, but should I have told her the truth?
"What should I have said?"
Day pumping the life back into my body and my brain caves so deep into me.
It was too cold on that day, when she came up to me.
Whispering, "I would like to stay." What should I have told her?
Sin so deep yet I wish only truth, what to do?
It was nice, her warm body, once mine;

Once mine, now gone and faded; candle lit and lighting my way.
Only I could have changed that day, blood and torment.
And her face, the taste I wish never to replace; that gift I once gave to her.
Now I wait for the night to fade and the day to die.
Death becomes my eternal vice.

Should I have told her, should I have kissed her?
Body sweet warm on a cold day; it was late "would you like to play?"
Always and forever was the last thing I'd say.
She who was once and now forever gone.
The screams and deathly decay my hopes.
The rusted walls of faded torment.
The day after day I scream, today I bleed.
What should I say? What should I do?
"Should I have kissed her, make love and lose."
It was cold on my walk back home, now there's nothing for me to say.
Should I have told her what I said, I wanted it right away.
We fade, one thing left for me to say.
There is only one thing left for me to say...
"I would like to stay."

That Day

There was a day in which I was not this dead.
There was a day in which I did not live.
There was a day that I watched you die.
There was a day in which I did not cry.
And eyes wide open to the lies you told.
And death wide shut, to the very thought of you.
And never shall the ever be. Away from grace and in depth I swing.
And never to the thought of you. "Why am I here?" Dead and confused.
Was I not the one who lived to love?
Was I not the one you loved to live for?
Was I just a freak, just dead rotted meat?
Was I too far gone or just that ignorant?
Was I that much of a loss, must I lose again?
There was a day in which I was not dead.
There was a day I did not beat my head.
There was a day I loved to love.
There was a day in which I did not die.
There was that day, I held you, not cried;

Now with eyes wide open to the lies you said.
Now with death shut open to the nothing you lived.
Now with nowhere to hide I run so far within.
Now with no one alive, I sit here and weep, not die.
The truth is I want to live not die.
The truth is I want to scream, not cry.
The truth is I want to cut but never bleed.
The truth is I live with pain, it sets me free.
There was a day in which I could not see.
There was a day in which I did not bleed.
There was a day when I felt that dead.
There was a day that you held my hand.
There was that day when I felt alive. "I want to live, not die."

Cry For Help

Somebody, rip out my eyes so I can see something more.
More than what lies beyond this hill.
Somebody, take me away and leave to the gray.
This body of frail facts and numb nerves.
Somebody, pull out my soul and wipe it on the curb.
It's all just a simple break down; somebody, hear me.
I scream so loud and wish to burn, so I can think of nothing more.

I cut open the roof of my mouth and bleed.
As endlessly on the bed you made for me.
I can't cut out the memory of when you loved me.
I die and weep inside hoping to get out.
Someday I may be the same as I was once before.
But for now I just lie here and burn wishing someone could hear me.
I wish I were not so dead and away from ever being sane.

It's not the same. It's not that way.
I loved a love that shall never be, truly I failed me.
It's not what you think. I am human; I am just dead rotted meat.
Please set me free, take me more into the pit.
Shove me behind the wall and drown in the loss of wit.
Someday I may get out of this hell.
Will anyone ever take me back for what I am? I am a demon, I am a man.

I did kill myself and forever ran, so deep into this hell.
A shady side to the last one in mind;

332

A slow set to the right way and mind drip.
Swing me above the stairs and kiss me goodbye.
I was once here; I was once alive.
I cut out my own teeth, to think of more than my heartbreak.
I'm broke, I'm dead.

I would love to take a swim in the lake of fire.
But it has frozen over, "I just can't win." Will I ever get a break?
Will I ever not break my own tongue on the rock of spice?
Will you ever open the door and see what I hide?
Please come on in, welcome sin.
Somebody may think that I'm insane.
But I'm just a man driven deep into this haze.

Ask me a question and I ask you to just go away.
Fade me nothing more and I'm away.
Staring deep into this hole in my hand.
Hoping to find a way home, I want hope.
With you I was at home, with you I had a reason to breathe.
Now under water I scream, letting out all the air; leaving without a care.
I wish you were here, with me.

Now I must live with the fact that I'm but second best.
I know it's over and spent, as is the monster named I.
To take away the light and for you I wish to die.
So helpless I weep crying and dying for someone to hear me.
"Please hear me." I just need to see a better point of view.
But in the end all I found was you.

I wish someone could hear my cries, I wish I could live not die.
I want an angel of a better drive.
Her pain I lost and my death I gained.
This is a cry for help. I seek a new hell. I want to love and live.
So as I swallow back the blood in my mouth.
I know now, "we could have never been."

Now All Is Clear

So this is where I would like you to just lay back and take a breath.
The soul of one has formed to sum and none of you will ever know.
Unknown to the very thought of you, that I may not be as evil and torn.
I love the sight of you and an angel's kiss on my soul; a way for me to live.
A way of what I've known once but fear now so, so much; I feel so stuck.
But there truly is more in life than just pain and loss, there is gain and love.
Even though sometimes it is hard, even if I was once torn apart by my heart.
I should have listened to my head; I should've walked away when you said.
But all is done and forever gone, just a bad dream as all seems to be.
But no more will I be blind, "what a lie."
No more will I not try to smile.
It took a while but now I once again feel alive, not another love or drive.
Just a notion that has been answered and I finally have what I need, hope.
So please just lay back and relax.
Take the time to love and live, to breathe and think.
But we all know who I am, it won't last forever; but for now I feel good.
I just need to remember. I'm not the evil spawn of hell you think I am.
I am just a man, and would like to tell you, the past could be put to rest.
Maybe someday it will but for now I lay under this hill, waiting to awake.
Someday I'll inhale and be taken from hell, but until then I'll just wait.
So for now I think I've cleaned the slate. I know now what I need to do.
Just once again stop, once again take a walk and be nothing more than, *Me.*
Nothing could be more for me to want.
Than the angel of love on my side but that's just a dream.
And no matter how much I beat myself it will always hurt.
No matter how much I feel I will burst, I will.
There is nothing that I can do to stop the pain.
All I'm left to do is find a way.
To live on and take it all in and maybe I could be happy.
Maybe someday I could be loved again.
But for now I just need to wait, and breathe.
I need to get my life together.
I need to bring together my soul; that I should hold.
I can never love anyone if I don't love myself; "I don't."
So I just need to breathe. I know that at times I am a demon.
I know that at times I cut myself. I know that at times I wish for hell.
To stop all the voices in my brain, but that's my pain.
For now I just need to clean the slate.
And wipe away all my tears, push back my fear.
If I smiled, then maybe I will be seen by someone out there.
Maybe someone can care;

Please someone help me through these times.
But for now I think I will just unwind.
See, I know it was my fault that all was torn and broken before my eyes.
I know that in the time I've taken to write this.
I could have missed another one.
All the years spent trying to gain back my love; I lost the one girl I loved.
But what could I do, she moved on and I should too.
So now I do, done, have and won.
All is not as gray as I say but for me it's just another day, for loss and pain.
I've learned to live with it, but that doesn't mean I'm happy.
I just know now what to do. I'll just be myself and stray from hell.
And wonder what lies ahead of me.
Maybe I could be happy, or truly I will die alone.
I know I am just a human and hope to someday be looked at as a man.
As who I am, just a child grown within.
In heart-take of the day I lost the one I loved.
I could never stop thinking of her but my eyes are open and I can see.
It's all clear now and truth will set me free.
I just need to be, "Me."

One Last Kiss Before I Die

What started off as a smile, soon turned to an assortment of un-satisfactions.
What started off as a kiss, turned to a world of pain and loss.
What started off as a song, then turned into a war of forever being just me.
What started off as a life, now is just the death of a poet.
What started off as a child, now is a man that wishes he were known.
What started off as a whisper.
Now a screaming voice in my brain eating at my soul.
What started off as a drip; now rushing blood from my wrist.

And I would just like for you to listen, just one day of knowing who I am.
And I would just like for you to open your body and soul.
And taken away from the grace we knew.
Shoved under earth and burned in youth.
Please just take the time and open your mind.
"Remember, you loved me once."
Please just take my life and end the fight.
I'm growing tired of all this pain. I'm numb now and forever will be.
In God's eyes I am just a freak;

I would like just one last kiss before I die.
I would like one last thought set aside.
When I held the angel in my arms, warm and close to me.
Why couldn't I see the things to be?
The voices of pushing the steel under my skin.
In the lust of sin I smile; now knowing that this is my life.
What started off as a smile.
Is now a death of my heart and fire in my eyes.
What started off as a kiss.
Now the death of my forever just being alive.

I would like it if I could be held one last time.
I wish I could be loved one last time.
I would like it if I could be human in the eyes of the world around me.
I would like it if I could be remembered.
But forgotten I fear I am already.
I would like it if I could rip the paint off the walls.
And see the whole picture.
I would like it if you would kiss me one last time; just before I die.

And the words were ripped from behind my teeth.
I was raped in the fears of my dreams.
She was only my heart and love. Now I'm gone and burned in the sun.
Will no one remember this face when it's gone?
Who will be there? Will no one remember these words when I'm gone?
And recall what I had to say.
Will you ever let me love again God?
Or am I damned to a forever being by myself?

The moon gives her gravity kiss; a smile on her lips and a breath of decay.
And in the ground I would like to stay, smiling at the devil's laugh.
Knowing that nothing's left, well... There's just nothing for me.
And I would like one last kiss before I die, to take you to hell with me.
I wonder if I will ever be remembered, for more than loss and pain.
I would like to be remembered as - just me.

Wingless

Someone has taken my wings. Someone has left me here to bleed.
I'm seeing the light fading. I see the world dying, gone and decayed.
Someone has taken my wings and let me to fall tumbling into the stream.
Gone faded memories of the last thing I said; when I never turned my head.
Cold steel under my flesh. If only God would give me one last chance.

Weak minds of our young mother earth I adore.
Weak minds of the youth I held, and smashed my hand in the door.
Was the torment just a better way to pass the time?
Was the torment a new way to live a lie?
When I was a human, I knew only how to destroy.
Now I'm a demon and I know only her voice.
And no one can help the damned and no one will.
Wingless fading away, behind the clouded haze of mushroom death.
I find the faded memory of the nothing you left.
I fight to stay on my feet but I'm falling now; under six feet.
I fight to be the only one heard. I fight because I'm the only one burned.
Who loved you, the boy you hold or the man who died?
Who loved you, the child you hold or this demon inside?
And I am going to eat your heart. I am going to tear you apart.
You were my only way, a path I died to gain.
But you pissed me away and now you're going to pay.

Someone has taken my wings, someone took my heart away.
Now in hell I stay, wishing for another day but all I find is pain.
Millions of spiders crawling under my skin, winding deep into my sins.
No one wishes to help me. I'm screaming so loud, trying to see.
Wingless, I wait for the big nothing in front of me.
Wingless falling - burnt decayed and left only to remember that day.
I loved once but who truly cares? I died once and fell deep into despair.
My last breath and thought was a "fuck you!" And I hold that true.
My last dream of being away but I can only find the maze.
Wingless I burn today, wishing for a better way; I am away.
No wings, no soul, no heart, no love; I live and die with this every day.
Speak up my loves... Set aside the notion and just watch me fall away.

Drive

One last reason, one last drive.
One last reason, one last time.
And no one was there to pick up the pieces.
No one was there to care about my cries.

One last reason, one last drive.
One last reason, one last time.
And no one cares to help me up.
No one cares to shut it up.

We have driven the darkness within.
We are driven and in a twist of lime...
The shadow was and always shall be.
In the drip of the *Never* and I now set it free.

One last thought, one last try.
One last hope, one last cry.
And no one was there to help me up.
No one cares about this poor *fuck*.

I sit here in a pool of blood, over my head.
I sit here and wish I were above and not so dead.
I sit here hoping the coin to land on heads.
I scream my last breath and now I burn.

On no open end of the fact.
That I was human and now that's past.
On no open end of the truth, that there is only pain for me.
I hope my last drive will set me free.

One last hope, one last drive.
One last thought, one last time.
And you don't care, not for me.
You don't care - not to set me free.

One last reason, one last drive.
One last reason, one last time.
In set with the lime dripping down my spine.
The dirt so dry and the sky so dull...

I'm Still Burning

Now I unlock the things I hide. Now I unwind the dreams I fight.
No one is caring who I am. I'm just a human, I'm just a man.
As I run down the streets I know, trying to find her under the snow.
She was the angel I spent all my life to find, but now she's gone and I unwind.
Hanging onto the last little thread called my faith.
I swing about in the loss of grace.
Knowing who I am, but cast away from the world.
I unlock the memories inside.
I find no more of the face in which I hide, behind the slime and dirt.

Here under our earth I weep, grasping the last tears from my cheek.
Here in the wonderment of the everything I once said.
Now I am a man, still lost within.
Where am I going to hide the rest of my life?
I already threw everything away.
I find nowhere else to go, under this hill and beneath a frozen lake.
In the tears of knowing that I will no longer have a face.
I fade away from grace because I found the light in darkness.
I didn't think I would have to lose you too.
How can I call you a love or a friend, when none of that is true?

Over years of beating my head.
Now nothing is left but me and the floor stained red.
Over the road I trip, finding that nothing is left but me alone on this street.
Looking for a love to seek, finding that everyone is gone.
"But really it's me."
I left the reality called yours and found a world I call mine.
Life was a lie, now I unlock the things I hide.
I unwind and hang on to this last thread called faith.
I hang on under a hill and beneath a frozen lake.
There I lay and sway with only me.
I couldn't find her, the angel under the snow.
She's gone now, to where; "I do not know."

Now I unlock the demons inside.
I unlock the open doors and all the things we hide.
Now I unwind and swing on this last remaining thread.
"Now I'm a man and nothing is left."
I creep away and wish for faith and still my fate lies on the face of a coin.
Here I turn and spin winding deep into sorrow, remembering the lies you said.
I loved an angel once but now I die within;

Keeping only truth close to me.
Here I wonder forever in my purgatory.
Weeping tears of joy that I'm still alive.
A free man in the wonderment of the fact
That I still burn alive; forever that's my life.

Now I unlock the things you hide.
And I will rise in the dawn of knowing you're gone.
It's locked forever under the snow.
The leaves were gone and no path showed.
I looked forever to find my love and friends, but the truth is.
"I never had them."
Forever I was alone even when they were around.
If only I knew what I know now, maybe she would still be alive.
Maybe if I would have said no, "I would have lived."
Now I weep red on the white snow bleeding still and forever-always will.
I'm burning and learning.
That I've unlocked the door to you, "but I shut it for now."
I know which path to choose.
The frozen leaves point me within; I'm a man now.
I unlock the child within. "*You could never win.*"

Holding My Face

Every time something falls out of place, I stand hopeless ripping off my face.
Wishing for a better you, knowing that it could never be true.
Hoping that you would hold my hand, finding that I am a human too.
I only fell into hell. I only cried when you died. I only live for revenge.
Now on sweet lips I can breathe again. Now tomorrow shines the better you.
But all has fallen out of place and I stand on the edge, ripping off my face.
I was so far from grace, at her side and her hand I will never know.
It will never show, it will never be known.
I tore away my face to find a better place, so now I'm home.
I am human too. I am alive, smiling without you.

The times and times I tried to love but all was shoved beneath the hill.
The hours and hours I tried to awake from the pain.
The miles and miles I fell out of place. After years, I tore off my face.
I held the torment in my soul but now once again I am alone.
Holding nothing but me, holding my face in my hands, ice-cold I bleed.
It was only to tell you how I felt but you drifted so deep into hell.
I never knew I could hate you so much;

I never knew you were that far and out of luck.
The lies and lies, the time and time, the mind and mine; it all broke away.
I hope you can be alive. I wish I had someone at my side but I never will.

I took my time, I've gained my revenge and it is so sweet on my lips.
And as the demons and love fades, I start to remember the sight of light.
I can remember the taste of warmth and love.
But I stand now alone and done. I am done trying, I am done crying.
I will never win. Never let it win. I am done dying, "I win."
I will never take away what you want, it is what you need.
Now I am free, "I am Me!" I will never take away the feel.
I lay under this hill, bleeding numb but alive.
I sit here awake and feel so alive. Don't bother to be the one to say you cared.
You and I know that you were not there; I know you don't care.

Every time something falls out of place, there I am ripping off my face.
Every time I feel alive, I remember that that's a lie, so heartless I sing.
Though I am alive under this hill. I know that you swim in hell.
Every time I feel that dead, I just stand and turn my head, "as have you."
But I know who I am. I am human and alive with revenge, "I win."
You can't say that you're not mad. I know your every move and thought.
Remember, I was once a part of you but now and forever I choose to breathe.
Every time something falls out of place, there I stand ripping off my face.
Fading deeper into myself, where I want to stay.
Alone in this abyss and cold today.
"So now I'm home, I am human too, I am alive; smiling without you."

Once Upon A Yesterday's Love

Do you remember the day I kissed you for the first time?
Do you remember the days when you held me and cried?
Do you remember the days when we were alive?
Do you remember the days I kissed you and felt so alive?
Do you remember the days? When I loved you and would never leave?
Do you remember the days when we were happy? Were you happy with me?
Do you ever think of how it could have been?
Do you ever think of how we would have lived?
Do you ever wish that you were with me?
Do you ever think of how it could be? Did you ever think it would end?
Did you ever wish it to end? Did you ever feel my love?
Did you ever think of what we had done?
Do you remember our first kiss? Or our last touch;

Do you remember telling me it would last always and forever?
Do you remember watching me die?
Do you remember laughing while I cried? Do you remember why you lied?
Do you remember why I left you and died?
Do you ever think of how it could have been?
Do you ever wish it would have never ended?
Do you ever feel this dead? Do you ever wish to hold me again?

I have once held an angel in my arms.
Only to watch it burn to ash and blow away.
I have once loved an angel but that was yesterday.
Now I must stay awake because I have a story to tell.
Of the pain that I have once endured but now she is gone.
I sit here asking all, so many questions.
Here in inquiry I stay, wishing for a better day.
I once loved a love that failed as have so many before it. I feel so worthless but still I rise.
I sit here in question, a dark day and in the bright night.
I live to live and love to die.
I wish she could hear me but that is only a dream.
She is gone now, forever from me but what is there for me to say?
What could I do to stop the pain?
I love this pain because that's all I have ever known.
To lose all that ever mattered to me.
But now I am older and have earned so much to share.
I've learned a way to leave this hell.
It is quite easy I say, I must only save this day.
I must awake from my pain.
Truly it is all I have to hold at this time.
As she lies there happy in his arms.
As I scream beating my skull in blood and death wishes.
I wish she could hear me now.
I wish I could just awake and be out but truthfully...
"Where is the fun in that?"
I ask you so many things but as always; I'm only asking myself.
I need an ear to listen. I need a hand to hold.
I wish I were a little younger but now I feel so old.
The days are growing longer but I sleep them all away.
I know that I loved her, "but that was yesterday."
I know that I'm a monster, watching my angel fade away.
It was no fun to watch my heart be raped in my chest.
By the people I loved but now I have a family.
I have all that I earned; I gained the path and tool,

But who are you to say otherwise?
I think I will awake now and see the light.
I once held an angel. I once loved her true.
But now I've grown up and feel less confused.
So to you, the one who stands at my side.
Take my hand and now we are alive...

Deep Gaze Into The Past

Gaze deep into my heart and give me back what you stole.
Gaze deep into my heart and take me further into this hole.
Gaze deep into my soul and know that I am only myself.
Gaze deep into this hole and watch me burn and smolder.
I do feel much older. I know that I have done my time.
I do feel much older, as I lay back and pass my time.
Years spent on the notions of being a man of my word.
I still hold myself true to that thought, "I shall have my revenge."
The years spent on the only things I ever knew.
The years spent on trying to find a better view.
If only I knew that it would have ended this way.
Maybe my heart I could have saved, and yours too.
But there is nothing for me here, no reason to awake.
Only revenge and the drive to be myself today.
I took in all the pain and hurt, I felt the burn.
And who are you to say that it was okay? Who were you to me?
I spent years trying to be a better man for you.
But now I stand here waiting for the sun to rise.
I feel like just another face in the crowd.
How could I have let it cloud my judgment?
I feel so hell-bent and what a whore-sent thought of you and me.
I will no longer wait for you to wake, the angel is dead and it's too late.
I am the demon you made me out to be; true I am a monster indeed.
I tried to tell you at the start, but you just wouldn't listen to me.
Could you have ever walked in my shoes?
Could you have ever thought that we would lose?
I tried to hold you, but watched you fade.
I tried to hold you, but was overwhelmed by the haze.
It was hard to rip out my heart, and watch it burn.
It was hard to rip out my eyes and feel the burn.
I know who you are now. I wish you were alive.
So time after time I cut open my tongue and watched it bleed.
So many souls I had to watch fall before me;

It was hard to hold my love dead in my arms.
And watch these frozen tears roll down my face.
I kissed her while she wept; it was all because of me.
I feel so out of place sometimes but can never find somewhere to stay.
I hate this world, it just eats at me.
I wish I had someone on my side, someone to guide me through the dark.
The gray abyss called my chest; it is all I have known.
So now I ask you to just take me home, in my grave where I wish to stay.
Alone holding nothing close but me and sweet revenge, "it's here."

Things I Knew

There was a day I awoke and knew that nothing would change.
There was a day I slept and was betrayed, by the ones I loved.
There was a day I took a blade to my wrist.
I lie here bleeding and wondering if I will ever be missed.
I miss the days I held nothing but my love and friends.
I'm grown now and can remember only pain and sin.
I wish I could have held her that one last time.
I wish I could speak to her and never cry, the time is flowing.
I fear the growing pits of pain and death in my soul.
As I carry this load on my back. I feel a lack of reach to the world.
If I could remove their knife, would I bleed and die?
If could remove their knife, could I breathe and move on in life?
The years spent on the only thing I ever knew; to feel lost and confused.
But I have grown and feel more like a man, I can see now.
And I look into the time sand; I watch it roll down crumbling on top of me.
A million hammers beating me soulless, till nothing is left.
But there was a day that I did not cry, when I had it all at my side.
But it's gone now and it broke my pride, and left me with only hate.
I bitch here all day of the nothing that I need.
I've had it all in front of my face but I was just too blind to see.
I wish I had the strength to die and give up, "but I never will."
My life of revenge drives me so close to the edge and I scream.
I wish I had a heart to stab but I bleed now, only the time sand.
I know I've grown but who are you to me?
I want to breathe, I want to love, I wish to die. I lie here and cry.
I had so much stolen from me at such a young age.
But I'm much older now, and that was yesterday.
I've thrown away all in which I cared for but what more should I have done?
I sit here and wish it were done. I am done trying to please you all.
I am done dying, I had fun trying to live but I failed;

In the grave of my brothers "friends," they now mean nothing to me.
In the eyes of that lover, she is dead now. Was taken from me.
The truth is so easy to see but what is it that you want from me?
I tried to make you happy, but lost everything instead.
I tried to be the one who cared. I was the one who cared.
Who else was there, who else wishes to rip out their hair?
I stand on the top of my sanity, screaming in tongues I do not know.
I look down at you, remembering all the things I knew.

<u>*Release*</u>

So here I stand now on her grave, remembering the joys of her grace.
Now here I am, weeping on her grave.
Remembering the last touch of her cheek and face.
Now here I am weeping on her grave.
Knowing of what I've done, so forever I hold the blame.
Here I am lying on her grave, holding in the tears; inside it rains.
Now here I stand, remembering that day.
It fell deep and I took in the haze; in the dark, I release.

I took an ax to that whore and cut it open piece by piece.
The blood runs down my face. So here I am standing on her grave.
Knowing who she was and remembering that taste.
And it sure was a daze, falling further into my maze.
Knowing the dawn of days of this haze I made.
Now here I am weeping on her grave. Knowing that she's gone and I'm away.
The smile I adored, her young innocent grace.
Now she lies bloody in her grave, *decay - and I release.*

I took a walk to free myself of the shame; in her smile - an angel of God-sent.
I took a walk to set myself free of the haze.
It crushes me so deeply unsane and never shall I ever be saved.
I weep numb sound, blood rubbed on my face.
I took a walk to free myself of the pain.
I stay here weeping on her grave.
I knew it would take me far from faith.
Dripping deep into my mouth, and her soul - I release.

It took some time but I'm okay.
I know that it was hard; as I stand here on her grave.
The smile that drove me so insane.
The lips of lust and sin that drove her so deep *within - Her grave.*
I took an ax to her flesh and I tried throwing the bloody ax into the lake;

It froze over and stayed, now in this haze I sway.
I took a walk to free myself of this pain.
But here I am weeping on her grave.
I release the thought of being with this.
I release the dream of dreaming of youth.

Sometimes I wish it would just fade away.
And here I stand watching my soul slip away.
Knowing that nothing will ever change.
Knowing that it will always be this way.
Now here I am, I stand weak and gray.
Burning in time-sands and into salt I fade.
Wishing that she were here standing on my grave.
But I'm okay; *now I release.*
No, I'm okay; watching my eyes burned in my head.
Watching the blood pour from my mouth.

But what more was there for me to say.
I stand here weeping on her grave.
I took an ax to her flesh, and cut it open piece by piece - God!
The taste I will never forget and in the blood of the love I put into the ground.
Now I scream, to hell I am bound.
Stuck to the floor like a pill, washing away the feel of ever being alive.
Now here I stand, weeping over that day.
In the hell that I made I sway, in hell I stay.

But now I know, it can never be the same.
I took a walk to free the strain.
I dream of dreaming of her soft lips.
Remembering our last kiss, oh what an awesome gift.
So here I stand, weeping on her grave.
I remember the last words as I touched her face.
Here I am, lying on her grave.
I will hold you always and a day, forever in our haze.
Now here I am, I can just barely see.
It was hard to do... Setting her soul free, *now I release.*
"I fall."

When I Was Numb And She Left Me

On the last hope - I was numb and she left me.
Only a tear came to my brain.
Only a whisper into my soul, I took the blade.
I grabbed my head, and now she's dead.

I'm sorry that I had to cause you so much pain.
I was numb and she drove away.
I asked you then and still I do.
Will it ever stop, forever I am confused.

I was ready but I fell away.
I was ready but now away.
I wish I were alive, she is dead now.
God! "Dead!?" Why!?!

When I was numb and she left me, I could only feel the pain.
Over years of hate and torment, now my life is burnt away.
I was dumb, so numb and cold. It was cold when she drove away.

All is over now and I am burnt away.
All is faded now and forever will stay that way.
I watched her die, I felt alive but now I scream without a hope.
Here I wait to free my body and soul. So here I wait, numb and cold.

No Fun

It was not fun, to watch her die. It was not fun, to live a lie.
The fall again, into a pit of despair. I want to love, I do not care.
Please wake me, give me back my life.
Please hate me, do not waste my time.

It was not fun, to watch her die. It was not fun, to live a lie.
The fall again, within my sin and soul-loss. I want to love, I do not care.
Please wake me, return what you stole.
Please hate me, I'm not a fool.

"It's no fun being a dead-man alive."

Just Another Question

Do you think I could be enough for you?
Do you think I could ever be the only one for you?
Do you think you could ever fill this hole in my chest?
Could you ever pick up the pieces and leave nothing left?

I wonder day by day if there will ever be one out there for me.
I wonder day by day if I could ever be the same with you.
As once I was with all the rest.
I wonder if you could put up with all my shit.
I wonder if I could love you as much as I once loved them and more.

Years spent on those feelings of pain and regret.
I want to smile with you. How could I be happy?
I fear losing another person close to me.
I want to smile with you, but I fear the results I might create.
Do you think you could deal with all my pains?

How so deeply insane I can be at times, but could you love me still?
How deeply upsetting it can be.
To watch me beat my head against a brick wall.
Could you help save this soul, before there is no coming back?
I want to be happy, but I hate myself so much sometimes.

Do you think that we could dance through the night? *Until the sun rises.*
Do you think we could smile even when things get bad?
Do you think you can help save this broken man from crumbling away?
I want to just smile and hold someone close to me.
But I fear what may come to be.

I like having someone to talk to, an ear to listen to my pain.
But I feel that at times, it drives you away.
I want to love and live; it's hard for a dead-man to love again.
I know that time with you is well spent and I hope it to be years.
"God I hope it."
Just another question before I stop this little rant.
Do you think you could be happy with this shell of a man?
Do you want to spend time with a broken soul?
Will you help me to smile, even throughout the bad?

Just another question before I go now.
In the end, do you think we will still hold each other's hands?

<u>3:00 am</u>

I've spent so much time spilling my heart down onto these paper sheets.
Only to watch them age and crumble in my hands, they burn and I die.
I've spent so much time beating my head on this desk just to pass the time.
Tears and blood, in my heart I draw a picture of the true person I am.
I've spent so long trying to tell the world who I am; "*Who we are.*"
There is no reason to kill yourself, over the troubles of an everyday life.
There is no reason to live on and on in this endless fright of being myself.
I fear who I am and what I have done, to those people close to me.
The truth is there; the blade has a handle and I shove both into my spine.
She was a thorn in my side, that I could never be rid of and never will.
Why do I still speak of those failed loves and nonstop pains?
Of my youth that I lost. It's quite a pointless act.
To scream endlessly into the dark abyss of the night.
It's 3:00am and I sit here awake.
Weeping over the things I've lost and shoved out.
I want to just be a normal man.
With a family of my own and a hand to hold.
I want someone to guide me out of this hell, this war I seem to survive.
Maybe I should just go to sleep; my eyes burn and I've run out of tears to cry.
It's been far too long for me to still feel like this, I threw them all away.
So now I think I will just wait for tomorrow; I need to fill this hollow.
It was so hard to watch them all die; gone they turn to salt and fade away.
It's 3:00am. I think I need to sleep, I think I need to breathe.
There is no reason to kill yourself over the losses of our youth.
The truth is; we have the rest of our lives ahead of us, I want to live.
In the past I die, in my today I weep and wish for light; I want to be alive.
I've spent so much time on these damn things.
Screaming and no one hears me. I wonder if I will ever be heard.
I wish I could be there but I need to face the facts.
I'm just a kid, I'm just a man, I need only a hand to hold.
I would like a shoulder to cry on.
A light to guide me out of the hell I made for myself.
It's 3:00am. I think I need to sleep, "damn it!"
My clock just broke, and I see the sun begin to rise.
I've spent so much time, spilling my soul onto these paper sheets.
Only to watch them fade away.
I think now I will go to sleep, and wake when the pain subsides.
I think I will go to sleep now and tomorrow I might find some light.
3:00am and only this paper and pen to comfort me.
"Damn" I need to sleep. "*Good night my reader.*"

Break Me Off Another Hit

You can't hold my hand forever mom.
You can't bring me back from the dead.
You can't wash out the blood stain.
In my soul I contain the forever push out and shove down.
You just can't be there when I die.
You just can't stop the suffering in my mind.
You can't hold my hand forever mom.
You can't bring me back from the dead.
You can't wash clean my soul.
The stain I contain of my sprit crushes me deep inside.
Break me off another hit; just one last drag before I die.

You can't wipe away the words I said.
You can't wipe away the blood I've shed.
You just can't wash clean this child in dread.
I fear the watching her fall from my arms.
You can't stop this monster; you've created an unstoppable killing machine.
You will never be further than the wars of the mind.
I find that you were already gone from the start.
You just can't be there when I die.
I wish so much I did not have to watch her die.
Break me off another hit; just one last drag before I die.

It won't always be like this.
There might be another side to the coin I call my life.
It won't always be like this; someday after I die I might be missed.
And who would spend their time.
Wondering about this sad man writing his life away?
It can't always be like this.
Someday I might find a reason not to shift my wrist.
It won't always be like this.
Someone might care about how I feel.
I would just like one more drag.
One last inhale before I drift deeply into hell.

I would like it if we could all just go our opposite ways.
But this rings true today.
I would like it if we could just stop this hate.
My pain is covering my every being.
I would like it if we all could awake from this haze.
This maze is far too much for me;

I would like it if I could hold your hand.
But will you ever return the feeling?
I would like it if I could just so forget this feeling.
Of being a man of hate and revenge.
Just break me off another hit; one last smoke before I go.

You can't hold my hand forever mom.
You can't bring me back from the dead.
You can't wash out the blood stain, my soul corrupted and breaking away.
You just can't be there when I die. Please, don't ask me why.
You can't hold me down forever World. You will never be the one to win.
You can't wash clean my slate.
Not until I have my revenge, "it's what I live for."
Just break me off another hit; just one last drag before I die.

Break me off another hit, just one last kiss before I die.
Break me off another hit, one more shot and then goodbye.
Break me off another hit, just one last smoke before I go.
Break me off another hit, just one more stop before I'm home.
Just break me off another hit, just one last smoke before I die.

One Last Drink Before Noon

We are what we were made to be.
I am what was made of me; who do you think you are?
I am who I try to be. I am what is inside of me.
I know now what it means to be a man.
We know what we were made to think.
We are what we feel in deep; inside our heart and soul.
I know now who I truly am.
I know now what it means to be a man of my word and heart.
I tried as hard as I could to stop the pain.
But they didn't listen; it drives me insane. What more could I say or do?
I can feel the end, one last drink before noon.
I would like to tell you that I'm okay. But that's a lie and far from sane.
I would like to tell you that I love you still.
But it's over now and buried under the hill.
And we hold the truths that should have been told.
What I know now I should have said.
But it's far past me now, and I turn my head.
We are much older now and far from the end.
I feel like I'm melting, turning into nothing more than just a puddle of tears;

I feel it bursting, into nothing more.

Just a man living his fears, I feel it's coming soon.

As once told to me by a man inside.

In the dawn was the trust and in the death within snow.

I can remember that day.

I was driven to be what I am today but now I'm much older and less insane.

I feel much bolder; I feel less at a strain.

But I still have a very long way ahead of me.

I know that death is just one part of eternity.

It's inevitable and we can never change it.

We know only what we were told to think.

We follow and are led over the edge and away we fall.

We are who we choose to be, "as for me" I would just like one more drink.

Please don't get up, please just stay there.

And enjoy my torment and suffering, "smile."

The end of all things will come to be, or just maybe for me.

I know the rising noon comes soon.

Over years spent on trying to learn and live, love and hate.

I've come to a conclusion, "I'm me."

I'm nothing more than what I started with. Just a man and a very neglected kid.

My youth stolen by those who I loved, but now I am a man.

"Look what you have done." Sing me another nursery rhyme.

Lay me to sleep and I pass away my time, until I fade away.

I am who I am because I choose to be.

We are who we are, who we were made to be.

We feel only what we want to feel, and know only what we learn.

We are ourselves, so don't try to tell me that I'm just trying to lie.

Once upon a noon wish and down falls the light.

When the North Star rises and falls.

When the moon kisses my cheek and I lay to sleep.

Forever I feel the angels weep.

Over the murder of the sheep called man; I laugh and smile.

We are what we chose to be, so before noon I would like one last drink.

Just one last drink before noon. One last dream before I awake.

I want to stay, before I have to leave and say my goodbyes.

I would just like one last toast to the midnight sky.

One last drink before noon, one last dance before I die.

One last dream before I awake, "I cry."

I never wanted to be the man you hate, but I'm me and we're too late.

Upon noon, the end to all things. I rise my glass and kiss goodbye my past.

Just one more thing left now for me to say. One last drink before noon.

"Here's to yesterday."

We All Fight

Hand to hand, head to floor. I spit out the mud and fall forever more.
I drift and sway, I melt in my grave, in the time sands I wait.
We all fight, an endless fight; a battle that only we can see.
We all fight; I fight this war inside of me. I fight only to keep my sanity.
Can you feel the burn and shove-down; can you take it onto your own mind and soul?
Could you wipe clean my wrist and wash the blood off my face?
We all fight to keep ourselves alive. We all fight an endless fight, our lives.
I wish to stop all this pain but it's far too hard and I seep further away.
Over the flesh that was given to us, must we do what we think is right?
Under the flesh that was given to me I seep the torment and open myself free.
In the darkness of being a man of my word; "*I told you I would die alone.*"
Here I write away my heart and soul, to whom - I do not know.
Someday, over the hill they'll play. Singing and laughing away their days.
Someday, I might win this fight. Someday I might find the darkness in light.
Somehow, I must tell you the truth to all these words.
But for now, just watch me burn.
We all fight to keep things right, by you and me.
We all fight to save our sanity.
I found my worst enemy, staring me in the eyes.
In the mirror and bloody fight; as wolf is I and sheep are man.
I feast upon the flesh and smile over the dead.
And as I watch her body decay, I remember that day.
I saw the outcome and washed it away.
In the yesterday knowing that we were once one.
Now I fight the biggest fight of my life; "myself."
The little children of the world, the ones we over look.
Those are the ones like you and me. We all fight, just to be set free.
I want to live not die but who am I to say? I wish to breathe again.
In the open air and throw my arms free. I want to be set free.
We all fight our fights and no one can help.
It is a dark place between heaven and hell.
I want to be the one you come to for guidance.
But who am I to you, just another page.
We all fight to save our lives, so why does everybody hate me?
We scream yet are never heard. It is only to keep things right.
It is only to shadow the darkness with light.
We all feel the feelings I feel. I am but another face in the crowd.
We are one and the same.
Someday we might stop the fight and live on and be so free.
"As for me," I fight on indeed.
Until the day comes when everything falls right into place;

It may be years, "so for years I wait." We all fight, we all die.
It is hard to lose all that was at our side. We all live and we all cry.
It's not a weakness but a new strength on our side.
We all live and we all scream.
Just until the day comes when we never have to worry again.
Until that day, I will fight and stay.
I wish I could never break but that's far from truth.
We all fight, to keep our youth but someday we will grow up.
And it will all be okay.
But until that day we fight to keep things right, by you and me.
I fight my worst enemy, "Me." Until the day comes when we are all free.
"We all fight to keep our sanity."

My War...

It was forever beating me down to the floor.
And I was forever being the nothing more.
It was forever beating me to the floor.
Now I wait here forever more to see her face.
I did beat me to the floor, now here I stand; fighting my war.
To be a man, to dig myself out of the sand.
In the ground where I need to escape.
Somebody help me flee, somebody set me free.
I wish to never feel this feeling again.
I want to be the one alive. I want to have someone at my side.
Please someone help me!
In my war I wish to leave. In this nightmare I find the beast.
What a creature of the damned I am.
What more would you like me to say or do?
My war in my mind, the drive over the edge.
The torment of my soul. I need to find a home, in this hole I lay.
In the pain I write today, of the years spent on the one thing I know.
This war in my mind, a foe I wish I never knew.
This torment of my soul, I need someone to hold.
Please guide me out of my head.
Please guide me somewhere else instead; I wish I could see.
My war of being a human under your disgusting ways.
This body is mine and you're too late. My war of the forever is now.
The some-said, side-set monster in my brain; driving me away.
My war of the dead is here now and the notion of us is forever gone.
I wish it were here. In the opening of her mouth, it drove me away.
In the torment of my heart, the crushing of my brain;

I am the one thrown to the side. I am the child with demon cries.
I am the devil that you do hate. I wish I weren't here now but you're too late.
My war of being just me, this forever wishing to set my soul free.
I need to see; I will and have become what the world has made me.
I am just a monster wishing to be free.
I am the nothing that you threw away. I am the nothing that you gave to me.
I am the whore you thought I would be. I am not what you want, I am only me.
And in this war, I fight the monsters in me.
In this war I fight you and me. My war of the forever is now.
And I would like to tell you how I feel but who cares?
My war of the forever is here and you're too late.
The clock was a fake. You are a freak like me.
We are the nothing that was cast aside but I was pushed away.
And now here I stay, wishing for light.
How many people must die to set your mind straight?
How many more ways can I die? How many more faces must fade?
Before I find the one who is right.
Through how much more darkness must I search before I can find.
Just a little light and "how much more must I fight?"
In this war, in my life, in my soul, in my head, in my heart.
I'll fight until I'm dead. The ink of the man, the demon is who I am.
I wish you could see me now. Here I stand, waiting for the time to come.
I want to let you know. I did what was right.
In this war where I fight; the monster inside.
The demon in mind, myself and you.
I want to watch it all fall from my eyes and mouth.
I wish it to all fall and I scream out loud.
I tried to tell you who I am, in this war where I must stay.
I wish I could love but now too far away.
My heart they did take but you could help me find.
My soul they did shake but now I am fine. Where do you think we'll go?
Will we ever find us a home? In my grave I wonder why...
Why is it so hard to tell you what I feel?
I do fear the loss of it all again but you are here now and I'm a sin.
I am the devil that you all hate. I am the monster but you're too late.
I am the angel, inside and alive. I am the lover that you cast aside.
I am a warrior, a soldier of my mind and soul.
In my war, I fight myself so cold. In my war, I watch the world fall.
In my war; where you all fall. I wish you were here now but it's all too late.
I have become the monster I wished to be.
Now here I stand in this war; I set you free.
In my war I fight myself and you.
But you're too late, and now you're dead too.

This Knight's Next Stand

Just one foot in front of the other and step by step I take in life.
On I move in this fight as the Moons of Saturn beat me down into the ash.
On I move in battle, holding together my flesh, with my sword at my side.
With my love in my mind I move on to show you who I am.
On in the nightmares I beat my head; on and on I move again.
To find an outcome and hope in night...
Truthfully, I am the knight who seeks the better side of the line.
I seek the love I left behind.
Someday I might find a voice in me, one of straight utter exactness of my being.

Now I stand upon the platform in front of your eyes.
Here I stand waiting for my time.
This is my next stand; to fight for what is right.
To never back down in fear, I fear you no more.
And as so many times I laid bloody on the ground, to this hallow I am bound.
This is my struggle of being a man of my word.
Someday I will be with you my love, until the stars fall from the sky.
I will be with you my love forever, you with this knight.
And so many more dragons I must slay.
So many more miles I must walk in a daze.
Every monster I fight brings me just that much closer to you my love.
"I'm coming home."

So I look down now, watching the blood flow beneath my feet.
I watch the ashes cover me deep.
I fight on and more; to be with you once again.
This world I will crush and I move on again.
This is my next stand, another fork in the road.
Where now will I go? I fear that I do not know.
Somehow I feel that it will work out in the end.
But here in fright I lay; beating on my grave.
How much harder will it be?
I want to be alive; I want to set my soul free. "Set me free!"
Once in the land of my childhood.
Might I find the true things to be? Under and above me.
Once in the light of the dark that I fight, might I find another reason to breathe?
I want to feel that warmth, as another blade is shoved into my chest.
I scream once again! And no one is here to help me.
I feel so cold and I fall to my knees. I pray to you my God "set me free;"

Lord, I wish to know why I'm here.
I wish I could know why I must live in fear.
So many enemies I have made, my nemesis is only me.
This war I fight, "a pointless life."
I want to be the one to make me sane.
I want to be the one, holding true that day.
Here I am, the knight indeed. Here is my next stand; to set myself free.
Now I am a true man, now I have seen the path but far from being on my way.
So many miles more I must take in today.
I have left the battle but the war is far from over.
I'm coming home, to you my angel.
I am coming home to the one true woman I love.
As in the blue sky may lay the tool of the weapon I need.
Here is my next stand and I set me free. I am a slave no more.
To the world and our king. I am a knight of my word and I fight to be free.

I feel the love of my dove in heaven flowing above my soul.
We will be once again, "I'm coming home."
This is my next stand, to take me on the right path.
To be myself and come home to you.
This is the knight I am and no one can stand in my way.
Forever I shall fight to be free and safe.
I will take this vow to my grave.
I will take this honor into my soul but my heart I leave for you.
I am a man of my word and I will be with you once again.
I love you forever in this knight's dream.
I will forever be the man of my word.
I will forever be the man who loves you forever true.
This is my next stand. This is the path I did choose.
I will now be on my way; as to the moon's gravity kiss upon my cheek.
I shall be on my way. I will move on again.
This knight's next stand, to take me onward into her arms.
I am the knight of my word and you can hold me true to that.
I shall be with you again my love.
Until then I march onward upon this path.
"I'm coming back..."

Six Feet Away From Light

A small child leaning over the ledge, trying to see if there'll ever be an end.
A small child wandering in his head.
Trying to find a new grip, "because he lost the last."
I am that small child, lying deep in myself, wondering if I'll ever be held.
A dark cloud forming above my head.
Under this sea I take another breath.
And the rainbow forms another noose.
The words break free and I am loose.
Here under the ground where I lay.
Here under our earth where I wish to stay.
I am a small child leaning over the edge.
I am trying to find a better end to this day.
Six feet away from light, I stand six feet away from life.
Hoping to be set free, here beneath a tall tree.
I swim in the knowing of who I am and what I've done.
Here under our earth I wait, till the dark day is done.
I will not rest until it's complete.
Where else would you like me to be?
I wonder if I will ever be free; I need to stop the push.
I stand six feet away from light.
In this darkness I swing and fight; in the darkness I scream.
Here in this darkness I wait.
As once swung above the staircase; now lays in the grave.
Six feet I am from light, I stand six feet away from life.
Awaiting my death. I am a child sitting here holding my breath.
Never finding a place to call my own.
I beat my head on this stone, here lying under the dirt.
Sleeping under our earth, I want to seek but will never find.
I've lived with neglect, but now I'm fine.
I'm not that smart but I know who I am.
I will never let go, until the end. I am a child looking over the edge.
I am a man standing on the ledge; "just waiting."
Can you tell me who you are? Can you tell me who I am?
Six feet away from light? I want to stay here. I want to be the one alive.
I wish for my revenge in this darkness I fight. It has been a long time I say.
It has been a hard path I say. Indeed it will be much worse.
If I am the man I say I am. Here waiting under six feet.
Here I lay, "just dead rotted meat."
In this darkness I want to seek but fear what I might find.
In the head-bent skull I call mine.
Six feet away from light, six feet away from sight,

Six feet away from truth; all I lost in youth.
Where did it all go, where will I go on from here.
What will they say when it's all done?
I lay here bleeding from my mouth.
I sit here waiting for an answer to the questions I asked.
It is scary here, laying in the dark with only my heartbeat to listen to.
I am a dead man waiting to die.
It is scary up there, in the bright sun light.
With warmth and our mother earth.
I want you to know that I will do whatever it takes to get out of this hole.
In the dirt I live, in my soul I decay.
In the red blood that I bleed, I write today.
There was a world I called my own but now I feel so out of place.
You stole it all and shoved me away.
In the ground I weep, six feet away from sane.
In the ground I weep, six more feet away.
In the world I've left, will I ever be there again?
In the love I felt, dead and buried with sin.
In this dark I wait, until all will fall into place.
In the dark I wait, six feet away from light.
In the hurt I hate; you raped my heart in my chest.
Now I rip it out for you and scream.
So many faces, voices ringing deep into my ear.
I wish it to go away, fade away with me.
In the ash I lay, of the dirt I called myself.
I am a child leaning over the edge, wondering.
I am a child looking over the ledge.
Wandering deep in my head; "am I not alone?"
I scream beating my head, wishing for a better end.
Until then I will wait, here under the slate.
I rock back and forth in myself.
Winding deeper into my own hell; I wait more and more.
Six feet away from the light, just six feet away from life.
I lay wandering if I was right.
Will I ever feel the same again? I think I won't...
The next shall be washed clean of sin.
Six feet deep within, I wait for the answers I seek.
Six feet away from light, "and I sleep."

Only To Watch Her Scream

I need to take a quick breath before I crack.
I need to just sit back and relax.
I need to stop falling back into my memories.
I need to not feel so forgotten.
I loved an angel once but now I live for only revenge.
They shall all fall, all within.
I only wanted to be with her forever in our love.
But now we're gone and that is done.
I only did this to watch her scream; I only loved her.
"What more would you want of me?"
I only did this to watch her scream.
I love the fear that I made, as I watched her bleed.

I need to take my time before it's all gone and I'm buried away.
I need to stop freaking out on the thought of the scars on her knees.
What do you want from me, what do you want me to see?
Please answer me, answer me!
I only did it to watch her scream. I only enjoyed the pain that I caused.
I stayed there at her side because I was a lover and she still cast me aside.
I feel the torment of being there with that knife.
I fell aside into the lake of the *Never.* I knew it would be forever.
The holding of her soul in my hands, but she's away.

It was all just a bad dream. It was only to watch her scream.
I seep the sound I love but it was all just bad timing.
It was only because I cared. So I love the look in her eyes.
It was all just a lie to see if the outcome I thought was right, "*I was right.*"
I can still hear her scream at night, in my memories I hold the truth.
Under the frozen lake lies the tool.
I was a fool to think things could change.

I did what I felt had to be done and now she lies dead in her grave.
I did what I knew was right by me. Now I feel I can set her soul free.
I want to tell you how it really happened.
But I don't think you will listen to me.
It was hard for me I say; to watch the angel I loved just crumble away.
Into the dirt and within our earth, where she should stay.
I want her to be okay. I did it all, only to see her face.
And I feel I will never wipe clean the images in my brain;

I took an ax to her face and watched her drop like a fly.
I walked in just to see and I knew I was right.
I was right but now just damned.
I wish it were only a dream but I awake every day with that same pain.
I walked in not ready to see what I saw.
Her lust and lies drove her into her grave.
I wish I could have saved her before I did what I did.
I wish I had never met her but I did.
And now it's done and buried within.

I took an ax to the room, just to watch her scream.
"Who would have known I was right?"
I wish I never had to always be right but now we're too late for that.
I did it all, just to watch her scream and enjoy the sound I seep.
I love the pain I have caused.
And enjoy the torment of the demons stabbing my brain.
Voices and faces spinning all around my head.
Now I wish I were with her once again.
But never again, never ever shall I be saved.

I need to take a quick breath.
I just need to relax before I break down and crack.
I just need some time to gather all my thoughts.
I just need to wash clean my hands, but I know what I did was right.
To save not her body but soul. I was right for what I did.
And I hold that close to my heart.
Black, ripped out and thrown onto the floor.
I did it all, only to watch her scream.
Who would have known I was right?
"Who could have known besides me...?"

Backwards Soul Fuck

Holding the tool in the middle of my hand. I drop down to my knees and freak.
Holding the truth deep in my soul. Grabbing the blade and seeping it within me.
Over the notions of how I failed and further I fell deep into sound sorrow.
I sit here and dream of tomorrow; hoping that I will awake with her next to me.

HOLDING THE NOTHING DEEP IN MY HEAD!
FALLING FURTHER INTO MY BED!
KNOWING THE NOTHING THAT I LIVE!
I SEE FOREVER THE BEATING OF ME!
I KNOW WHO YOU ARE NOW AND IT KILLS ME INDEED!
I JUST WON'T LET IT BE!
HOW CAN I *LIVE*, KNOWING THAT YOU'RE SOUL IS DEAD!
"I SCREAM!"

Fading to the nameless section of my head; the hole I once called home.
I sit here and sway back and forth; forever in the memory of a love that failed.
And deeper I dug myself into hell, feeling so forever stuck.
In this eternal backwards soul fuck. I want to be the one on your side.
But now and again I am cast away; fading forever in me.

AND I PULL THE NAILS OUT FROM UNDER MY EYES!
I BLEED AND CRY!
I WISH I WERE HERE AND NOT AS LOST INSIDE!
I WISH SHE WERE HERE AND ALIVE!
I PULL FROM MY BACK YOUR KNIFE!
AND TUMBLE BACK INTO MY BRAIN!
NOW AND FOREVER I FEEL SO OUT OF LUCK!
IN AN ETERNAL BACKWARDS SOUL FUCK!

I watch the leaves flow out from under me.
I'm falling with no one to catch me before I hit.
I sit here waiting for an answer to all the shit I took but in the dark I remain.
As I rip off my own face and let go of the past.
I feel my soul die just a little more.
I just can't take knowing of what you have become.
I wish you were here with me.

I WALK AWAY WITH BROKEN PRIDE!
I WALK AWAY WITH MY HEART ON MY SLEEVE!
I WATCH THE YEARS PASS!
AND FEEL THAT I COULD HAVE SAVED HER AND ME,

I WANT YOU ALL TO KNOW!
I HAVE AWAKED FROM THE PAST AND FEEL SO ALONE!
NOW I FEEL SO DEAD!
IN THIS BACKWARS SOUL FUCK, IN MY HEAD!

I know now what I should have said, and I did.
I did throw it all over the ledge, into the dirt.
I watch the world fall from my head.
I watch the angel crawl, on and over the edge.
I am singing to the wind and moon.
I feel the rising anger at the dawn of noon.
I feel the torment in my brain.
Stuck in this memory and it eats me away.

I HAVE TRIED AND I HAVE CRIED!
I WANT YOU TO KNOW THAT I DID CARE!
I WATCHED IT END, I HELD IT DEAD!
I KILLED IT ALL AND BEAT MY HEAD!
IN MY SOUL I FEEL THAT YOU'RE TOO LATE!
FAR TOO LATE TO SAVE ME!
IN THIS BACKWARDS SOUL FUCK!
I FEEL FOREVER STUCK AND DECAYED!

I wanted you to know how I feel every day.
But you don't care; you just walked away.
Holding a new face in your hands. Holding a new heart within your grave.
I hope you know what you are doing. I don't know why you hate me so...
I loved you then but now I feel so numb.
I know who I am now and you're forever gone.

And I know now the words that flowed from my head.
Rocking me to sleep...
The truth is, I cared too much and now in eternal torment I am stuck.
I lived with this then and have found no luck.
I live on forever in a backwards soul fuck.

"That's all I have."

"Don't Read This One!"

" Well - I told you so..." And how could I put this at first?
How can I put this in words? Take one step back, turn and hit.
Pull the bullet out of my cheek and shove your finger into the hole.
Can you feel the gaping sorrow deep in my soul?
And the teeth are broken back one at a time.
Why are such things happening you might ask from time to time.
The raped angel lying bloody in herself.
Shaking and cold from the morning dew.
The monster watching, lusting over the corpse of the sheep that we choose.

And I fill my mouth with blood.
I feel the hot pointed steel shoved under each fingernail.
You pull them back and watch me laugh.
So I whisper softly into your ear, a bullet into your brain.
A thorn shoved into each eye. I love hearing you cry.
And why, dear God why! Oh why was it so tight around my neck?
I kicked off to but swing above the stairs.
Free falling into despair, loving each second of it.
You found it lying at your feet; you stole it and thought it was sweet.

Don't you ever think you can stop what you did not begin!
You will never be with me again.
And with pleasure I pull out my tongue and cut it in half.
Hoping to get a reaction from God.
Will there never be a stop to what I have made?
Will I ever not destroy but create?
I feel the doctors cutting off the burnt flesh.
I will never grow it back. I am naked to the world.
All elements sticking to me like there is no tomorrow.
I fear the hallow beating me dead.
I wish I could have been there, when he chopped off his own head.
"What a sight it must have been."

He took an ax to his skull and chopped it bloody in the snow.
I smile still over the thought.
Do you think me to be wrong for thinking like this?
I told you to walk away in peace; now I fear you shall leave in pieces.
Thrown into a garbage-bag and cast away like the trash you are.
I think so little of you, you fucking whore.
I feel the needles stuck far too deep into my legs.
My body shakes and I lose all control;

I spin fast in a whirl, throwing up on myself.
It was the blood I drank, or just the dead meat I ate.
And you are too late to stop me.

I warned you and gave it some time.
But it's too late now and you are out of time.
It was far past the line and I seep the mushrooms into my head.
I melt and spin and spin; the colors smell so great when the sun is just right.
It's far too late to change your mind.
I cut open the roof of my mouth.
I bleed and watch it flow down the drain.
Yes I think you and me are insane.
For staying here on what we call earth.
In purgatory I lie, for all the sins I write today.
I will never change; I know who I am.

I will never be forgiven for what I have done.
And I like the fact that you're still that dumb.
We are and always have been this way.
I live here now and forever will stay.
In the notions of being a man and demon within.
I look to the sky and kiss it goodbye.
Because I know what I did and I enjoyed every second of it.
I will never quit! It's too late to save yourself.
You're breaking each bone in my body and laughing at my pain.
I know you hate me now and it will never change.
The teeth are on the flesh and I rip it and scream!

I warned you about this...
Have you just not listened to a damn thing I said?!
I warned you about the eating of your own flesh.
The break of bone above skin and the drag of meat.
I pull on the rib that sticks out of my chest.
I pull and pull until it snaps and nothing is left. I eat at my own remains.
In the dark I am the monster of a man, and in my soul I was raped.
In my flesh of being a man.
"I am just a little different than you would think."
I told you not to read this one but look what you did.
It's funny to be both a demon and a man of sin.

"Things like this will never change."

This Thorn In My Side

My eyes rolling into the back of my head.
At night tossing and turning, feeling like I am dead.
Nothing stopping the pain; inside myself bleeding.
Unwinding in my head, "the memory of her."
She drove away and I screamed, laughing within my soul.
Knowing that all was lost and away. She became the thorn in my side.
No matter what I say or do. I can never forget the truth.
And never shall the voices be stopped.
In my head dancing and singing demons on my brain.
She was my eternal love and emotion-set.
I set her so deeply into my soul and held it true.
Now I can never wash away the stain.
The blood running down my face. I wonder why!

Here I lay bleeding, remembering that thorn in my side.
The love that I lost, my heart that I killed.
Nothing will ever fill the hole inside of me.
Here I lay bleeding; she's now happy without me.
I can feel the white cloud overwhelm me.
The memories that bring a tear to my eyes.
I toss and turn and feel that I will never be alright.
I feel like I'm at such a loss of light.
Now tumbling back into the past year spent.
And memories darkened by the evil of us.
I rock myself tumbling back into my pit of despair.
Falling into a world of my love and cares.
I can feel the white cloud overwhelm me.
I feel the memories that bring a tear to my eyes.

And I fall tumbling back into the past years.
The times of peace, love and care. Now I awake in the same place.
Holding a hand that I can remember; feeling warmth and free.
The love of a kiss on my cheek.
The warmth of a hand on my chest, the feel of her and me.
I can remember the times when we held each other so close to our hearts.
I said I would never let go. I held her so tight and skin against skin.
We were one and so free; the memories I wish I could forget.
We were in love, and nothing was going to be in my way.
I can remember the softness of her face.
Hugging her so close to my heart.
Holding her so tight to my soul, but now I am alone;

How many times have I awaked to an empty room and house, remembering her grace?
How many times have I walked aimlessly through the streets?
Hoping for hope and to see her face?
I fall to my knees, knowing that she is free.
I feel so dead in myself. I feel so dead and in hell.
How much more can that one girl haunt me?
How can I be rid of this thorn in my side? Here I lay and weep.
I wish I could sleep just one night and not feel like I'm alone.
I want to get over the thought...
Of her leaving to throw her life away. "*She threw her life away!*"
I want to be over it but I feel like I am so out of place.
She broke me good and left me alone. Now here I wait.
Until the day comes when I am standing above all of it... "And I do."

I feel that I will never be rid of this thorn in my side.
The pain that I have caused and made. I made it so easy to hate me.
I made it so hard to ever love again; I wish I could and win.
But nothing is here but a thorn in my side.
And the feeling so sick when I see her face.
I watch her hold his hand and she is so happy and alive.
I wish she were dead or I was away but now here I lay.
Bleeding and feeling like I will never be alright, but I am.
I know that the past is my worst enemy.
And myself is my nemesis that hunts me down.
It beats on my skull, ringing so loud in my soul.
The demons dancing on my brain.
I loved a girl once; now this thorn in my side.
I want to be rid of it and feel so alive. I walk aimlessly through the night.
On the road of leaves and into a sunrise.
But I have never forgotten the feel of her and me.
And never shall I, as I walk alone upon this road of leaves.
I smile because I know that she threw her life away.
And I gained my own, *I am myself.* I feel that all happens for a reason.
And the reason of this is clear; she is gone from me now.
And I stand on top looking down. Remembering that we were once alive.
"Now I stand free." "I rip out this thorn in my side and bleed."

Zombie Smiles

Cool fog lingering above the scattered blades of grass.
On the headstone lies my name. A midnight owl flying above our beds.
Screaming deep into our souls and heads.
On this hallow ground lies the eternal peace.
Of freedom of the dead; here laying peaceful rest.
No one out in the cold midnight haze.
The no one standing in the respectful house.
Here lying under the ground, the truth of what you did.
You can never hide it forever.
The ground trembles and breaks open and I am let out.
"Wet decay of rotten flesh."
Arms reaching for the moon, body limp and falling.
Cracking, breaking under itself, now I - the walking dead.
The stumbling over the rotten meat falling off of my bones.
Now here lying with stone against bone.
In a wonderment of why I walk again.
I'm now the living dead. I rise and seek human flesh.
Not here for peace, only revenge.
I don't know anymore, of who I once was.
Maybe a kind man of my word, or a demon from hell.
I know I have a mind from hell.
And my body now seeks murder and destruction.
"I shall find you."
Now I have awoken and feel an endless pain.
My hands cracked open and no blood to flow and drain.
I search now hoping...
To find all of whom put me there in my grave.
I shall find you soon.
I am a zombie... a decayed walking piece of rotted meat.
I stumble over my own flesh and seek.
I howl at the moon, I moan so low and deep.
I feel no more love and hate, only pain and pain!
I want to be there resting and asleep.
But now I have awoken and you I now seek.
Cemetery gates locked, I break open the chain.
I walk down streets I knew so well; not much has changed.
I come upon their house and I can smell there lustful deceit.
I drag myself to the back door.
And I know they are happy and asleep.
I know why I am here, to feast upon their flesh and souls.
A red door, locked and a window open;

I crawl my way in and head to the bed room.
My eyes come upon a child lying there in her crib.
I haul myself to the master room.
They're sleeping, unknowing of their certain doom.
I move myself to the bed side and lick my lips.
I hear the baby start to cry.
The mom and dad are far too intoxicated to even hear her scream.
I fade back to the child's side.
And she gazed deeply into my eyes and I know who she is.
The one part left of the woman I loved.
The one woman who put me in my grave.
The baby laughs and giggles, I hunger for the soft untainted soul.
I want to feast upon her flesh. I grab the child and hold her in my hands.
She only looked into my eyes and didn't question a thing.
I grabbed her tight, and held her close to where my heart used to be.
I felt a tear come to my eyes. I looked at her with a zombie smile.
And she only laughed at my rotted flesh and decay.
I stole the child and took her to a peaceful place.
A home where she will be looked at as a person.
And her mom and dad awake and just had another drink.
Unaware of anything, "anything." And so I slump back into my grave.
Knowing that my revenge was sweet, and I did what I had to do.
I saved one soul, and left to be damned the other two.
I think I can go to sleep now and rest.
So the sun begins to rise and the fog now morning dew.
I feel the peaceful rest and I can relax.
I hear them screaming, wondering where their child went.
But now she is happy and free with a new family.
I lay in my grave with a zombie smile.
Now my soul can be set free; I am now free.
I lay back and rest my head against the soft leaves.
Cool in the spring, and now I sleep.
And on the hallow ground lies the respectful dead.
I rest at the top of a hill and beneath a tall tree.
And the child can grow now.
And hopefully be a pure soul and stay clean; "I know she will."

For that child stared into the eyes of death and smiled.
I know that she will be better than the rest.
For I stood above her with zombie smiles.
And held close to me the last love I would hold.
Pure, innocent and sweet.

The Enemy In The Mirror

I can feel it pounding down on my skull, the nail shoved into my brain.
My head is spinning and I just can't seem to get a grip on reality.
I am feeling shoved deep into a personal hell; a torment of being myself.
I can still taste the burn in the back of my mouth.
My throat stings and I can't see. In a pool of blood I awoke.
Not knowing whose it was. "Who I am," and where I've been.

And there she lies dead on the floor.
Dripping pure her blood and grace of heaven.
And I would find the man who did this and bring him down.
"He shall pay for what he did."
And I see her face; her eyes staring back at me.
A look of fear and doubt at me.
On the kitchen floor she laid dead and her body stiff.
Her lips white and once red.
On the kitchen floor, I wish forever more I was with her.
"And that bastard will pay."

I just can't get a grip; I feel so sick and my body aches.
I stumble my way to my room.
I plummet down to the floor and I begin to remember telling her.
I will love her forever more and I just can't stay on my own feet.
I just can't get her face out of my head, "I want her back!"
I shall watch him bleed and die.
He will lie there bloody at my feet and I want him dead.
I look so deeply into the mirror and the enemy I can see.
Truthfully I know now what I did.

There lying dead on the kitchen floor.
Her body stiff and her skin pale and faded.
I know that I am the enemy in the mirror.
I can begin to remember what I did.
A ring collided against my face and I feel that I grew to be such a disgrace.
And I said I loved her, I remember saying I will never hurt her.
But now she lies dead on the kitchen floor and I miss her so much.
I know I lied and I would never harm her; but I did, I did!

And the enemy in the mirror calls my name.
He tells me to rethink that day.
The enemy in the mirror calls my name.
He tells me to grab the blade again;

I want nothing to do with his face.
I want to be rid of this place, "I need to get out."
I said I would love her forever and I still do.
But as she lies there bloody and dead.
I grab the bottle and beat my head.
I am sorry for doing what I did; I know I did.

And the enemy in the mirror grabs my neck.
He wants me to rise again and murder.
I rush frantic down the hall, into the other room.
I want her back, "give her back to me!"
But in the bedroom mirror lies my biggest fear.
The killer in the mirror was me.
And true as can be, I held it all in my hands.
Stained red with her blood; "I'm so sorry!"
The killer in the mirror haunts me so deeply.
He wants me to kill again.

I rush myself to the blade in her chest; I grab it tight...
So I shove it deep into his chest and the glass shatters tumbling down.
Breaking into hundreds of pieces and he screams so loud.
I stand there laughing with a knife in my heart.
As he lies broken there dying bloody at my feet.
I lie down bleeding next to my love; "I am sorry."
I never meant to hurt her.
But the enemy in the mirror drove me over the edge.
That crazy bastard; I am so glad I got to see him die.
And I look into my loves eyes.

So true I loved her, "*loving her so true*;"
And I will forever hold this blade in my heart.
I bleed lying next to my love.
Holding her hand, knowing what I did "*and I am sorry!*"
I never meant to hurt anyone, but now in hell I burn and scream.
A million times a day I die and I get to enjoy watching her stabbing me.
I am just so happy I get to see her again and loving you so true.
I fall down dead and I scream.
The enemy in the mirror now dead...

Fingers Smashed In The Door

It must have been all of the sleep still in my eyes.
I just couldn't see that clear, as all the truths laid on the line.
I was just too blind to see and as it crumbles down tumbling onto my soul.
It crushes me weak; I scream!
I rushed so frantic to stop you from throwing your life away.
But now, "what can I say?"
I rushed to stop the door before it slammed in my face.
My hand reached to grab, now bloody knuckles and broken past.
My fingers smashed in the door, "I tried to stop it!"
Should I have said what I said?
Now alone I wait for an answer to this endless pain!
Deep in my heart I contain the memory.
Of a past slammed in my face and fingers smashed in the door.
I scream, crying louder than her.
But nothing changes the fact that I did what I did, and that's that.
Here weeping over my broken fingers.
Knuckles bleeding onto the floor; I beat my head on the door.
I tried to stop her from throwing her life away.
I tried to be with her just one more time.
I tried and tried and died and cried.
But nothing will ever change the fact that I am forever alone.
What can he give that I can't?
What makes me such a freak and a demon that you hate?
I rushed to stop the door from closing, and shoved my hand in the way.
Only to find that it will still break.
My world was a place I could go to be free.
And where everyone knew me; now faceless I scream.
But I have my life and broken fingers.
I have a knife in my back and I just can't reach it.
I tried to help you up but my fingers smashed in the door.
I just could not get a grip, and I lost it!
But here I try to regain the power.
I tried to be the one to make you happy but lost my place.
And here I beat my head on the door and scream.
As my fingers were smashed and broke open.
I wish I could have stopped her from closing that door.
I wish I could have stopped her in time.
What makes him such a better person?
"Did he fight to be at her side?" Did he die to stay with her?
I feel like I am at such a lack of reach to the world.
And so much has changed, some for the good;

I lost her and them; all that I held in my hands.
But now alone I can finally think straight.
I reached out my hand to stop them from leaving.
Now all I have is a broken heart and hand.
My fingers hurt now day after day and I can't believe it all ended that way.
"Such children we were." And she cried.
And I watched my world crumble out from under my feet.
Now I fall every day, I awake in the bottom of my purgatory.
Waiting for a voice to call me out of myself.
I want nothing more than to see where I went wrong.
And now I feel I know; "such children we were."
I rushed to stop them from closing the door.
And reached out my hand; my fingers smashed in the door.
Could I ever take this blade out of my spine?
And remove this thorn from my side.
My hand now broken and I am afraid to touch anything again.
I fear I might be the same, now what more is there for me to say?
As I sit here dwelling in my shame; I hate myself today.
I shoved my hand in the door when I should have walked away.
I should have moved on sooner.
But it is all in the past and just makes for good writings.
It's just a story of my youth I lost.
I should have just enjoyed what I had and left the rest to be.
But I just couldn't let any of it go, I wanted it all to be so good in the end.
But I ruined it all for me... Now all I have are these writings.
But now I stand on top of the world and remember.
Remembering the words that we spoke; now I throw them away.
I tried to stop her from getting away.
I wanted her to stay but that was yesterday, "Now I have myself."
Here I sit remembering the days of fun and joy.
My youth I burned out of my head; I wanted to forget.
But I know now that it was just the things that we all go through.
And I should have let go sooner.
I rushed to stop the door before it slammed in my face.
I reached out my hand and broke each knuckle.
My fingers smashed in the door, I should have just let it all go.
But I tried and that's more than they can say.
My fingers smashed in the door.
I tried to hold on for one more time but that was yesterday.
Now I wait for my hand to heal.
I sit here remembering my youth that I threw away but I'm still so young.
I have the chance to make right with the next.
And maybe something so much more. As I pull my bloody fingers from this door.

Tomorrow

I truly never thought that I would see this day.
To come and pass us by like a cool spring wind.
I truly will miss your face, and maybe someday we will meet again.
"Goodbye until then."
And so many times I spoke of the pains.
Of being the man I say I am; "I truly am."
Today comes the thrust into our forever.
Being the people we will be; "always and forever free."
And the days just pass me by and I hope to be there.
Standing at your side in the end.

And so here I take my walk today.
And I can remember the smiles of our yesterday.
So many years spent on those things.
And miles walked to get me where I stand now.
Here on the brink of tomorrow.
I watch the sunset and the moon rise, "such sweet grace."
Here I stand; now a whole man.
And so glad you get to be here standing with me.
And over the times I wept; the hard days in the past.
Now I can smile knowing what's next.

Tomorrow holds the path.
Of being the whole people we will forever be, "you and me."
Here standing on top of the hill.
I look back and a tear comes to my eye.
I can remember all the pains and loves of my youth.
The yesterday now passing us by.
Here on the brink of tomorrow.
Here my revenge was held sweet.
But I would have been nothing.
If it wasn't for you helping me.
"I thank you all."

Soon we will be away, and all of this.
"Just a memory in the book - a faded thought."
But I will always remember the day I stood here.
As a whole man for the first time.
Here I am looking at all of your faces.
And they are etched into my mind.
I will never let go of the one thing I hold close to me;

You - and all of the days past.
I will never forget the times we spent and the fun we had.
"I hold it forever in me."

Tomorrow holds the rest of our lives.
And I wish I could be there with you at the end.
But I am glad you are here with me now.
As I walk on this road of leaves.
And into the sunrise of tomorrow.
Now all can be set free.
We are who we fought to be, "you and me."
It brings a tear to my eyes, to think it's over already.
"But it has just begun."

Into tomorrow I lead the path.
To accomplish all we can and to make it right.
I know now all happens for a reason.
And that reason is in front of me now.
I will never forget you all.
Forever and always I hold you close to me.
As now my life is set and I walk upon this road of leaves.

"Until we meet again... Goodbye."

Extras:

By Jonathan William Haubert

Spanning from the years 2001 through 2005 Wars of the Mind Vol1. (Upon the Road of Leaves) follows the story of Jonathan W. Haubert throughout his high school years and into adult hood. The Wars of the Mind series had truly begun as nothing more than a collection of rants, rhymes, lyrics and poems all handwritten on notebook paper either in class or late at night. What the Wars of the Mind series would ultimately form into is an epic chronicling of poetic adventures spanning decades.

Wars of the Mind Vol. 1 (Upon the Road of Leaves) is a story of relationships, friendships, family and the inevitable acceptance of loss and death. Upon the Road of Leaves is symbolic of the paths in life we all walk. Sharing in the emotional pains of loved ones and using life experience, Upon the Road of Leaves welcomes the readers to share in the battle of the mind and the soul...

Jonathan W. Haubert Would like to thank:

Mom and dad for all the love and support. My big brother Jason.
My two sisters Rebekah and Victoria, My Grandparents.
"Count Your Dead" And all of my greatest friends.

I could not have done this if it wasn't for you.
All of you are what keeps me going, and to anybody who picks up this book
And holds it true to your heart. "I thank you all..."

I have never grown, I have never changed
My body may age and decay
Yet I'm still the same

"I'm just a child."

Coming Soon:

Wars of the Mind
Vol. 2: (*Beneath a Frozen Lake*)